THE EM
OF
THINGS

SELECTED WRITINGS 2003 - 2013

C.J STONE

Typeset by Jonathan Downes,
Cover by Dave Hendley
Layout by SPiderKaT for CFZ Communications
Using Microsoft Word 2000, Microsoft Publisher 2000, Adobe Photoshop CS.

First published in Great Britain by Gonzo Multimedia

c/o Brooks City,
6th Floor New Baltic House
65 Fenchurch Street,
London EC3M 4BE
Fax: +44 (0)191 5121104
Tel: +44 (0) 191 5849144
International Numbers:
Germany: Freephone 08000 825 699
USA: Freephone 18666 747 289

ISBN: 978-1-908728-36-4

www.cjstone.co.uk

In memory of our Mum, Mary Stone, who passed away peacefully in her sleep, April 20th 2013, after a long illness.

"Pleasant dreams."

Acknowledgements.

My thanks go out to the editors of the various magazines and newspapers who have printed my work since the loss of my Guardian column. To Marion Williamson at Prediction, to John Nurden at the Whitstable Times and to Leo Whitlock at the Whitstable Gazette, but especially to Tania Ahsan, who first took me on at Prediction, and then again at Kindred Spirit, and who has been a constant source of encouragement for me ever since. Thanks Tania. I'd probably have given up years ago if it wasn't for you.

Thanks also to my family: to my Dad, Eddy, to Joe and Emma, to Helen and Matthew, to Robert and Louise and family, to Julia and Peter and family, but particularly to Sluggy Slimebucket – you know who you are – for time spent at the park and for all the fun with words. Remember: I'm not insulting you, I'm describing you.

Special thanks to Fraser and Angela and Chloe and Isobel for being such a lovely family, to Dave Tong and Mary Gidlow for the friendship and the breaks, to Paul Allen and Robert McDonald for putting up with me, to Ruth Hoskins for the reassurance of touch, to Warren Hughes for We're Here Because We're Here, to Dave Hendley for the cover, to Eric Lipin for the Amanae, to Julie Wassmer and Kas Kasparian for the strength and inspiration, to Vanessa Winship for remaining a friend, to Lois Davis for being with me through the years, for reading through the text and for giving me sound advice - and finally, to all the guys at the delivery office.

At least we took a stand. They won't forget us in a hurry.

Introduction.

This book has been compiled from stories from a number of different sources: from my column in the *Whitstable Times*, which ran from 2000 till 2008; from my column in *Prediction* magazine which ran from 2003 till 2008; from a short-lived column in *Kindred Spirit* magazine, which appeared in 2009; and from my column in the Whitstable Gazette, which began in 2009 and continues to this day. Other stories appeared in the *Independent on Sunday*, in the *National Federation of Occupied Pensioners* magazine, in *The Big Issue*, and in *Kent Life*.

Many of the stories, however, have never appeared in print before and have only ever had an on-line existence, where a few of them have enjoyed moderate success. The story called "Vlad the Impaler", for instance, has had, at the time of writing, approaching 29,000 hits. That's not bad. Knowing that my entire collection of on-line stories has been seen by over 177,000 people has been a major boost, even if most of those people just stopped by on the way to somewhere else. At least some of them must have spent time with my work. I know that because many of them left comments.

For a while, in fact, if you put "Vlad the Impaler" into your search engine you would have found my story at the top of the page. It was number two after the Wikipedia entry; until Google decided to smash it, that is, and to undermine any possibility of me earning any money on-line, by withdrawing me from their Adsense programme. Which is no bad thing really. The money was never any good anyway. I think, in my entire on-line existence (from 2008 to the present) I only ever earned about $100. That's $20 a year, or about 0.1 cents per hour at a rough estimate. I was never going to become rich that way.

And for any of you out there considering a future as an on-line writer: beware. Google have total control. They are judge, jury and executioner. They are proprietor, ad agency and editor. There is no appeal, and once you are cut off from your source of income, you stay cut off. Such is the new "free" world of the digital age: one global Leviathan controlling all advertising revenue on the World Wide Web. No appeal process. No regulation. No come back. No law.

They did me a favour. I was using my on-line presence as a replacement for real publishing. Looking at my stats, counting up my hits, had become a substitute for seeing my work in any real, physical form. And in a way, that devalued it; not just financially, but spiritually too. There is something about on-line reading that diminishes the work. It appears as nothing more than electronic drizzle. The words pulsate with the frequency of a cursor on a computer screen. Bundling up the work into this form, in order to make a book out of it, removing all the links and the fancy graphics, the jpegs and the YouTube videos, has given the content of this book new weight. It is real at last. I am real.

So you will read a whole host of stories that have appeared nowhere else. Mothers Club in Birmingham. Robin Hood's Day. Ranters Lane. The Stonehenge stories. LSD Refugees. Requiem for a Dreamer. We're Here Because We're Here.

I could go on. Possibly half of these stories are being published for the first time. And I think you'll find – I'm not being vain here – that a substantial number of them deserve recognition: they deserve their place in history.

Just to mention one: We're Here Because We're Here. If I'd only ever written one story in my life, and I could choose which one, it would be We're Here Because We're Here.

It was given to me by Warren Hughes, a colleague at the delivery office where I work. He gave me the outline one day, and asked if I would be interested. He thought it might amount to a line or two in the local paper. But it was always much more than that to me. It took several weeks before I had enough material to make anything of it, and several more to write it, but, once it was written, I knew I was in the presence of something real.

And then, after that, well what was I to do with it?

I sent it off to a couple of papers, received no reply, and then gave up. It has had a sort of ghostly existence on-line since 2008, and it had made me a number of friends, but it really hasn't had the recognition it deserves.

The same goes for a number of the other stories. Bear Nation, for instance, is a chapter from a book that was never finished. There are several more of those tucked away on my hard-drive. And The Home Front is series of columns I wrote for a newspaper which didn't exist. It ought to have existed. In a parallel universe, maybe, it does exist. But meanwhile, despite the quality of the writing, despite the warmth and good humour in a situation that was actually very painful for me, no newspaper or magazine, in the UK, or anywhere else in the world, has ever published these stories.

And more fool them.

Even amongst the stories which have had a previous incarnation on paper, there are substantial changes. So the story called "Drug Problem or Drug Solutions?" – another one of my on-line hits - is actually made up of a series of columns I wrote for the *Whitstable Times*. And the first two stories from the collection called "Money" are sets of 350 word columns from the *Whitstable Gazette*, stitched together to make some sort of sense, I hope. Of the four stories that make up "Tales of Ordinary Magic", from *Kindred Spirit* magazine, only three of them were ever published, while the story "Every Day is New Year's Day" is actually two stories written in succeeding years for my column in Prediction magazine, and updated for my website in 2012.

Which is where the largest group of stories in this book came from: from my column in *Prediction* magazine. There are stories from *Prediction* scattered throughout this book, from the chapter called "Time", to the one called "Therapies", and I will always be grateful to Tania Ahsan, the editor at the time, for taking me on. It was that 1,000 word column, once a month, for nearly five years, which kept me from going insane: which kept my word count going up and my self-esteem from going down; not to speak of earning me a little pocket money along the way.

As in any collection, there are some inconsistencies here. I've tried to create a narrative of sorts. I've interspersed story pieces with opinion pieces, in a way which I hope balances them out. There are more stories than opinions, and what opinions there are, are meant to illustrate the stories. But some of the facts are dated. Some of the columns come from as far back as 2003. So in one of them Gordon Brown is still the Prime Minister, and in another Michael Howard is still refusing to deny that he had ever smoked marijuana. I hope these minor blips don't detract too much from the overall impression.

You can think of it as like a decorated room. Yes, it's got new carpets and curtains, and a lick of paint on the walls; but the objects on the mantelpiece are vintage now, the clock doesn't tell the time any more and the pictures of the kids show them when they were young. There's a certain nostalgic appeal. You can't throw away old photographs just because the children are grown up. And I can't throw away my work just because some references are out of date.

The bulk of it, however, remains contemporary. Just to point out the story from which the title is taken: *The Empire of Things*. It was written in the aftermath of the riots of 2011, but acquired new relevance after the death of Margaret Thatcher. I chose it as the title of this book because I believe it genuinely describes the state of our current world.

The story is made up of snippets collected from facebook in the days following the riots, with added commentary. So that's how up-to-date it is: a story constructed and informed using facebook. But the theme is very old and the story still holds true. We are being duped by our world, and by the culture which controls it. We are being mislead and misdirected, misinformed and misrepresented. It's like a magic show. The magician makes a great display on stage to dazzle our senses, while behind the scenes, hidden away and in secret, he's messing about with the end-result to make sure it comes out to his advantage.

That great dazzling display is the Empire of Things of the title: the shallow and the superficial, the empty materialism of our contemporary world-view.

All I am asking of you in this book is that you take a deeper look, beyond the surface, to what lies elsewhere.

Memories

1. My Earliest Memories

My earliest memory is of my Dad. He was leaning out of the window wearing a cap, waving as the train pulled out of the station. I thought he was the train driver. It was only on reflection, many years later, that I realised it was a Navy cap he was wearing, and that he wasn't a train driver at all, but a sailor.

I was perched up in an oversized pushchair, on a platform of Birmingham New Street station. The reason I know this is that my Mum told me about it, about the first time Dad came home on leave, and us going to the station to wave him off, him leaning out of the window in his uniform, and me bundled up in this huge pushchair, several sizes too big for me.

"You looked so tiny," she said.

"I know," I said. "I remember it."

"You can't remember it," she said, in disbelief. "You were about two weeks old."

But I do remember it. Not directly, but indirectly, through a recurring dream I kept having all through my childhood.

I could see the cap, and my Dad waving out of the window, and the slow chug of the train as it hissed and laboured out of the station, sending out sprays of steam, and I remember being proud and excited because I thought my Dad was driving the train.

But then again there were probably many such leavings and returns in my Dad's Navy career, so it could have been another time I was dreaming about.

We lived in Main Street in a little back-to-back with a small kitchen in an alcove behind the stairs. It was very dark in there.

Mum used to lie in bed in the mornings and I would clamber in beside her, trying to wake her up. "Five more minutes," she used to say. I was walking by then.

I remember the smell of hot tea steaming in a cup and a bowl of cornflakes on the kitchen table. The cornflakes went slimy if you left them in the milk too long. I didn't like them when they were slimy.

I remember the stairs going up with the tiny kitchen behind, lit by a single bulb that only seemed to add more darkness to the darkness. And I remember the outside too, bursting with light. The pavement and a big car parked up by the kerb. The smell of oil on the road. I lost my toy lorry under the car. I remember lying on the pavement looking under the car trying to reach the lorry. It looked so small under there, so lost and far away.

I was about two and a half years old.

It was just me and my Mum and occasional visits from Dad. Whenever Dad came he would bring me presents wrapped up in paper.

Main Street wasn't a main street at all, but a little cul-de-sac leading off the main road to a dead-end. Mum tells me there were workmen there, building a school, and that I would wander over the road to watch them work. Also that there was a lady across the road who I would visit and who would give me bread and jam. It was a different era, a different world. There was a pub on the corner and when Dad was at home they would sometimes go and sit in the pub of an evening and leave me at home. I was perfectly safe.

After that my Dad was posted to Malta, and when I was about three years old we went over there to live. It was where my sister was born. Memories of Malta are vivid and colourful, but all jumbled up like a pile of washing in a washing basket. It was air and sea and high, dry hills. There was a game of marbles in the dust and the local kids winning my marbles from me and my Mum chasing them all down the road. There was a pair of sharp-cut brown Italian shoes which I hated. I walked home barefoot one day and lost one of the shoes on purpose. My Mum never did find out what happened to the shoes.

There was a barefoot girl with brown legs walking in front of me in a flowery dress one day who suddenly bent over and lifted her skirt to show she had no knickers on. I've been following that girl ever since. I'm still trying to catch up with her to this day.

There was a cave whose walls were alive with tiny, red insects. My uncle Robert took me in there, but when we saw the insects we jumped and ran out again screaming.

There was a church with a picture of Jesus on the wall. Jesus had sandals on his feet. That's all I remember: Jesus' sandals.

There was a big harbour and a sea and a wall and – strange memory this – my Dad stripping down to his swimming trunks and carrying his clothes and me on his back, crossing over the sea to the other side.

And there was a man diving in the water to catch me.

I don't think the first memory ever happened.

As for the second, in later years I heard the story. I was in one of those little inflatable boats bobbing about in the water by the shore when the tide and the wind suddenly took me, and before anyone had time to do anything I was several hundred yards out. My Dad dived in the water, but I was already sailing out to sea. Luckily there was a headland before the open sea, and a man saw me from there and dived in to catch me, so I was saved.

And then a memory of something that didn't happen, but did happen.

It was after my sister was born. I was given a present, a great big, yellow lorry. "Your new sister brought you this present," Dad told me.

I was so angry I threw it in the harbour. For years I carried that memory around with me like a guilty secret: about the yellow lorry which I threw in the sea. I must have been very angry with my sister.

Many years later, when I was all grown up at last, I spoke to my Mum about it. "I was very angry when Julie was born," I said.

"No you weren't," she said. "You were delighted. You used to want to hold her all the time."

"But what about the lorry she brought me which I threw in the sea?"

"She never brought you a lorry," she said.

But in my head all of that is really true.

2. Mothers Club In Erdington

*Mothers Club in Erdington, Birmingham, an early psychedelic **music ve**nue, opened on the 9th of August 1968 with a performance by Duke Sunny, and closed on the 3rd of January 1971, with a blockbusting three-band show by **Quintessence**, **Stonehouse** and **Happy**. The following is a personal record of that club, and that era.*

*John Peel: "People are amazed to hear that for a few years the best club in Britain was in **Erdington**."*

*Roy Harper: "Oh blimey - that was the first club outside London that meant anything at all and that's why there's been this long association with **Birmingham**. I played there about six times between 1968 and 1970. I have always enjoyed playing here." **Brum Beat Magazine 1995***

I don't know now who suggested we go to Mothers. There was a gang of us, just sixteen years old, and all into this "new" music. Alan Greensall and Robert Russell and Kevin Nurrish and Colin Walker and me: all sporting our brand-new centre-partings as our hair crept unceremoniously over our ears, with little bum-fluff moustaches staining our upper lips. This must have been 1969. The year previously we'd come back from our Summer holidays to find psychedelic graffiti slapped around the walls of our school, in swirling, colourful letters. All you need is love. Turn on, tune in, drop out. Make Love not War. They were heady days, in more ways than one. Hippies never referred to themselves as hippies at all. They called themselves "Heads".

So, anyway, whoever first suggested it, we all trouped off to Mothers, the Mecca for psychedelic music in Birmingham at the time and the only place to see the new bands. The thing is, none of us knew what to expect. We were discussing it beforehand, wondering what to wear. I mean, in those days people still went out fox-trotting on a Friday evening. They dressed up in suits and ties to make a night of it. So, of course, that's what we thought we should do too. We put on our best suits. Mine was a four-buttoned Mod-suit made for me by my grandfather. And Robert Russell's, as I remember, was a two-tone suit of shiny grey. I had on a pair of brogues.

As soon as we got to the queue we knew we'd made a mistake. No one else had suits on at all. They were in battered jeans with triangular, flowery-vents to make them flared, with ragged patches all over them, which hung about the heels sucking up the dirt. And some of them were wearing old stripy blazers or duffel coats two sizes too small. And bangles and beads and badges. And they all had hair. Cascades of hair. Puff-ball frizzes of hair, like mini nuclear explosions on their heads, and beards and sideburns and moustaches to make our feeble attempts look like a joke. It was like we'd walked into a foreign country. Hair country.

It was after that night that I started to dress down, and my Mum became embarrassed at the strange incomprehensible monster I was turning into. She just couldn't understand why I ripped my jeans on purpose, and put patches all over them, when she was quite happy to buy me a new pair. Ah Mothers: they never do understand, do they? So there were two kinds of Mother now: the cool, clubby sort; and then the other sort, the one at home who continued to remind you that you were still only a boy really.

The queue shuffled grumblingly down the alley into a side-entrance, and then we were shepherded into a gloomy room. It was five bob to get in. That's five shillings to you, or 25p. It was five bob for the lesser bands, and twelve and six (55p) for the top-notch superstars. *Pink Floyd* recorded parts of their live album, *Ummagumma* there, and *Traffic* had their world debut there. *Led Zeppelin* played there, as did many of the top bands of the period.

I remember posters on the walls and the tang of beer. The walls were painted black. There was a set of creaking wooden stairs with posters all the way up. Posters on the ceiling. The bar was as the back, behind a partition. We bought our pints (although we were far too young and certainly didn't look old enough) and went to sit at the front. There were rickety chairs lined up. Dancing was scorned, unless it was Idiot Dancing, that crazed head-shaking twitch that made the performer look like he was just developing Parkinson's disease. Then the band came on. I forget who they were, except they played harmony guitars. They glanced out at the audience and said, "hey look, the straights are here." We were looking over our shoulders wondering who they were talking about. It took a second before we realised it was us. We took compensation from the fact that they called us straights rather than schoolboys. At least it implied we stood for something.

Actually, on reflection, and after much consideration, I think I do remember the band. They were called the *Blossom Toes.* I even went out and bought their album. They are one of the forgotten bands of the 60s now, which is a pity, because they were good. I know that Robert Russell and Alan Greensall, budding guitarists both, spent the evening straining forward to watch the guitarists' fingers leap about the fret-board like Chinese money-lenders with an abacus. And afterwards we had curry and chips from a takeaway (that was the height of exotica at the time) and then walked home. It took hours. We lived virtually on the other side of Birmingham, in Sheldon.

When I got home my parents were still awake. My Dad shouted at me. He said, "what time do you call this?"

I said, "I dunno, what time do *you* call it then?"

He said, "don't be so cheeky." It was the beginning of youthful rebellion for me. Mum couldn't sleep, he told me. I guess he was irritated that me being awake was keeping Mum awake, which was keeping him awake.

After that we started going to Mothers on a regular basis, almost every Friday night, and sometimes on a Wednesday too, if I remember. We saw a string of bands. *Black Sabbath* were virtually the resident band there. *Black Sabbath* were from just down the road, from Aston.

There was the *Edgar Broughton Band* with their homage to Captain Beefheart.

I remember *Blodwyn Pig*, who were some sort of off-shoot from *Jethro Tull*. And the *Soft Machine*, who were so intellectual that they took their name from a William Burroughs novel, and who appeared at the proms one year. I liked *Soft Machine*.

John Peel was DJ-ing one night. He was already balding, though his hair dangled limply over his shoulders. He was wearing stripy fingerless gloves. He played the whole of one side of *Anthem Of The Sun* by the *Grateful Dead,* and never spoke a word. Psychedelic DJs were far too cool to speak, though it made you wonder exactly what they *were* being paid for.

We saw the *Battered Ornaments*, who were Pete Brown's band, and the *Deviants*. Pete Brown was a poet and wrote the words to several Cream songs. *The Deviants* had once been Mick Farren's band, when they were called *The Social Deviants*. Mick Farren had an underlying political message. He later went on to write for the *NME*, and to found the free festival movement with his Phun City benefit festival for the *Oz* defendants, and has since become a freelance writer of some renown.

In those days several of the bands used to ritually destroy their equipment as the finale of the set. It was a radical statement against the perversity of materialism. *The Who* did it first, then Jimi Hendrix. *The Deviants* were so radical that they destroyed their drum kit at the *beginning* of the set, and had to play rest of the night without. Far-out, man. *Cool.* This was probably intentional as they were not a particularly good band.

And that's all I remember of Mothers. A cultural eddy in the current of time, some passing moments from the late sixties and early seventies. Will it ever be the same again? Will anything ever be the same?

After I'd finished writing this I was telling a friend about the club. We were talking about our first hangover. I told him about Mothers and how one night I'd woken up with cramp after drinking beer for the first time.

"Mothers Club?" he asked, puzzled. "Why would you want to go to a Mothers Club?" He was confused. He had visions of groups of Mothers sitting round discussing knitting patterns and child care arrangements.

"No, Mothers as in Motherfuckers," I told him, faintly embarrassed. But the spell was broken. I could never hear the name 'Mothers' again without thinking of the knitting.

3. A Photograph and a Memory

I was born on the 16th June 1953 in the great industrial city of Birmingham in the West Midlands. I had a very happy childhood. I went to University in Cardiff in 1971 to study English Literature, having got 2 Bs and a C in my A levels.

This photograph was taken about two years later. I'm in my early 20s. I'm sitting on the roof of Cardiff University main building overlooking the concourse in the centre of town, within walking distance of the Arts Block building and the Art Gallery & Museum. In order to get to the roof I've had to climb through an open window from a corridor on the second floor. It's strictly out of bounds and I'm very nervous.

I'm wearing a white linen jacket with a red and green felt flower in the lapel. Around my neck is a green scarf on which is embroidered a racing greyhound. I have on monkey boots and brushed cotton loon pants. My hair is quite long and, as yet, without any sign of grey.

I thought I cut quite a dashing character, colourful and flamboyant, though really it was a disguise to cover up my innate shyness.

I'm clutching a camera case. The camera belongs to my friend Lois who took the photograph. Later that year Lois and I were married. It was a marriage of convenience. Lois, being from Zimbabwe, needed a British passport in order to stay in the country. I agreed and it is a measure of the time, and of my attitude, that the reason I gave for the marriage was so we could throw a party.

Lois and I are still very good friends.

There's one curious anomaly in the photograph: that ring on my right hand middle finger. You can see it more clearly when the photograph is enlarged. It looks distinctly out of place since, in my own mind, I'm not the sort of person who ever wears a ring. It has taken looking at the photograph for me to remember it.

It was given to me by my parents to mark my 18th birthday, which means that by this time I'd been wearing it for at least three years. It's a gold signet ring. I remember my grandfather wearing a similar ring when I was a child, but, up until this moment, I had no memory of me wearing one.

That ring marks a change. At some point I must have taken it off. There was a decision involved. Before that I was the sort of person who might wear a ring, like I might wear a scarf with a racing greyhound embroidered upon it, or a white linen jacket with a felt flower in the lapel. After that I became the sort of person who never wears a ring. I was fixing my character, tethering it like a boat to a dock, in order to secure it.

In fact over the years I've not just tethered my character, I've built the dock around it. This is how we become who we are. Bit by bit, year by year, we build the structures that define us, in repeated patterns of behaviour. We grind them into our souls. We say, "this is me, this is mine", referring to our habits of thought, our likes and dislikes. We define our tastes. We weigh ourselves down with opinions and anchor ourselves with beliefs. We start to say we know who we are.

I look at that young man on a roof outside Cardiff University library, and I remember some things about him. I remember how nervous he was that day. I remember his friends and where he lived and how he spent his days. He smoked a lot of dope back then and read a lot of books. He was searching for something, something hazy and ill-defined. For his character, perhaps.

But his character was never a fixed thing. It was more fluid and playful back then, more sinuously alive. Sometimes he was sunny, sometimes he was serious, like the flow of days around him. Sometimes he was in strong pursuit of an ideal. But the character was more like a river than a building, free-flowing, sparkling, rolling easily around the objects in his landscape, always moving, never fixed. More natural, in fact.

And then one day he took his ring off and he thought, "I'm not the sort of person who ever wears a ring."

And he's been building on that moment ever since.

4. My Son Joe

Joseph was born sometime in the early hours of the morning, September 15th 1980. It was one-thirty in the morning. Or at least I think it was. I have a clear visual recollection of the clock on the delivery room wall - one of those standard, circular hospital clocks with clean black figures and hands - and it reads just after one-thirty. I can even see the slim, red second-hand ticking round. It's just that I can't be sure whether it's a real clock or not. I may have made it up.

That's the trouble with memories. You never really know where they're coming from.

I have other memories too. I can see the flushed effort on his mother's face as she forces down and down to the cheer-leader chants of the nursing staff. "That's it dear: push, push." I remember thinking that it looked like mighty hard work, that's why they call it labour. And one funny incident. One of the nurses handed me a glass of water. "Thanks," I said, taking a sip and setting it down on the side. The nurse gave me a curt, disbelieving look. It was only later that I realised that the water was meant for the woman on the bed, not for me.

Later I remember the surrealistic image of his head popping out from between her legs, poised in a moment of *Monty Python* silliness, before the rest of his body slithered out like a blood-flecked snake from its red lair. And I remember the look on his face too, like one of those Buddhist demons, all crimson fury, as if he was fuming with indignation that we had dared exorcise him to this place, when he was perfectly happy where he was.

Mostly I remember the moment when he was laid upon his mother's breast, and how she glanced from him to me. There was something indescribable in her eyes, like some glint from another star; something warm but wise, elemental but kind, strange but friendly. All-embracing. Call it love.

There is no other word.

There were only three people in the world in that moment. No one else mattered.

And then, when it was all over, and his mum was taking a well-earned rest, I was cast into the neon emptiness of a Scunthorpe night, and I felt strangely bereft, strangely choked. Why Scunthorpe of all places? Because that's where we lived at the time. Or rather, we lived in Barton-on-Humber, about 15 miles away in what was then South Humberside. So Joe has "Scunthorpe" as his place of birth, both on his birth certificate and on his passport. Poor Joe. Of all the legacies of an itinerant life, this one must be the most peculiar for him, the most difficult to comprehend. Because that's all it is to him, a mystical place-name on his birth-certificate. He's only ever been there once.

I rang up my parents from a telephone box and told them the news. They congratulated me. It didn't help. I felt very alone. Later I slept on a wooden bench in Scunthorpe bus station, and awoke in the grey dawn to the sight of oil-stained concrete and scattered crisp-packets.

Well I may have got the details wrong here. I may be romanticising. But one thing I am sure of. One thing I know for certain. I know how it felt for me. It was as if, in being born, Joseph had changed the world forever. I remember thinking exactly that: that this one, small, bright new life had breathed new light into the world; a new perception, a new thought. It was a spiritual thing. He was like Jesus to me. I was absolutely certain about this, that the whole world had changed because of the birth of this one child.

Which it had, of course. But only for me and his mum.

After that they came home, and there were several weeks - months maybe - in which I had a pang in my chest like a hot dagger. It was difficult to know what this meant. It was a very corporeal kind of a feeling. Not mystical or emotional. Of the body. Maybe the body is the soul in another form. Maybe what hurts is what is real. But a baby is a very demanding creature. All tongue and arse and lungs. An innocent dictator, he stands over everything, a little Hitler making raucous, unintelligible speeches about the Motherland. Ein Volk, ein Reich, ein Fuhrer. Gimme, gimme, gimme. I want, I want, I want. Sometimes it became very hard to bear. Sometimes, I'm afraid, I even resented him.

But there were compensations too. There were the Arabesque swirls of a black, wrought-iron candle-stick holder hanging on a hook on the back of the bedroom door, and Joe's reaction: how he would look at it and point and laugh, as if this was the best joke in the world, as if this mundane object held some immense secret and he was trying to impart it to us. And the song I used to sing, rawly and croakingly, into his ear, as he lay with his head on my shoulder, as I danced about trying to get him to sleep:

Wouldn't you agree, baby you and me
We've got a groovy kind of love?

It was a song I'd loved as a child.

We moved around a lot in Joe's early years. From Barton-on-Humber to Bristol. From there to Whitstable in Kent. From estuary to estuary, for some reason. It's because I'm a Brummie. Brummies always have a fascination for the sea.

And, despite the moves, life developed a routine. It was one of those things. Always, "who's going to look after Joe today? It's your turn to get him up." "No, it's your turn." And in the following years his mum and I drifted apart. We no longer knew whether we were together because of each other, or only because of him. I became sullen and depressed. She was much younger than me. She'd had Joe at a very early age. Maybe she longed to have her own young life back. Eventually we split up.

This is a very ordinary kind of a story, of course, and I'm sorry if you've heard it before. It is the story of the late-twentieth century. Where it is maybe a little different in our case is in the situation we found ourselves in when we split. We were living in a commune. I'd had enough residual hippiedom in me to have been able to engineer this situation. So, while his mum continued her college course in London, Joe stayed with me. And - being sullen hippies, all of us - child rearing was a shared occupation. Later, again, I moved out of the commune, but the shared child-care continued. So that was how Joe was brought up, shuffling between a shared house in one part of Whitstable, my council-owned maisonette in another, and his mum's flat in London.

It's a surprise he isn't completely mad. He told me he'd been counting the times he'd moved. Thirteen times, he reckons, in only a few more years.

Where we can thank that commune is that Joe never felt the split like a schism in himself. He never felt like he was forced to choose between the two adults. Because there were many more adults in his life. I was only one of them. His mum was only another. So: no problem really. He could navigate his way between the emotional reefs with a certain grace. He had other people to refer to.

Which kind of brings us up to date. Joe is grown up now, and he lives in London. He is currently working in Photography. The other people in the commune have moved away, though he keeps in contact with them. His mum travels the world. She is also a photographer and is married. I still love her, though not as a lover any more. As the mother of my son. We all seem to get along.

And Joe is a typical young man. Smart-casual, with a concerned, interested mind, he rides the storms of life with a sort of controlled insouciance, aware of himself and of all the people around him. He's not at all like me. He's not at all like his mum. He's not at all like the other people in the commune, though he's learnt a lot from all of us. In my case, what I've had to teach him has been mainly negative. How not to live your life. How not to fuck up your relationships. He's learnt his lessons well, being self-possessed and extraordinarily loyal. It's like he has learned the courage to be ordinary.

A credit to his Old Man.

Tales of Ordinary Magic:

Columns from *Kindred Spirit* magazine

Somerset Meadows is a nice place to live.
CJ Stone *sees all sorts of things through his window.*

1. The sun came up. Again.

"Are you a druid?" she said.

"Pardon? Whatever gave you that idea?" I said, slightly bemused. It's not often you get asked a question like that. Not in the stairwell of one of the blocks on Somerset Meadows it isn't.

Her name is Mrs Rivers. She's quite deaf. She screws up her face and watches my mouth when I talk, but she doesn't hear what I'm saying. It's easier and more polite to listen than to talk, so that's what I do. I listen. And I never did find out what made her think I was a druid.

So she launched into this story, about the time she lived in Salisbury and went to Stonehenge for the solstice. This was in 1964, she said. It was very different in those days. There weren't any fences and you could mingle freely with the stones. She went with a friend but they got the date wrong so there was no one there. But then they went back the next night and that's when it all happened.

She was laughing while she told me this.

"And then the druids turned up," she said. "They all had on those white headdresses, you know, and they were blowing trumpets, up in the air. No one seemed to know what was going on. We were all just milling around waiting for something to happen, and then the sun came up and we all went home."

I laughed. Not much has changed, I thought. The last time I went to Stonehenge for the solstice the sun came up and we all went home too.

After that Mrs Rivers and I smiled our goodbyes. I carried on down the stairs while she carried on up, and we've never had occasion to talk about Stonehenge again.

Somerset Meadows is where I live. It's a cul-de-sac consisting of a number of red-brick blocks set in spacious communal lawns.

There are no gardens in Somerset Meadows. Every so often a man comes and buzzes round on a sit-down mower cutting the lawn and there are benches lined up on the sunny side of the blocks where people gather in the summer months to drink tea and chat. The small flower beds lining the blocks are tended communally. You get to know your neighbours very well around here. Your neighbours are never very far away.

It's also full of old people. I don't quite know why that should be. It wasn't designed with old people in mind. Not everyone is old. I just think that, not having gardens to tend, and with a residents association to take care of the external repairs, it tends to suit older people.

Also I think that some people have been here since it was first built, way back in the 60s. There's a lot of infirmity and the occasional death to witness. I've been meditating on mortality ever since I came here.

But I liked Mrs Rivers' story. She went to Stonehenge thirty five years ago, nothing much happened and she still remembers it. How like life that is.

Well what actually happened is that the sun came up. The sun comes up every day, of course, but we're not always around to witness it. What made it memorable for Mrs Rivers is that she was at Stonehenge and she saw the druids. They blew their trumpets in the air in the eye of the sun in order to celebrate the moment, turning it from a mundane event into a magical one.

Which reminds us: there's nothing mundane about a sunrise. It's a cosmic event, meaning that it takes place in the cosmos. It's part of the vast interweaving of the universe in its infinite play, complex and precise. It is only our perspective that makes it appear mundane and it is by our intent that we restore it to its magical glory once more.

This is the essence of magic: the time, the place, the people. In this case, summer solstice sunrise at Stonehenge with Mrs Rivers as a witness.

And by restoring the magical significance of a sunrise to its place in the cosmos, perhaps we restore ourselves too, as witnesses to the interplay of forces before our eyes, in our own very significant lives.

2. The life of trees

I used to see her looking up at the tree outside my front window. She would pause beneath it most days and look into the leaves, lifting her face towards them as if basking in some invisible radiance. She couldn't see very much, of course, being mostly blind, but she could see movement and tell dark from light and I imagine she would sense the shimmer of the sunlight from the surface of the leaves through the interplay of shadows beneath the branches.

Sometimes she would catch a leaf between her fingers. It was as if she was communicating with the tree, talking to it, absorbing its presence in all its seasonal moods.
There are a number of trees in the communal gardens at Somerset Meadows. She would talk to

them all in the same way, pausing beneath each one as she went on her way.

She was my next door neighbour. I live at number 23, she lived at number 24. Until about a month ago, that is, when she died. I don't know how old she was. In her 80s I'd guess.

The last time I saw her she was in a wheel chair, with a pale blue blanket wrapped tightly around her, being lifted into the back of an ambulance, with an oxygen mask pinching her face, looking very pale, very fragile.

I was sitting at my computer in my living room. I put on my shoes to go out, but by the time I got out there the ambulance doors were already slammed shut. Another neighbour was standing outside, arms folded, wrapped up against the cold, waiting with an air of patient expectation.

"What happened to Daphne?" I said, joining her.

"She had a funny turn last night," she said. "She collapsed. They think it might be a stroke."

"Did she ring you?"

"Oo yes," she said. "We always ring each other if we're in trouble."

"Let me know how she is," I said.

The other neighbour is called May. She lives at number 22. Daphne and May would sit on the bench outside my back windows in the summer, watching as the shadows lengthened into evening, drinking tea and putting the world to rights. I never knew quite what they talked about out there on those benches outside my window, except that is always seemed to involve a lot of laughing.

One interesting aspect of living in a flat in a communal garden is that you can't help but notice what's going on. Hence my close observation of Daphne when she was communicating with the tree. I wasn't being nosey. I was just looking out of my window.

Hard not to notice, too, when she was being hauled out by the ambulance men, trussed up like a turkey on a Christmas morning, with an oxygen mask slapped unceremoniously on her face.

I see a lot of ambulances in Somerset Meadows. I see a lot of people being bounced up and down in wheelchairs with oxygen masks on their faces.

It's like the waiting room for the next world around here. I'm considered a wild young raver being all of fifty-something years old.

But I liked Daphne, very much. She was always ready with a cheery smile and a kind word. She couldn't see me, so I would have to address her to get her attention. I guess this is why she liked trees so much. People move around and you can't tell one person from another, but trees are always recognisable being always in the same place.

And despite her blindness she was active right up until the end, walking resolutely everywhere with her white stick, talking to all the trees on the way.

At first the prognosis was good. She'd had a minor stroke and would soon recover, May told me. But then, suddenly, she summonsed her entire family to her bedside. After that she had a second massive stroke, and she died.

So she knew before the moment came that it was time for her to leave, and she was able to say her goodbyes to her grieving family.

The tree outside my window has dropped its leaves for the winter. That's why trees never grieve. They are stoically aware of the cycles of death and rebirth.

3. Alien nature

Steve is an old friend of mine. He's 6'2", balding, with a blaze of white hair about his shoulders, and a bright green beard.

He says he is an alien.

When I first knew him I thought this was some kind of a joke, a metaphor for how he felt in relation to the rest of the world. Later I began to realise that he meant it.

One day I gave him a lift in my Morris Minor. Steve got in and I asked him to do up his seatbelt. There was some puzzled fumbling lasting at least half a minute. He had one half of the seatbelt in one hand, and the other half in the other, and he was waving them about in the air. It was like he didn't even know what a seatbelt was for. I caught this look on his face - bewilderment and consternation - and I laughed.

"Come here," I said, and did the seatbelt up for him.

That's when I decided that he really might be an alien after all. It was clear that the very concept of "seatbelt" was something alien to him.

Steve says that he always felt out of place. As a boy he loved nature, and was always out and about, wading in ponds and rock pools, or wandering around in the woods, observing the life there.

He used to collect creatures too: caterpillars in jars, and field voles and shrews, and exotic things he'd get by mail order, like silk moths and stick insects. But human beings always puzzled him.

The other boys also collected creatures: but whereas Steve collected insects in order to observe them and watch them grow, the other boys caught insects in order to pull their legs off; and whereas Steve collected newts in order to breed them, the other boys collected newts so they could throw them on the grass and flick knives at them.

So it's a matter of opinion whether it's Steve who is the alien. He is perfectly at ease with the other creatures on this planet. Maybe it's the Earthlings who don't belong here.

It was Steve who introduced me to V. That was what he called himself: "V". I never met him in person, though I used to exchange letters with him for a while. Well I say "he" and "him" but this is really for ease of expression, since, according to his own testimony, he is neither male nor female, but some kind of a galactic gynandromorph.

V claims to be an alien, or - to put it more precisely - a Kaiana, an interstellar deva, the earthbound fragment of a being called Aona, with whom s/he will merge at some future date, and emerge, like a caterpillar out of its chrysalis, as some entirely new species of being altogether.

I used to like writing to V. It's not often you get to receive letters with such unusual concepts in them.

I never quite knew how to picture him, however. I mean: what does an interstellar deva look like? Do interstellar devas ever go shopping, for instance? What would it be like to stand behind an interstellar deva in the shopping queue in Tescos? These are the sorts of questions that interest me.

Steve used to have one of V's paintings on his wall. It was very well executed, hyper-real. It was of an intergalactic female-type creature, blue with white hair, with scales instead of nipples, very attractive in an alien sort of way, giving you this arch, sensual, come-to-bed look.

Steve said, "if you look at her before you go to sleep, she will come to you in your dreams."

I think this might have been Aona, the creature with whom V hopes to merge one day. But despite the fact that he never made it clear – in fact did everything in his power to disguise it - I was never in any doubt that V himself, in his Earth-bound incarnation, was a man.

One day he wrote to tell me that he'd been having trouble with his wisdom teeth. It had been a very painful experience, he told me.

"Who invented teeth?" he asked peevishly. "Nature is very inefficient."

In the end I think that V was alienated from his own body.

4. One day in the Co-op

I first caught sight of him in the second aisle in the Co-op where I'd gone to get bread and milk. He was shuffling about in his pyjamas, looking confused. He was holding a tin of something and looking at it, studying the label. Then he wandered to the front desk and back again, still holding the tin, eventually putting the tin back on the shelf.

I caught all of this out of the corner of my eye while I was grabbing my bread and milk from the shelves. I didn't want to look directly at him. It seemed impolite somehow.

You don't often see strangers in their pyjamas in the Co-op. Or anywhere else, come to that, except maybe in a hospital or a mental institution.

It's funny how the brain can construct such huge, elaborate story-lines out of the flimsiest of material. In my head he was some lost old guy so fragile and out-of-touch that he'd wandering in off the street in his pyjamas and then forgotten what he was in there for. He was obviously ill. Why else would he still be in his pyjamas?

And then I got to the counter and they were all dressed in pyjamas too.

"What's with the pyjamas?" I said to the check-out woman as I handed her my bread and milk.

"It's for charity," she said.

"That's a relief," I said, laughing. "I was wondering what was going on there."

"I know," she said. "Someone just came up to me and said that there was some old feller messing about with the groceries."

"That's what I thought," I said. "He was shuffling about looking confused to me. I thought he must have escaped from an institution."

At which point she broke out into peals of laughter and called down the aisle to the person concerned.

"That's three now," she spluttered, holding up her fingers to indicate the on-going tally. "This one thought you was mental!"

By which time everyone in the shop was screaming with laughter. It's not often that a shopping trip can turn into a comedy routine.

But it got me thinking about the nature of reality. We do this all the time of course. We build stories on the basis of appearances, without ever really knowing what lies behind. We are dupes to our own belief-systems and we construct appearances to fit in with them. This is the process by which we build our world. The assumptions are all implanted in us at an early age. They are the assumptions given to us by our parents, by our school, by TV and the media. After that we shape our perceptions to reinforce those assumptions in a continuous feedback loop. If we see anything unusual, we alter it to fit in with our overall world-view.

The shop assistant wasn't old. No older than me, in fact. I'd made him old because he was wearing pyjamas. And he wasn't confused. He was aware of my reaction to him, and was observing me.

So it wasn't only a comedy routine, it was a sociological experiment. That's why he seemed to be lingering about. He was making observational notes in order to tell his wife that evening.

Stage magicians play upon this propensity of ours to confuse reality in order to construct their illusions. They set up diversions, making a grand display of gestures, while all the real work is going on quietly in the background.

This is what they call "sleight of hand." One hand acts as a diversion, while the other gets on with the business of messing about with the cards. Politicians and advertisers use the same method.

You wonder how many more of our in-built assumptions are false; how much more dynamic and alive our world might appear if some of the deadening influences of routine were removed?

Who says that the trees can't sing, that the wind isn't alive and that the sun isn't beating down on us with its boundless intelligence? Or that shopping in the Co-op can't always be a comedy routine?

It's all a matter of perception.

"It's toffs and tramps next week," said the check-out woman, indicating the charity box for my donation.

Maybe the next time I walk into the Co-op I'll be a little more aware.

Time

1. All This Crazy Gift of Time.

It is precisely 8.07 am.

I'm sitting here, in front of my computer with a deadline looming. I have about four hours to get this story finished. Sometimes time can seem too short.

Prisoners, on the other hand, talk of "doing time". For them time is a punishment, a burden. They talk about it as a "stretch" as if time was being dragged out longer than it should be, like a vast elastic band. Time can seem to go on forever.

Albert Einstein said that time was relative. He meant that time goes at different speeds depending on how fast you are travelling. The closer you get to the speed of light the slower it goes, which implies that, at the speed of light time would actually stop and that - theoretically - going faster than the speed of light would mean going backwards in time.

Except that, according to Einstein's theory, nothing can go faster than the speed of light.

Einstein's theory is very technical, involving all sorts of mathematical equations. I tried reading it once. I couldn't get past the first sentence. But Einstein was a great populist and sometimes offered simpler explanations of his theories than the ones found in his books. Here he is with a more colourful explanation of relativity: "Put your hand on a hot stove for a minute, and it seems like an hour. Sit with a pretty girl for an hour, and it seems like a minute. THAT'S relativity."

He's right, of course. When you are enjoying yourself time goes tumbling by. But everyone remembers that last hour of school before the school holidays, the interminable tick, tick, tick of the clock upon the wall as it inches its way slowly forward, minute by minute, second by second, towards that final moment of freedom.

Then you have the school holidays and before you know it they're over and you're back at school again.

Sometimes there just isn't enough time. A modern person is always rushing around juggling a variety of commitments - work, play, lunch, dinner, love, friends, acquaintances, social life, work life, contacts, engagements - in a hectic round of schedules and arrangements, measuring out their lives in the pages of their on-line diary.

"Can you give me fifteen minutes at 3.30 on the 31st, or ten minutes at 2.20 on the 21st?"

"No, but I can give you ten minutes at 12.30 on the 13th or fifteen minutes at 5.15 on the 5th."

It's enough to put your brain in a spin.

And with all this hectic rushing around, what time is there left for yourself?

Time is like a scarce resource that has to be rationed out. We have everything we need in life except the time to enjoy it. In the past there was more time. People had time for each other. Their resources were scanty and their food was rationed but there was plenty of time to go around.

So what has happened to time? Is it running out?

Some people say that time is money. I don't like that idea. Does that mean we have to go out to work to get time now? That we can't have time unless we've earned it?

Sometimes we have to MAKE time, at other times we have to TAKE time. Making time is a creative act, a way of getting things done even when we don't have the time to do them. Taking time is a necessity in our busy lives. It's about allowing time for ourselves. People also talk about stealing time, as if time doesn't really belong to us.

One old hippy singer from back in the 60s, Kevin Ayres, wrote a song called "All This Crazy Gift Of Time."

> *Does the world seem good to you?*
> *Does the music get to you?*
> *Does the wisdom of your heart*
> *Show you how to play your part?*
>
> *All my blond and twilight dreams;*
> *All those strangled future schemes;*
> *All those glasses drained of wines,*
> *All this crazy gift of time.*

I like that. Time as a gift. Time as something you can do something with.

I think this is the image of time that I would like to leave you with.

Time as the gift given by the universe for you to play with at your leisure. Not time as money. Time as fun.

2. Every Day is New Year's Day

A happy new year to you.

Also, a happy new day, a happy new hour and a happy new minute. A happy new second. A happy new breath. A happy new moment. A happy new everything.

Because - if you stop and think about it - the whole world is reborn at every moment, with every breath you take. There is only ever the present. What is past has already been done, and cannot be undone. What is in the future hasn't happened yet. So there is only now. Only this one moment.

This moment encompasses all that went before, and all that is to come. It is the culmination of all the decisions you have previously made - all the accidental encounters, all the lost opportunities, all of life's strange turnings, those twists of fate - and then it is also the seed for what is yet to be, what hasn't been decided yet, the beginning of a new life and new opportunities and new journeys, just around the corner.

It is the collective decisions we make - all of us together, the whole of the human race, in this moment, at this crucial time in history - that will finally determine what our future will be, and each of us individually has exactly this amount of responsibility, that we must make our own personal decisions, but that we must make them with integrity and love. Whether it is a good world in the future - one that our grandchildren and our great grandchildren can enjoy - or whether it continues on its current descent into madness and absurdity, is still a matter to be decided.

Me, I'm a great believer that the small things in life count, small acts of kindness in a hostile world, the cheery smile in the supermarket, the friendly word, all those little acts of generosity and concern. I think these things matter. It's the accumulation of all the small things that make the big things that make the difference.

There's an old Zen saying: "Before enlightenment, chopping wood and collecting water. After enlightenment, chopping wood and collecting water." A modern version would probably sound more like this: "before enlightenment, washing up and going to the shops, after enlightenment washing up and going to the shops."

It's the approach you take to these mundane matters that makes the difference: whether you undertake them with anticipation and joy, or as just some task to be got out of the way before you get on with whatever other distraction is claiming your time and your attention. It's how you use your time that matters.

Time is actually a great mystery. Do we even know what it is or what it is made of? What is it for, exactly?

According to Einstein, for beings travelling at the speed of light time would not even exist. A being made of light could travel back and forth in time the way you and I get on a bus or hop on a bike to go to the shops.

There is one theory that as the universe is expanding so time is unravelling, which means that if space ever did collapse back in on itself, then time would run backwards again.

That is entirely possible. Thus we might have to live our lives all over again, but backwards this time: from death to birth, instead of the other way around. And who can say, really, which way is the right way? Life is a journey from one mystery to another, whichever way round you look at it.

Of course, whether you think now is the right time to wish anyone a happy new year or not depends on which calendar you are using. For instance, January in the Gregorian calendar is actually Tevet in the Jewish calendar, and the new year is not due for another nearly 300 days, on the 1st and 2nd Tishri, when the year will become 5773.

According to the Southern Buddhists, new year is the first three days of the full moon in April and the year is 2555.

According to the Muslim Calendar, new year will be November 15th 2012, and the year will be 1434.

According to the Julian calendar new year is on the 14th of January. The Julian calendar was the calendar used in the West until 1582, when it was replaced by the Gregorian calendar. Some Eastern Orthodox churches still celebrate new year on the 14th of January and some stubborn traditionalists still use the Julian calendar for all of their dates.

In fact it is possible to celebrate new year in almost every month of the year. It depends on what part of the world you come from and which belief-system you ascribe to.

According to Robert Anton Wilson, the great anarchist thinker and writer, the year is now 6012, his personal count beginning with the birth of Hung Mung, a mythological ancient Chinese philosopher who supposedly answered all questions by shouting loudly, "I don't know! I don't know!"

Thus Robert Anton Wilson's satirical version of a calendar system begins with an uncertainty.

Later he revised his views, saying that ALL calendar systems, including his own, were attempts to impose a single vision on a complex world, and he started using a variety of different systems at the same time. So a Robert Anton Wilson article might be dated in any one of about twenty different ways.

What most of these different calendar systems have in common is a starting date. That is, they are linear and progressive and whoever devised the system had to choose a day on which to start calculating the progression of days and months and years that lead us up to today's date. Thus time is perceived as a line. It goes from the past to the future, from something that is fixed and known to something that is as yet unrealised. It goes from young to old, from youth to maturity, from ignorance to wisdom. At the same time it goes from strength to weakness, from vigour to decrepitude, from imagination to habit, from creativity to decay, and it is a process which can never be reversed.

But time might not be like this at all. Time might go in circles.

One particular Celtic version of the new year came in the form of a story. The young Oak King challenges the old Holly King for the love of the goddess, and kills him. This story is commemorated in a garbled form in the ancient carol, the Holly and the Ivy, and is repeated, in reverse order, in the summer, when the Holly King defeats the Oak King.

Thus the cycle of the year is seen as a story of death and rebirth, endlessly echoed through time. Birth and death: it's all part of the same process. The birth of the new year, and the death of the old.

Which, of course, is exactly what it is: death and decay giving way to growth and rebirth, and all of us spinning in a merry dance through the cycles of seasons.

Actually it is this notion of time which we celebrate in our modern version of the new year, which we commemorate by our new year's resolutions. We celebrate the idea that the year can become new again. We celebrate the rebirth of the year.

Shall I tell you my new year's resolutions? I will wish everyone a good morning, even when it's not. I will look at the stars whenever the night is clear. I will always be good to myself. Have a great new year, whatever year you think it is!

3. Robin Hood's Day: A Medieval May Day Festival

Lythe and listin, gentilmen,
That be of freeborn blood;
I shall you tel of a good yeoman,
His name was Robyn Hood.

A Gest of Robyn Hood: *unknown date, possibly 1450*

Robin Hood is not a man, though many men have called his name. He is the spirit of the wildwood in its budding time, Jolly Robin in the Green, the force that makes the green shoots grow, that hisses in the foliage like love's electricity, that sizzles and crackles with the laughter of life, with the joy of the blossoming of the Earth's goodly store.

He is the spirit of the Maytime in its fruitfulness and splendour, the spirit of England, the

Summerlord, King of the Summerlands, where summer's sun always shines. The spirit of mirth and playfulness, of sport, of dance, of jest, of love. He is there with the lovers in their secret tryst, with the dance of the birds in the merry air, with the players of sports in their triumphs and losses, with all that is light and lively and fanciful and free.

His day begins on the first of May and continues through to Whitsun, and is accompanied by music and laughter, games, feasts and festivities. Dances and plays are performed in his honour, jests and japes and buffooneries. Not for nothing is his name Jolly Robin. Jolly as the sunshine. Jolly as the Noontime. Jolly as the Moon in May.

May Eve, the young men and women light fires, while the young men make bowers in the woods out of bent sticks interwoven with leaves and decorated with flowers for their lover's tryst. Robin Hood's bower. Later, in the dead of night, the lovers will steal away, to embrace, to kiss, to delight each other in their youthful beauty. Children born of these marriages - Greenwood Marriages, no need for the clergy's permission - are called the Children of the May, or Merrybegots, and especially honoured, as blessed by Robin Hood.

At the dances Old Fat Friar Tuck lifts his cassock to reveal a monster phallus strapped to his groin, as he dances obscenely with a Maid. This is the song he sings as she runs away screaming delightedly:

> *Here is an huckle duckle,*
> *An inch above the buckle.*
> *She is a trul of trust,*
> *To serve a frier at his lust,*
> *A prycker, a prauncer, a terer of sheses,*
> *A wagger of ballockes when other men slepes.*
> *Go home, ye knaves, and lay crabbes in the fyre,*
> *For my lady and I wil daunce in the myre,*
> *For veri pure joye.*

Robin Hood and the Friar:
from **The Mery Geste of Robyn Hoode**
William Copland 1560

Bishop Latimer, writing in the 1580s, tells of a day that he came to preach in a certain parish. "I found the church door fast locked," he says. "I taryed there half an houre and more, and at last the key was found, and one of the parish comes to me and sayes, Syr, this is a busy day with us, we cannot hear you; it is Robin Hoode's day; the parish are gone abroad to gather for Robin Hoode."

Such was affection the common people felt about Robin, that they would refuse to attend church rather than miss his day.

As a man Robin becomes an Outlaw, a man who, moved by pity and a love of humanity, rights wrongs, corrects misdeeds, turns the world upside down. He is the Lord of Misrule, the

Abbot of Unreason. His enemies are the corrupt officials of the Establishment, the greedy clergy, the tax-gatherers, the cowardly soldiers who obey orders, not because they are right or just, but because they fear the Tyrant's weapons.

Robin is a fighter for social justice, a friend to the poor, to the common people. Indeed he is one of them. A free born Englishman, a yeoman, not a slave or a serf, but not a Lord either. Not Robert, Earl of Huntingdon, but Robin of Loxley, who fights with the staff and the bow, skilfully fashioned from oak and yew, gathered from the greenwood that is his home. With Maid Marion and his Merry Men, Will Scarlock and Allen-a-Dale, Friar Tuck, Little John and Much the Millar's Son, he sports and carouses, drinks and eats and laughs until, called to action, he leads his band to the high road where the enemy's convoy flounders, and by courage and by stealth steals the stealers riches, to return them to their rightful owners.

His religion is the cult of the Virgin Mother, whom he loves to the point of death. When he steals from the clergy he calls it a gift from the Virgin.

There is not one Robin Hood, but many. Anyone can be Robin Hood. All you have to do is wear his mantle and call his name. He is the Earth's rebellion against greed and corruption and the desecration of her beauty. Whenever a man was driven to theft by the forces of Old Corruption, to the life of an Outlaw, he would change his name to Robin Hood. And in times of great rebellion, when many men were Outlaws, many bands would roam the land giving themselves the names of Robin Hood and the Merry Men.

The Robin Hood story is always the same. It goes like this. Robin is out in the woods where he meets a foe, usually on a bridge across a stream. Little John, Much the Miller's Son, Will Scarlock or Friar Tuck. So a battle ensues and Robin Hood loses. Robin Hood always loses the battle against his Merry Men. Always it is he who falls in the water and who struggles out, laughing and wet. And then, having won the battle, the foe falls to his knees and calls Robin "Lord". Thus Robin is the loser whom everyone calls Lord. What does that mean?

Or he is standing, leaning beneath the oak on a sweet May morning looking mournful. Little John will come up to him. "Are you sad, my Lord?"

"Not sad, bored. I want company."

And he will give instructions to the Merry Men to go up to the High Road and to kidnap a passer-by, so that Robin can have company.

And they will go to the High Road and kidnap a "guest", and then treat him with all honour, and feed him, and carouse with him as the day is long. And when the guest is fed, Robin will speak. He will ask for payment for the celebration. "What do you carry in your bag?"

And if the guest is greedy and conceals his riches, Robin will take it. But if the guest is honourable, and tells the truth about his wealth (whether he is rich or poor) Robin will reward him with more. And if the guest is in trouble and in need of help, then Robin will help. And if the guest has been dishonoured or had his lands taken away or his money stolen, or if he loves a maiden who is held captive by a Lord, then Robin will move all his forces in aid of the guest, and he will restore the honour or take back the land, he will restore the wealth, he will free the maiden, he will be a friend for life.

His heart is generous and true and his Englishness is not exclusive. He shares equally to all who come to these shores, for it is England herself, the landscape, the hills and valleys, the rivers and the trees, its gorgeous greenery, its abundance and beauty, which gives Englishness its special quality. And if the English themselves have grown sad and separate down the years, it is because they have forgotten the spirit that moved them, the spirit of laughing kindness, the spirit of bawdy revelry, the spirit of rebellion and fair shares for all, the spirit of Robin Hood. For, though Robin is as English as English can be, his is the Merry England of old, and he can be worshipped anywhere, so that even the Scots and the Welsh (who have had cause to hate the English at times) have always loved Robin Hood.

And since Robin Hood was born in England, and is spoken of and written of in English, in the first new flowering of the Nation's language - in the Maytime of English - and since English is now the common World language, spoken and written in every nation on the globe, we give you all Robin Hood. Robin Hood of the Greenwood, of the heathlands and fells, who redistributes wealth, who takes from the rich to give to the poor. For this nation which first gave birth to the scourge of capitalism and the factory system, also gave birth to its opposite too, to the idea of socialism, to the idea that the Earth should be a common treasury for all.

This is Robin Hood's contribution to the Earth. He is our herald of the return to the Summerlands, where we can dance and sport and play like freemen again.

Jolly Robin. Under the Greenwood Tree.

4. Stonehenge and Civilisation

How long is a piece of string?

I took my son to Stonehenge to watch the midsummer sunrise. It was the first time that he had seen the monument close up. He was not all that impressed. "It's not as big as I thought it would be," he said.

I can't blame him for that. Compared to a modern skyscraper Stonehenge does, indeed, appear small. It has to be put into context for the sheer scale of the achievement to be understood.

The people who built Stonehenge probably hadn't invented the wheel yet. They knew nothing of modern engineering methods and had nothing but stone axes and bone shovels to create this extraordinary monument.

It probably took over a thousand years to build, from its first to its last, and was in constant use for several thousand years after that. Indeed, you could say that it has never really gone out of use, if my visit to see the sunrise with Joe can be counted too. Who are we but the latest in a long line of visitors come to admire and wonder at this mysterious structure?

The question then has to be: why? Why did these ancient people go to all this trouble, dragging these huge stones over all those distances to make a circle in the middle of nowhere? What, exactly, is its purpose?

This, of course, is the subject of much debate.

Was it a temple or an observatory? Is its purpose religious or scientific?

The problem with questions like these is that they seek to divide the world according to modern concepts. Why not both? Maybe the people who built it were neither one nor the other, but both. Astronomer-priests, perhaps. Engineering-magicians.

What is clear is that whoever was responsible for it may have understood some very remarkable things. For example, if the work of the Scottish engineer Alexander Thom is right, then it was built using a unit of measurement (the so-called "Megalithic Yard") which turns out to be an exact proportion of the circumference of the earth. In other words, the people who built Stonehenge not only knew that the earth was round, they even knew it's exact size.

The usual response when confronted with information like this is disbelief. People either deny it completely, or they ascribe the knowledge to some outside source, such as alien beings from another planet, or to supernatural intervention. What we cannot believe is that our ancestors may have had access to sources of information that we have since lost.

This is because we think that history is like a piece of string. We imagine a straight line from some technologically inferior past to a well-informed present. From dumb to clever, from stone axes to mobile phones. But any clear understanding of the process makes it obvious that it is more like a wheel. History goes in cycles, from dumb to clever and back again, on a regular basis.

So, for instance, in medieval times we thought the world was flat, that the sun went round the earth and that the king had a right to rule his subjects absolutely. We were dumb. The ancient Greeks, however, two thousand years before that, knew that the earth was round and went round the sun and that people fared better as a society when they were allowed to make their own decisions democratically. They were clever.

The people who built Stonehenge, over five thousand years ago, only had stone axes. But they knew the size of the earth. They lived in wooden huts and cooked food on an open fire. But they understood how to measure the stars.

Meanwhile we've invented TV, we have mobile phones and SatNav and we fly all over the world in jet aircraft. But all we watch on TV are variations of Big Brother, we've lost our sense of purpose in life and we're busy messing up the world for future generations.

So who, now, is truly civilised?

5. Bonfire Night & Halloween

> Then would I never tire, Janet,
> In Elfish land to dwell,
> But aye, at every seven years,
> They pay the teind to hell;
> And I am sae fat and fair of flesh,
> I fear 'twill be mysell.

*From **the Ballad of Tam Lin***

Have you noticed how bonfire night has spread itself out over the last few years?

When I was a child bonfire night was just that: one night when we would gather in the back garden by a bonfire to watch a few spluttering fireworks before we went to bed. Occasionally we might be taken to an organised bonfire party in some large park somewhere, and watch a spectacular firework display from a roped off space, an agonising distance from the source of heat, while zealous fire-fighters roamed about looking efficient, making sure everything was safe. That was never very much fun, being far too safe (and cold) for any real pleasure.

But otherwise this was how it was. Rushing home from school full of excitement and expectation. Baked potatoes. Toffee apples. A box of fireworks that my Dad would ignite with manly glee. Hot chocolate for the kids. Beer for the adults. Sparklers that could write your name in the darkness. A flaming Guy. Sparks that danced like brief angels in the night air. The stinging smell of smoke. Warm woolies, cold noses, and an inability to sleep afterwards as other people's bonfire parties stretched on into the night. And we would watch and listen out of our bedroom window as the screaming surge of rocket-trails became gothic arches supporting the sky.

These days it all goes on for weeks. We have become gluttons for our own busy entertainment. It starts several days before Halloween, and ends usually some days after November the 5th.

Of course, bonfire night is a specifically English 17th century State-sponsored festival commemorating the victory of the Protestant Parliament against the Catholic opposition. In fact it is the commemoration of a failed act of terrorism, in celebration of which we burn an effigy of a Catholic. It would be like, in the aftermath of 9-11, holding a bonfire party in which we burnt a figure in a turban, calling it "the Bin Laden". Which would be funny, if it wasn't so plausible these days.

There are two major November the 5th parties in the UK: one in Lewes in East Sussex, celebrating the victory of parliament in which they have been known to burn an effigy of the Pope; the other, in Bridgewater in Somerset, marks a day known as "Black Friday", on the nearest Friday to November the 5th. The story goes that the supporters of the plot had set up beacons across the country which were to be lit if the act was successful. Unfortunately for the people of Bridgewater, predominantly Catholic at the time, a nearby beacon was lit accidentally, so they went to bed on the Thursday believing that the plot was a success. It was on the Friday morning that they heard the bad news: hence the name "Black Friday".

The Bridgewater party takes the form of a carnival, which processes though many of the West Country towns in the succeeding weeks.

The word "bonfire" may be a reference to "bone-fires", the burning of animal bones sacrificed to the gods in celebration of the turning seasons. Animal bones are full of fat and would sizzle and crack before they exploded. This would have been the prehistoric equivalent of a firework display, sending dangerous hot sparks high into the night air to mingle with the stars, and bone-shrapnel into the crowds.

Although in England we have moved the date to suit the anti-Catholic propaganda element, it is really an ancient festival recognising the coming of winter. Its historic date is October 31st, All-Hallows Eve, also known as Samhain. Traditionally it is the Celtic New Year, and was always celebrated with fire, with apples, and - possibly, in the dim and distant past – with some form of sacrificial offering. Hence the Guy.

It is the night that the dead roam.

In Scottish households an extra place would be laid at table to welcome the ancestors. And for all of you who think that Trick or Treat is an American invention: it is not. Its origins lie in the Celtic fringe. People would don disguises so that the visiting dead could mingle freely, and feel welcome in our midst. Who knows whose face it was behind the mask? Was it Uncle George just fooling around? Or Great Uncle Albert, long since deceased, longing to share the warmth of life with the living again?

You can see why. The time of year smells of death. It is ripe fruit and fermentation, rotting leaves and mushroom spoors. The smell of sweet decay. The winter nights are drawing in, and there is the sense of melancholy in the air. The light is in decline, and the dark is on the rise. In the eternal battle between night and day, the night is winning

The old Scottish ballad *Tam Lin* is set on Halloween.

The poem opens with a warning. The maidens are warned not to go to a place called Carterhaugh because it is haunted by an elf called Tam Lin, or Tamlane. No maiden goes to Carterhaugh, but she will lose either her gold ring, her green mantle or her maidenhead.

Now gold rings ye may buy, maidens,

> *Green mantles ye may spin,*
> *But, if ye lose your maidenhead,*
> *Ye'll ne'er get that again.*

But Janet refuses to take the advice and goes to Carterhaugh anyway, where she plucks a rose. Tam Lin appears, and asks by what right she takes what belongs to him? Because Carterhaugh is mine she says. It was given to me by my father.

Whereupon Tam Lin takes her by the hand and leads her to the bushes.

> *He's taken her by the milk-white hand,*
> *Among the roses red,*
> *And what they did I cannot say,*
> *She ne'er return'd a maid.*

Back in her father's house she comes down with a sickness, and her father guesses that she is with child. She admits that she is, but tells him that no man in the castle can lay claim to her, because the child does not have a human father. It is an elfin child.

She goes back to Carterhaugh and she plucks two roses, at which point Tam Lin appears, warning her that if she plucks any more she will kill the child. Tam Lin then tells her that he was once a human, but had fallen from his horse at the age of nine and been captured by the Queen of the Fairies. But every seventh year, at Halloween, he says, the fairies pay a tithe to hell, and he is fearful that this year it will be his turn. He asks her to rescue him.

> *This night is Halloween, Janet,*
> *The morn is Hallowday,*
> *And if ye dare your true love win,*
> *Ye have nae time to stay.*
> *The night it is good Halloween,*
> *When fairy folk will ride,*
> *And they that would their true-love win,*
> *To Miles Cross they must bide.*

But how will she recognise him, she asks? She is to wait at Miles Cross till the fairy ride passes by. She must ignore the first company and wait for the next. Then she must ignore the black horse, and the brown horse, and wait for the white steed as it passes by. She must lay hold of the rider and bring him down and not let him go. A series of magical transformations will occur. He will become an adder and then an asp, and then a burning lump of coal - which she must dip in first in milk, and then in water - and then a toad and an eel and a dove and a swan. The transformations vary, depending on the version of the ballad you are reading. Sometimes he is turned into a bear, and sometimes a lion, and a variety of other creatures. Finally he will turn into a naked man, and she must cover him with her mantle, and hold to him fast.

She does all that he asks, until finally she is holding the father of her child, naked, in her arms.

The Queen of the Fairies is not best pleased, but she has to admit that Janet has won the right to her own true love.

Thus the girl wins her knight and rescues him from Hell, and her child is given a human father.

In this way life is saved from death, and the earthly from the unearthly. There is a sense of ritual here, and of a charm being cast. It is a ritual of transformation. She must hold fast to her love in all his changing aspects. He has had his humanity stolen from him and she must bring it back. He has been under a spell since he was nine years old. There is something deep in this story, about the return to humanity after an absence, about the faith and determination needed to descend into hell to find true love once more.

The story reminds us of Orpheus, who tries to win back his wife Eurydice from the underworld. It is one of a nest of ancient myths which share this theme, and is a remnant of that most ancient religion: the cult of the dead, the worship of the ancestors, a religion which still has a huge, if mainly underground, following throughout the world.

Clearly this is a remnant of that most ancient religion: the cult of the dead, the worship of the ancestors, a religion which still has a huge, if mainly underground, following throughout the world.

In Romania, on All Hallows Day, the community gather in the graveyard with candles to celebrate the dead. Prior to that the graves will have been prepared, with fresh flowers and a makeover. On the night there is a hushed atmosphere of reverence, as people quietly commune with the departed, long-gone into the other world. Voices are subdued, candle-flames flicker over faces deep in contemplation, and the atmosphere is electric with expectation, as the quiet ghosts enter the world of the living for a night, and share secret whispers of grief with their loved-ones.

The blazing fire has its roots in our most ancient form of science too, sympathetic magic: the theory that like creates like. The fire is lit in commemoration of the Sun, whose waning light at this time of year was felt grievously by our ancestors, and its fierce light was meant to give encouragement to its return. As if the Sun had a personality, and could be appealed to in this way.

Well we can scoff now at such simple notions, while we enjoy the festivals as mere passing entertainment. But it is worth remembering that our ancestors were just as intelligent as we are. And while they may not have understood completely the workings of our Universe (how many of us do either?) yet in many ways they had a greater understanding of our place within nature, and a greater respect for the planet on which we enact our petty dramas.

Maybe they have something to teach us yet. Who knows?

6. Glastonbury Carnival

Within a couple of days of arriving in the town I went to the Glastonbury Carnival.

Actually it's not really Glastonbury Carnival at all. It starts in nearby Bridgewater around November the 5th, and then worms and snakes and shimmies its way through all the local towns over a succession of weekends. This weekend was Glastonbury's turn.

Jude was going to a party. She said, "when you get bored of all the mad drunks you can come up for a few drinks." I never did make it to the party.

I found myself a nice spot, just outside a pub where I knew the barmaid. There was a waste bin, on which I could balance my drink. And then I waited. There were thousands of people about. Many of them had selected their spots hours before. There were deckchairs lined up on the pavement up and down the High St. You could feel the excitement building up in the crowd. Some people were already line-dancing in the street.

I didn't know what to expect. I mean, I'd been given all the statistics. It's the largest illuminated parade in Europe, I was told. Each major float is 100ft long by 11ft wide by 17 and a 1/2ft high, with between 15,000 to 20,000 light bulbs, powered by megawatt generators. I wasn't sure if that was 15,000 to 20,000 light bulbs per float, or 15,000 to 20,000 light bulbs altogether. I tried counting them. I always got lost after about a hundred and fifty.

There were 130 entries this year, including 70 floats. The whole procession is three miles long.

It's all very well being told that sort of thing. But you have to see it to believe it.

I was starting to get nicely drunk by now, waiting for the Carnival to appear. I kept slipping back into the pub for another one. The bar staff were doing a magnificent job. I don't think they had a moment's rest in seven hours or more.

Some bloke slipped in by the waste bin next to me. He was using the waste bin to skin up. He offered me a dab of speed, which I took. Then I bought him a drink, and then he bought me a drink. And so it continued. He was from Essex.

The first figure to come up the road was a man dressed in a hooded cowl with a skull mask dragging a pair of coffins. That's when I knew that this whole thing was pagan. A festival of lights in the dark part of the year. Paganism simply refers to the beliefs and practices of the people. No need for Archdruids or High Priestesses. It's democratic. It has nothing whatsoever to do with religion.

After that it was a brass band, all dressed in Batman costumes. And that's when I started to laugh. It was a bunch of middle-aged men with paunches dressed in Batman costumes, with their spectacles stuck on the outside of their masks, pumping out a rousing show-tune on their instruments. Deliciously ridiculous. I never stopped laughing after that. No once, in all those hours.

After that the floats came. They were, as the statistics had told me, illuminated. But no amount of statistics can describe the effect.

It was like that feeling you had when you were a child and went to your first fair. All the moving lights, the bustle, the rides. The excitement in the very air around you, like sizzling electricity. It was like the Carnival Floats had got hold of that special kind of electricity, and that's what they were running on.

They were pulled by giant tractors, with the megawatt generators trailing along behind.

The images were crass, kitsch nonsense. But that didn't matter. It was all the usual stuff: scenes from Star Wars and Disney. The Black-and-White Minstrels. The Telly-Tubbies. There were a couple of Egyptian style floats, with pyramids and hieroglyphs and dog-headed deities. One Chinese float with ideograms. One Japanese, with Samurai. One or two Red Indian scenes, one Christmas scene. I was listing them all as they went by to my friend from Essex. "Look. That's the third Shamanistic float. There's another Egyptian one." But the images didn't matter. The point was, they were fantasies made real.

The people on the floats were either dancing or standing perfectly still, in a frieze. The dancing people looked the happiest.

One float went by and there was an adolescent girl in a skimpy Red Indian costume jiggling about for all she was worth.

My Essex friend said, "look at the tits on that."

"She's not a that," I said. "She's a person."

"Oooo PC," he said.

But I knew what he meant. My eyes were drawn to her too. And I realised that she loved it, that she was enjoying the attention, and that it was a sexual thing. Sexual but innocent. Sexy. I realised that it was liberating for her. And then I realised it was liberating for everyone else too. It wasn't just girls in skimpy costumes. There were middle aged men and women and adolescent boys, all half dressed in the blazing heat, all feeling sexy too, all enjoying the attention, the make-up, the costumes, the lights, living out a fantasy-world before our eyes, gloriously expressive, radiating energy.

"It's so human," I kept saying. "It's so liberating."

The Essex bloke had brought his partner over to talk to me. She was a witch. She said, "what path are you on?

"Pardon?"

"What path?"

"I'm not sure," I said, looking down at the pavement. "The footpath, I think. Why? What path are you on?"

"I'm a hedge witch and a pagan Priestess," she said.

The funniest bit came when I found myself dancing to *Ra Ra Rasputin* by *Boney M*. The float was a frieze of Russian Imperial life before the revolution. Rasputin was being brutally murdered before our very eyes. It was like a still from a bad B-Movie or a scene from a melodrama. I'd been dancing and laughing through the entire procession, jiggling away non-stop. But I was jiggling away even more now, with the sheer absurdity of the moment. No matter how crass the music, no matter how idiotic the floats, it was all so funny. There was a young woman dancing on the pavement in front of me. Everyone was dancing. I said, "you realise what we're dancing to, don't you?"

"Yeah," she said, "Boney M."

"Ra Ra Rasputin, Russia's greatest love-machine," I sang, joining in.

I don't remember much after that. I think I must have reached enlightenment.

7. Ranters Lane

> Behold, behold, he is now risen with a witness, to
> save Zion with vengeance, or to confound and
> plague all things into himself; who by his mighty
> angel is proclaiming (with a loud voice) that sin and
> transgression is finished and ended, and everlasting
> righteousness be brought in with most terrible
> earth-quakes and heaven-quakes, and with signs
> and wonders following.
>
> **A Fiery Flying Roll: A Word
> from the Lord to all the
> Great Ones of the Earth**.
> Abeizer Coppe, London 1650.

I've been looking for a word. It is something like "sacred". It is the idea of something being set-aside as special, or holy: separated from the everyday world by some particular quality or by mutual agreement. The word could be "sacrament": the notion of ordinary things acquiring a spiritual significance. Or "sanctification", the process of becoming holy. But it isn't quite any of these. The problem with all of these words is their association with religion and with the particular religious quality of holiness, and the word I am looking for does not denote holiness as such. Sometimes, indeed, it can mean its exact opposite.

No. The word I'm looking for is slightly more down-to-earth than that. It's spiritual, but not necessarily religious. It has something to do with the idea of creating a space, of setting aside that space for some special ritual activity. So, for example, at Christmas, during the ritual Mummer's plays in the Medieval period, the players would create a circle, perhaps by marking it out with a stick on the ground, or just making a circle in the air. They would enter that circle, and then it was understood by everyone watching that everything that happened within that circle had its own significance. It was outside of ordinary reality.

So Jack-the-Lad or Johnny Goodfellow would enter the circle and become St George, say, or Father Christmas or the Dragon. The characters would fight in that circle. The characters would die in that circle and come to life again, and it would carry ritual significance beyond the circle. The actor, meanwhile, would leave the circle and just become himself again.

But this isn't quite it either. We are all familiar with this process, since it is the same one that allows us to suspend our disbelief long enough to watch a play or a movie or our favourite soap and to get some kind of vicarious pleasure out of it. We know the characters aren't real, and that the actors are just actors, but we suspend our disbelief long enough to allow the plot to take on some semblance of reality, so that when the character suffers, we suffer with him, when he is elated, we are elated too, when he mourns, we mourn, and when he dies we too can feel the grief of the moment.

I still haven't found the word. I know it exists. What I am looking for is a word to describe Christmas.

So, yes, we set aside Christmas as special. We circle it around and make it different from other days. But it's not holy. It's like holy but not quite. It carries a special quality, an atmosphere if you like. There is a reverence associated with it. It is full of ritual significance. But it is not a religious thing, or not in the way that religious people would have us believe. Yes, it is the day of Jesus' birth, but it is also the day of Mithras' birth. Mithras is the sun. It is the day of the divine child, the day of the rebirth of the sun, associated with the midwinter solstice. It is the day when the sun begins to move again after it has stood still in the heavens for three days during the solstice period. So it is the day that the light returns, when the first vestiges of light are coming back after the darkest time of the year. And we light fires and candles and fairy-lights and Yule logs in commemoration of that, in order to encourage it maybe, as a kind of sympathetic magic. It is a very ancient festival indeed.

And we eat, of course, and we drink. It is a feast. A feast of plenty in the lean period. A feast of preserved foods, of brandy-soaked fruit and Christmas cake and rich, sultry, dark things. A day of drinking and feasting and pleasure. A day of excess. A day of ritual fecundity, bringing in the greenery from outside, with mistletoe as one of its symbols (surely representative of drops of sperm) and with kissing as its purpose.

And who doesn't like kissing?

In the Medieval period it was ruled over by the Lord of Misrule or the Abbot of Unreason who would turn everything upside down for the twelve days of Christmas in febrile acts of buffoonery, making the Lords servants and the servants Lords, and inverting the common order of things.

In Roman times it was the Saturnalia, the ancient festival of Saturn, celebrated for seven days from the 19th of December (thus including both Christmas and the solstice): a time of freedom from restraint, of merrymaking, of fun, of riot and debauchery, of alcohol and sex. Not a lot different from today, in fact.

The Saturnalia involved a school holiday, the giving of gifts and a market. There was a banquet in which the social hierarchy was reversed: the slaves were served by the masters and special clothes were worn.

The Nordic and Germanic Yule also involved a great feast. The peasants attended the temple bringing with them gifts of food and ale. As long as the ale lasted the feast would continue, sometimes for several days and nights. Trees were decorated and brought indoors, along with other greenery, including holly branches, candles were lit and presents were given.

One of the Norse sagas refers to Yule as "a time of greatest mirth and joyance among men."

Amongst the Celts it represented the day set-aside from the thirteen-months-of-twenty-eight-days calendar they practiced. Thirteen times twenty eight equals three hundred and sixty four, which is one day short of a year. The extra day was a special day all by itself, was noted as the day of the divine child, and took place on the 25th of December. At least according to Robert Graves it did, though I must admit you can't always trust him. But this is why, according to some authorities, the ancient Brits took to Christianity so well and so early: because they already had a notion similar in their own religious tradition - and why the early Christians (canny politicians that they were) adopted it as the sacred day of their own divine child.

And there is, indeed, something magical about the notion: of God being born on the Earth, being born in a stable, amongst the lowly creatures, of the poorest people, a carpenter and his young wife. I can still feel the resonance of all that, a kind of shimmering quality, particularly in the words of *"Mary's Boy-Child"*, a song I loved as a child.

> *Hark, now hear the angels sing, a new king born today,*
> *And man will live for evermore, because of Christmas Day.*
> *Mary's boy child Jesus Christ, was born on Christmas Day.*

It is still very special.

I almost found the word there, by the way. It was on the tip of my tongue, and then it faded again. It lies somewhere between the two words, "magical" and "resonance" (with a bit of "shimmering" thrown in), that I eventually selected.

But it is much more ancient than this, of course. It goes back, back, right back, to the very dawn of human history, to the earliest periods we have evidence for, to the time of the great monuments, of Stonehenge and Avebury.

A few years ago I went to see my old friend, the archaeologist Michael Parker-Pearson, at Durringdon Walls near Amesbury in Wiltshire, where he was conducting a dig. In case you don't know it, Durringdon Walls is the sister circle to Stonehenge, only about five or six miles away as the crow flies, and connected to it by the river Avon, which snakes its way past both monuments. It is where Woodhenge is situated; and, in fact, Woodhenge is really part of the same complex. If you stand on Woodhenge looking North to North East out over the landscape you will see what appears to be a large crescent hill, on which houses are built. In fact it is not a hill. It is a henge, entirely man-made, raised over many years by these ancient people with their antler picks and ox-shoulder spades, the largest henge in Britain. But whereas Stonehenge is orientated to the mid-summer solstice, Durringdon Walls is orientated to the mid-winter solstice. And Mike showed me what they found there: a huge fire, layers and layers, year after year, where whoever visited there or lived there, in the days when Stonehenge was being built, would roast pig. So there were layers of reddened soil and charcoal riddled with charred pig-bones. That was what they got up to. They overdosed on pig-meat, no doubt washed down with large quantities of alcohol. This is almost certainly the case. The people who built Stonehenge and Durringdon Walls are known by archaeologists as "the Beaker People", as a consequence of the large quantities of decorated beakers they left behind. It's the beakers that define them, and it's what they put in those beakers that matters. Personally I think it had to have been something other than water.

So there you have it: the origins of Christmas in a pig-eating alcohol fest of vast and extraordinary proportions, taking place in the Neolithic period, at the mid-winter solstice, when the sun stood still in the sky for three days, and huge fires were lit to encourage it to move again.

So, anyway, what all this amounts to is an introduction to the story of what happened to me at Christmas in 2005.

But first I have to go on another excursion, another diversion, by way of the Ranters, if you are to get the true significance of all of this.

Hence the quote from Abeizer Coppe, above, which opens this tale.

Those of you who know me will know that I am obsessed by the Ranters.

They were a sort of anarchist spiritual cult who flourished, briefly, in the period of the interregnum between the end of the English Civil War and the restoration of Charles II in 1660. They were Christians, but they took on a particularly radical form of Christianity known as antinomianism. "Antinomian" means "against the law". It refers to the doctrine of free grace, by which it is understood that Jesus came to overthrow the law, to forgive our sins and that therefore, we cannot sin any more.

It's more complex than this, of course: but that's its essence, in a nutshell.

The Ranters were the extreme left-wing, as it were, of this form of Christianity, the extreme left-wing of what would later become the Quaker movement, who considered themselves so free of sin that they would happily blaspheme in the Lord's name, would drink, smoke, rant, sing, dance, whore, eat, indulge, with absolute abandon, because, in their terms, everything is sacred. Everything is from God.

The quote from Abeizer Coppe gives you a flavour of the philosophy - "his mighty angel is proclaiming (with a loud voice) that sin and transgression is finished and ended".

The "word" to "the Great Ones" is a political warning. The Great Ones are the great and the good, the wealthy, the titled, the men of property, that the Lord will bring down, will level.

But there is also the notion that we are ALL God. That God exists in all of us. Hence Coppe's amusing repetition of the term "My most excellent Majesty (in me)" and "mine own Almightiness (in me)". It is the brackets (in me) which he repeats over and over in the text which is amusing: just in case you don't get the point. Coppe's God is Coppe, or some form of Coppe, some essence of Coppe (in Coppe) who utterly transforms the world, and Coppe, by his presence.

The Quakers would address each other as "Friend", hence their name: "The Society of Friends." The Ranters, however, called each other "Fellow Creature."

"Hail Fellow Creature!"

I wish they would come back and we could all call each other by that title again. It says everything that needs to be said about our condition on this Earth.

So there you have it: a sort of pantheist, ecstatic, radical-political, levelling democratic Christianity.

I first picked up on it reading Christopher Hill's great book, *The World Turned Upside Down* back in the 70s, and I've been following up on it ever since. As soon as I read that book, I knew that I was a Ranter.

The term "The World Turned Upside Down", which applied to the world of the Ranters, also, interestingly enough, applied to Christmas, and to the Lord of Misrule, who would invert the common order for the season. Christmas was the season in which the world was turned upside down.

The Puritans, who the Ranters were opposed to (and who eventually instituted a military dictatorship under Cromwell) abolished Christmas.

The Puritans were the political party of the rising merchant classes, the new Great Ones of the Earth, and they understood very well the subversive nature of Christmas.

It was the very slogan of Christmas that had helped bring about the revolution that overthrew the King, and, as they were well aware, threatened to continue into complete political reversal, into economic levelling and political democracy, which was the demand on the lips of large portions of the population at the time, and which had to be stopped if the financial and political gains of the merchant classes were to be consolidated into a state political system. It wasn't only the Ranters that were challenging the state. There were all sorts of cults and political and spiritual ideas stirring in the minds and hearts of the population at this time, and threatening to transform the world forever.

So, on with the tale.

As you may know, I am a postman, part time.

I do this to keep the roof over my head, to pay for food and warmth and electricity, and for the time I need to keep writing.

Christmas is the busiest time for postmen. There is a lot of overtime available.

One of the jobs we do is a form of county-wide sorting. A lot of mail gets mislaid. The sorting machines can't cope. So they bring in the ordinary post-person to sort it out by hand.

Thus it was, in 2005, that I was throwing letters into slots.

What we had to do was to read the postcode, and then throw the letter into a slot with that postcode above it. It is mind-numbingly dreary work, but essential, if you are to get your Christmas mail on time.

Some of the mail has been mis-sorted completely, so we are getting letters from all over the country. We throw this into a slot which is called "missorts".

And it was while I was doing this, just before Christmas that year, that a certain letter passed through my hands.

It was addressed to Zion Barn, Ranters Lane.

I looked at it and laughed. There's a name to conjure with, I thought. And I threw it into the missorted slot and forgot about it.

It wasn't until Christmas day that the full significance of that letter that had accidentally passed through my hands struck me.

As I began by saying: there is something about Christmas. We set it aside. It has a resonance, a quality, that imbues it with special meaning. We dress up for it. We eat a special meal. We associate it with profound things, like "peace on earth" and "good will to all men". It has emotional power, spiritual significance. It has its roots deep in history. From the Christmas dinner table, indeed, we send out messages of hope and reconciliation throughout the world.

- Help me: I'm still trying to find that word.

It is a Christian thing. It is a Northern thing. It is a pagan thing. It is a Celtic thing. It is a European thing. It is a human thing. You cannot ignore it. It is in the very air you breath on that day. In the atmosphere. In the psycho-spiritual atmosphere as it were, in the very soul of the people. It is sacred and profane. Spiritual. Mundane. High. Low. The sacrament of a sanctified meal. A meal in which we remember those without food. A home from which we remember the homeless. A welcome to strangers. The clinking of glasses. A toast raised on high. An offering to the gods. An offering to the sun. A sacred moment in time. A wish. A fulfilment. A hope. A transformation. A resolution. A charm.

So, then, it is Christmas morning and I am dressing up to go to lunch with my Mum and Dad. I have on my best shirt, my silver cuff-links that belonged to my Dad, with a yin and yang symbol on them, and a gold watch that belonged to my Granddad, and which makes me feel like I am part of a lineage, and there is something emotional in me.... maybe the cufflinks, maybe the watch, maybe just the moment.... maybe because it's Christmas.... something deep, profound... when it strikes me with all the force of God.... like a finger pointing down to me through history.... like a beam of light shimmering across the ocean.... like a spiritual message, just for me.... that letter.... that letter, I think.... no one in the entire world at that moment.... no one but me.... could have understood its message....

Bang!

It's like someone has struck me directly on the forehead.

Of all the postmen in all the world, that letter had to pass through my hands.

Zion Barn. Ranters Lane.

Who else could have understood it?

It's like a clue left in history, in a place name, the solution to a puzzle.

None of this is very logical. Bear with me. This is not a logical tale.

I kept thinking it was a message from God. That's all I could think. It's a message from God. But how was this possible? It was as if God was selecting me, at that moment, of all the people in the world, for some special attention. Of all the people, I kept thinking. Of all the people...

As if all of these historical events - the English Civil War, the Ranters, the Diggers, the Levellers – had conspired to address me at that moment, through a letter which had passed through my hands, and whose significance was only just becoming apparent ...

Of all the people....

It was like there was a presence in the room with me, an immanence, in the very fabric of being, like God was whispering in my ear at that moment, and that I had been selected....

Of all the people...

For a particular task. A calling.

I had no idea what the task was. Still don't.

I also know that this doesn't make sense, and, indeed, knew it at the time. It was a letter, that's all. Actually a Christmas card. There was an address, and as a postman there was a reasonable chance that I would have come across it at some time. Even now I know I can't explain this. I'd picked up the letter and thrown it in the slot, noting the address with some amusement, but it wasn't until Christmas day that it assumed all of its significance. It was to do with the lineage. Father's cufflinks. Grandfather's watch. The Ranters, those hoary old crazy men of times long passed, as it were, reaching out to me, telling me that I was a part of their lineage, that I was descended from them in some special way, to carry forth their message. That's all. A moment of excitement, of inspiration maybe. A moment of revelation.

My Grandfather lies dead in a grave in Birmingham. He was a Jew. My Father is thankfully still alive. The Ranters were English, but are themselves heirs to a strand of history which came through the Jewish religion. We call it Christianity now, but in other times, in times past, it has borne other names. They were called The Poor, The Way, the Children of Light. Nasoreans. Nazarenes. The Children of God. One strand of their tradition was Gnosticism – actually the original strand - and the spiritual creed they have passed down to us is this: that we are all God. That God is love, and that we are children of love. That God is knowledge, and we are children of knowledge. That is Abeizer Coppe's truth too. The Ranter's truth. The Gnostic's truth. "Mine Own Almightiness (in me)". And that this is how the lineage is passed on. Not through documents, or historical tracts (these are just the clues) but through the God that is inside of everyone. The God of freedom and justice and hope and equality amongst the nations, of equality between the races and equality between the sexes, of righteousness and righteous anger, of The World Turned Upside Down, of peace and goodwill to all men, of the willingness to sacrifice for the truth and for the good, and for a better world for everyone. The God of Christmas.

All this I got from the thought of a letter that had passed through my hands briefly a few days before, as I did up my cufflinks on Christmas morning 2005.

I've found the word I've been looking for, by the way. It is "liminal".

It's from the Latin, limen, meaning threshold.

It is a word commonly used in psychology and anthropology to refer to a state of mind or a ritual state that exists outside the normal conventions. A state between the states. It refers to the reversal of hierarchies, a state of uncertainty, a state of transformation, a moment of poise and clarity before the great change is to begin.

In anthropology it refers to the Rites of Passage by which boys become men. It is the still time of separation between the easy play of childhood and the responsibility of being an adult. In the Rites of Passage the children are divested of their childish things, even their names, and taken to a place of separation before they are subjected to trial. Having undertaken the trial they become adults. Then they are treated as adults. They are given an adult name, an adult task. They slough off their childhood persona and adopt their new grown up one. But the liminal time is the time between these times. The undefined time when they are neither adults nor children. The time of waiting. The time of potential. A moment of poise between the worlds.

That is the liminal time.

The time of the Ranters was a liminal time in history. It lay in the interregnum between the death of one King and the reign of another. A time of uncertainty, when the world was turned upside down, when everything was stirring, when no one knew what the new world would be like, when everything was up for grabs. The world could have changed decisively in that moment. It could have become a world in which all citizens had a stake. There could have been a democracy, and people were arguing for that. It called itself the Commonwealth, and people were arguing for that too. Look at the word again. It means what it says: Common + Wealth = wealth in common. That's what people were arguing for. They were arguing for an overturning of the normal world and its replacement by a new world, a world in which all men would be equal, and all wealth shared in common, the slogan of Christmas made real. When the Commonwealth was overthrown, the Ranters spun off into their own psychic space. The revolution, frustrated in the real world, took over their souls, and God erupted into their hearts making them all mad.

Examples of liminal beings in the human world are shamans, diviners, mediums, priests, monks, hippies, hoboes, gypsies and artists. Examples of liminal beings in the mythical world are mermaids, mermen, centaurs, sphinxes, ghosts and satyrs. Liminal beings in the literary world include cyborgs – half man, half machine – and Dracula – neither dead nor alive. Liminal beings are often dangerous. They draw us into their state of inbetweenness. They are neither here nor there. They are betwixt and between. Neither one thing nor the other. Half human, half animal. Half spirit, half man, they stand on the threshold between the worlds.

Father Christmas is a liminal being. He exists only for this one day, and is neither human nor spirit, but embraces the whole world with his gifts, crossing thresholds (and coming down chimneys) to do so.

There is something of the devil in Santa Claus, and he is really quite a threatening creature, as the popular song makes clear:

You better watch out
You better not cry
You better not pout
I'm telling you why
Santa Claus is coming to town

He's making a list,
Checking it twice;
Gonna find out who's naughty or nice.
Santa Claus is coming to town

He sees you when you're sleeping
He knows when you're awake
He knows if you've been bad or good
So be good for goodness sake.

In psychology liminality refers to a psychic state of transformation, between the dull certainty of our ego-lead world, and the possibility of creative disruption leading to a more inclusive state of mind.

In Celtic times Christmas day was a separate day from the rest of the year, a day outside of the monthly cycle, a time out of time. On this day the normal rules are suspended. The normal flow of time is suspended. Time stops for a day, to allow entrance from other worlds, other times. It is a time to remember the dead. On this day the dead come back to haunt us, to whisper to us, to bring us messages from other worlds. It is a doorway between the worlds, on the threshold of other dimensions, when we can change our fate. It is the day, therefore of our resolutions. These days we've moved the day back a week or so, to New Year's Eve, but in Celtic times Christmas day was New Year's Eve. It was the day after the old year had finished, and the day before the new year was to begin.

Other gods said to have been born on the 25th December include Horus, Osiris, Krishna, Dionysus, Heracles, Tammuz, Adonis, Hermes, Bacchus and Prometheus. What all of these mythical beings have in common is that they are all sons of a god born to a human parent, often to a virgin, sometimes in a stable.

They are liminal beings, half gods, half men, able to intercede on our behalf. They are the saviours, the redeemers, the ones by whose sacrifice we can be saved.

The Christian story predates Christianity by many hundreds of years, and the Christ-child has many names. Jesus, too, is a liminal being, part human, part divine, part of an ancient lineage. He is the messiah, a being who will lead the Children of Israel to the promised land, the Land of Milk and Honey. The Kingdom of Heaven. Born to a human mother, but of a spiritual seed. Born of a tradesman but of Royal blood. A miraculous child. He is born in a stable to represent his animal nature. Sometimes he is born in a cave. Out of the cave of darkness comes the light. He is the son of the Sun, our Father who art in heaven, the divine light who shines down on us all. He is the son of light who heralds the return of light to our darkness. He is visited by magicians and kings to show that the highest and most erudite must bow down before him. He is a harmless child and yet the most powerful man in the land fears him and loathes him and must commit acts of atrocity to be rid of him. Even the stars seek him out. He is the symbol of the divinity which is in all of us, our own child-soul of immortality, the divine spark of light that lies in the core of our being. The innocent beloved. The beloved of God. The children of God, for that is what we are.

I went to find Ranters Lane a few days later, by the way. It's not far from where I live. In the whole of the UK there is only one Ranters Lane. It snakes along between Cranbrook and Wadhurst near Royal Tunbridge Wells in Kent. In Cranbrook there's a Quaker Lane too, which implies that particular Quakers and Ranters might have found a home here, a place of refuge in this quiet corner of the country, away from London, the great city that spawned them. There's also a Ranter's Oak, which brings a clear picture to mind. These ranting preachers usually gave their sermons in the open air, often under oak trees. So we can picture our solitary Ranter there, beneath the overhanging branches of an ancient oak, with a small crowd gathered around him, pouring forth his fiery invective against all the injustices of the world: calling for the return to Commonwealth, for an end to Monarchy, for equality, for fairness, for democracy, for an end to old corruption. Listen to him. Can you hear his voice? He is making the same sermon to this day.

Stonehenge and Synchronicity

1. The Origins of the Stonehenge Free Festival

The Stonehenge Free Festival started in 1974. At least according to some reports it did. Actually people had been meeting at Stonehenge for the solstice for decades before this. There are photographs of solstice-night celebrations inside the stones dating back many years: to the early 20th Century at least. Some of the photos make it clear that there was a lot of merriment going on. There's drinking and partying and dancing, as well as formal ceremonies.

The link between Stonehenge and the solstice had first been suggested in the 19th Century and from the 1870s onwards people were turning up to see the sunrise. The first recorded Druid ceremony took place in 1905, conducted by the Ancient Order of Druids. Later they were joined by the Church of the Universal Bond, and the two groups continued to hold Mid-Summer sunrise ceremonies in the stones, on and off, right up until the festival was banned in the 1980s.

The festival simply extended these rites, absorbing some of the mythology of the Druid movement, while extemporising and elaborating on them with typical hippie extravagance, adding various elements to the mix, including turning it into a rock festival: a sort of organised camping spree and mass-gathering of like minded people frolicking and carousing in the sunshine while listening to rock music.

This wasn't a new idea either.

There had been outdoor Summer festivals of various kinds going on since the 50s. In the United States there was the Newport Folk Festival, which famously featured Bob Dylan's first electric performance in 1965. There were other festivals too, including Monterey in 1968 and Woodstock in 1969. The film of Woodstock came out in 1970 and became very popular amongst the hippie population at the time. Woodstock had started as a pay festival but had become so over-subscribed that eventually the gates were thrown open and it was declared a free festival. Joni Mitchell wrote a song about it, which was covered by *Matthews Southern Comfort* and reached number 1 in the UK charts in October 1970. There were also various free concerts held in Hyde Park during the latter part of the 60s and the early 70s, most notably the *Rolling Stones* concert held in July 1969.

After that there was Phun City, held on Ecclestone Common, near Worthing from July 24 to July 26, 1970. This was the first of the true Free Festivals, although it too, like Woodstock, had started as a pay festival. It was organised by Mick Farren, ex lead singer with the band the Deviants, a political activist and a journalist, as a fund raising event for the *Oz* defendants, then on trial for obscenity, but when funding was withdrawn the festival was declared free. The bands who had been booked were approached to see if they would play for nothing, the only one refusing, ironically, being *Free*. William Burroughs, the beat writer, appeared at the festival, as did the *MC5*, *The Pretty Things*, Kevin Ayres, the *Edgar Broughton Band* and the *Pink Fairies*.

The *MC5* were a high energy political band from Detroit. Very radical. Very raw. They were the first band to be described as "punk rock" - this was in the late 60s and early 70s - playing fast and hard, aggressive revolutionary music. They sang a song called *Kick Out The Jams*: "Kick out the jams, motherfuckers!" Steve Andrews went to see them but he wasn't impressed. "They were just another band making a lot of noise," he says.

But what made this festival so spectacular was less the concert, than the lifestyle elements that went into it. People came prepared to live outdoors for a few days, so there were benders and the like popping up here and there. Some people made tree houses. Steve remembers walking through the woods at night, and there were people in the trees. They were like wild people living in the woods. Natural people. There were little fires sprinkled about with people sitting around them, with candles flickering in the trees, so that the whole picture seemed to be like a scene from Fairy Land.

Steve also remembers seeing Kevin Ayres with his hair dyed purple on stage with Edgar Broughton. This was a good six or seven years before the hair-style innovations of punk made hair colouring normal practice: "My hero Edgar Broughton," he said, getting all excited. "Edgar Broughton on the same stage as Kevin Ayres, and Kevin Ayres with shoulder length locks dyed purple. And you could see this. It stood out. There's Kevin Ayres jamming with Edgar Broughton, wow!" No doubt this would have impressed Steve, who was always drawn to extravagant visual statements. In later years he began to dye his own beard green, a style he wears to this day.

The first Summer Solstice festival took place near Glastonbury in 1971. It was organised by Andrew Kerr, who had been the Personal Assistant to Randolph Churchill, son of Winston. Such was Kerr's commitment to the idea that he sold his house in order to fund it. Originally it had been planned to take place at Stonehenge, but this altered as he was lead by a series of "signs" to Michael Eavis's dairy farm in Pilton, Somerset. It became the model for all subsequent Glastonbury Festivals, but with this one marked difference: it was free. It was a visionary affair. Kerr was a dowser, and he dowsed the spot for the stage, which was a pyramid exactly 1/10th the size of the Great Pyramid at Giza. It was made of scaffold poles and see-through plastic which blazed with light once the sun had gone down. The idea was they were going to concentrate celestial energies through the pyramid and begin the process of healing the Earth. As Kerr said: "If the festival has a specific intention it is to create an increase in awareness in the power of the Universe, a heightening of consciousness and a recognition of our place in the function of this our tired and molested planet."

All of these different elements were filtering into the cultural mood of the time. It was a period of revolutionary spiritual and political ferment. People wanted change. They wanted change on the outside, and change on the inside too. The Vietnam War was still in full swing, and there had been mass protests in London in 1968. Also the famous Situationist political stand-off in Paris in May 1968 was still fresh in people's memory, as was the hippie conflagration in the United States. The notion of a gathering acting as a spur to consciousness and as a political protest had arisen out of the Acid Tests, the Be-Ins and Happenings of the hippie movement of late 60s California. Everything seemed on the verge of some vast, catastrophic change. The whole world was stirring.

Timothy Leary had famously said: "Turn on, Tune In, Drop Out!" at a press conference in New York on September the 19th 1966. No one quite knew what he meant by it. It was one of those sound-bite statements that seemed to promise a lot more than it actually said. At the time of the start of the free festival movement in the UK, Timothy Leary was on the run in Algeria, having been declared "the most dangerous man on the planet." That gives you some idea of the mood at the time. Leary was a college professor who had taken LSD and become a sort of impromptu guru for the whole of the counter-cultural movement. Hippies interpreted the "Drop Out" part to mean excluding themselves from the limitations of the capitalist jobs market and trying to find something more creative to do with their lives. They were squatting properties and attempting to live for free in London. They were experimenting with lifestyle options. Some of them wanted to get "back to nature", to live on the land in a simple and direct way once more.

The slogan for the Windsor Free Festival, first held in Windsor Great Park over the August Bank Holiday 1972, on land which had once been common land, but which had been seized by the Crown, was "Pay No Rent." That says everything. It was an assault on property and inherited wealth, while being an assertion of the people's historic common-law rights and an attempt to live outside of the constraints of the capitalist economy, all at the same time. Later, when the festival became banned and began its wanderings about the country looking for a new site, it was renamed The People's Free Festival, a name which was also adopted by the Stonehenge festival organisers, who were essentially the same people. Eventually the two festivals merged into one.

The man behind Windsor was Bill "Ubi" Dwyer. "Ubi" was short for Ubique, a telescoped word made up of two contradictory words: "Unique" and "Ubiquitous". Think about that. It tells you something about what was going on in Ubi's head at the time. It's actually a very profound thought.

The story goes that Ubi had had a vision at one of the Hyde Park concerts. He was on acid. He'd "seen" this great gathering of people at Windsor Great Park, on Crown Land, and had understood all the implications, both spiritual and political. He thought it was a vision from God. He was a sort of freelance anarchist and acid smuggler who had landed a job in the civil service. He used a civil service Photostat machine and civil service stationary and stamps to publicise his event. He sent a letter to the Queen, which was responded to in the usual polite but officious manner. It said that the Queen would be unable to attend the event as she would be in Balmoral at the time. Ubi took this to be an acknowledgement of the legal status of his festival.

The festival continued at Windsor over three consecutive years, until August 1974, when it was violently broken up by the police. Such was the outcry from newspapers at the over-the-top actions of the police in attacking what were perceived to be peace-loving hippies, that free festivals were virtually left alone for a decade after that.

Windsor was followed by Watchfield in 1975, a not-very-good festival which nevertheless has the distinction of being the only free festival ever to have been partially – if reluctantly - sanctioned by the government: Watchfield being a disused World War II airport which had been donated for use by the festival by the Labour Government of the time.

It was in the middle of all of this that Phil Russell, aka Wally Hope, had his vision.

Phil was a middle-class hippie of independent means, who, like Andrew Kerr and Ubi Dwyer before him, had seen the revolutionary spiritual potential of the idea of a human gathering. He too had had a vision. He was less political than Bill, but more of a Situationist than Andrew. There was a pranksterish element to his designs. He hooked up with some hippies who had a commune in Epping Forest. One of them was Jeremy Ratter, later to become famous as Penny Rimbaud, the drummer with the anarcho-punk band Crass. It was Penny who turned Wally Hope into an icon when he wrote a pamphlet about him which was given away with one of Crass' LPs. The pamphlet was called The Last of the Hippies and introduced the punk generation to the revolutionary anarchist ideals of the earlier hippie movement, of which Wally Hope had been a part.

The first Stonehenge free festival took place at the Summer Solstice 1974, between the second and the third Windsor festivals. It was a relatively small scale affair, consisting of maybe six or seven hundred people, and one band, called *Zorch*. These early free festivals were less like pop-concerts and more like experiments in out door communal living. There were geodesic domes built of sticks gathered on site where people met together to discuss their various ideas about the possibilities of "the new culture", as the movement was being described. There were lots of meetings. Phil was central to these. He was full of extravagant slogans and weird magical conceits. When he'd made a particularly poetic point he would pause dramatically and gesture to the sky. "Look," he'd say: "that cloud agrees with me!" And then they'd all look up and see some bright cloud formation which did, indeed, in those heady, strange moments, full of drugs and revelation, appear to underline his point.

Later, the festival over, he and whole bunch of Wallies stayed on to squat the site. They were all called Wally. This was another of the conceits, that they all bore the same name. There was Phil Wally, Arthur Wally, Chris Wally, Wally Egypt, Wally Moon, Sir Wally Raleigh, and Wally Woof the Dog. Everyone was Wally. As Wally Hope put it, in the 1974 Windsor Newsletter: "I look to the revolution to rename every citizen with one sound and the composite name of all citizens to be the analogue of the deepest terrestrial vibration so that when we are all called we will all hear."

In a way, they were one of the first of the tribal groups to appear in this period. They went along with the Merry Pranksters and the Diggers in the USA, and the Hyde Park Dwarves, who Phil had had some brief fraternisation with. They were like the White Panthers, but less overtly political. It was much more of a game for them. They were young and innocent, full of ideals and dreams, just kicking about in the park, having a great time while changing the world at the same time.

The Department of the Environment attempted to evict them from their squat and they were taken to court in August. The court found against them and ordered them to move, but Phil came out and announced to the press: "These legal arguments are like a cannon ball bouncing backwards and forwards in blancmange. We won, because we hold Stonehenge in our hearts. We are not squatters, we are men of God. We want to plant a Garden of Eden with apricots and cherries, where there will be guitars instead of guns and the Sun will be our nuclear bomb." That just gives you a flavour of Phil's rhetoric. After that they went back to Stonehenge, hopped the fence, and began a new squat on a new piece of land and the process had to start all over again.

Not much more than a year after this, having worked with increased diligence on the organisation of the second festival, Phil Russell was dead. He'd been arrested and sectioned just before the festival was due to start. While in psychiatric care he'd been pumped full of debilitating drugs. It was said that he compared himself to Christ and that his favourite book was Aldous Huxley's Island, which is a utopian fantasy about a perfect society. Those were the reasons given for his incarceration. After the festival was over, he was released again. He was suddenly "cured". But the drugs had done him irreparable harm and he was later found dead - choked on his own vomit - on the kitchen floor of his parent's home. It was assumed that he had killed himself.

We won't continue this story here. It's an old story, and it has been repeated many times. The circumstances surrounding Phil Russell's death are a mystery and it's impossible to say exactly what happened. There are many theories surrounding his death, some of them very plausible. Unfortunately the time is long passed when we can either prove or disprove these theories.

We can say this, however: that his was probably not the first human sacrifice to be associated with Stonehenge.

2. Synchronicity: the Magic of Imagination

> What are these
> So wither'd and so wild in their attire,
> That look not like the inhabitants o' the earth,
> And yet are on't? Live you? or are you aught
> That man may question?

William Shakespeare: Macbeth.

Synchronicity. It is a word invented by the psychoanalyst Carl Gustav Jung sometime in early part of the 20th century.

The first time he used the word publicly was at a memorial address for Richard Wilhelm in 1930. Wihelm was the German translator of the I-Ching. The word was used, in this context, as an explanation for how the I-Ching achieves its magic. Later Jung worked with the physicist Wolfgang Pauli to develop the idea into a full-blown theory.

It refers to a series of coincidences that appear to have some kind of meaning.

When two or more events conspire by their unlikely coincidence to lead you on a journey, that is known as synchronicity. Some people live by it.

Another word might be serendipity, a happy accident. Or you could call it "pronoia", the positive form of paranoia, meaning that the world isn't out to get you, it is out to guide you to a better place.

Other words might be "fate" or "wyrd" or "destiny".

Fate doesn't necessarily refer to something inevitable, as if the story of your life was prewritten in the stars, and all you have to do is to live it. Rather it refers to a kind of force acting upon the world, something primal and ancient that breaks in on the ordinariness of our lives. You know when it is there. Something happens and it startles you. You stand back from it shaken and amazed. The whole world seems to turn to you at that moment. It is like the eye of the universe is bearing down upon you. But it doesn't tell you what to do. Instead it asks a question. It asks what you will do next. Will you rise to the challenge, or will you fall? Will you be brave enough to stand up to your fate, or will you crumble beneath its challenges?

It may be the word "fate" and the word "fairy" are related, as is the word "fey". The Fey are spectral beings from another dimension whose job it is to question you, to prod you, to lure you, to tempt you, to challenge you.

Sometimes the Fey appear in the form of human beings, and maybe then they challenge you on an emotional as well as a psychic level, as Morgan Le Fey challenged King Arthur.

The word "wyrd" too refers to a form of fate. We spell it this way, with a "y", in order to distinguish it from the modern use of the word, as something just odd or out of the ordinary, although, in fact, they are the same word.

The weird sisters in Macbeth are weird in that they represent fate, not because they are old or ugly or strange. They are archaic beings, like the Fates of ancient Greece; and like the Fates, there are three of them. When they tell Macbeth his future, they do not tell him how he should act. It is hubris, his own vanity, which brings him down, not the weird sisters.

The wyrd is the web of life. It is the vast, all-encompassing fabric of being, which binds us together. It weaves the universe into a whole. We are held together by it, all of us, as one.

In Jungian terms synchronicity is an acausal principle which links coincidental events into a meaningful pattern. One example Jung gives is when he was talking about a dream in which a scarab beetle appeared, and a real beetle flew in through the window at the same time, which Jung interpreted as a sign.

Jung believed that the mind and the universe are connected on some level, that the mind can influence the universe.

The sceptic's argument against this is that the ability to read meaning into apparently random events is a product of the human brain, not a law of nature. But then, you ask, what is the human brain but a product of nature? So our tendency to read meaning into random events is a product of nature too. It is nature's counter-balance to its own meaninglessness, perhaps, to have created a being whose very purpose is to find meaning.

Perhaps the mind and the universe interweave with each other, like the warp and the weft in a carpet. Maybe this is the meaning of the magic carpet of Near Eastern imagination. It is like this: the physical universe is a linear series of complex causal events coursing through time, while the mind is the lateral perception of it, creating meaning across time. The mind and the universe interweave with each other, binding themselves into a pattern.

Thus we are instruments of meaning in a random universe. Synchronicity is not external to us, it is internal to us. It is not a law of nature, it is a choice we make. Does the universe have meaning? Yes it does. It has the meaning we choose to give it.

This might be the meaning of the word "destiny" too. A destiny is a destination. But there's nothing inevitable about a destination. It's somewhere you choose to go. You are not obliged to go there. You could choose somewhere else instead.

So that's it. We're free. We can choose to follow a synchronistic event, or not. It's up to us.

It all depends what we're lead by. Some people are lead by money. People who are lead by money are the slaves of the money-religion. The people who control the money-religion are money-priests. We call them bankers. They are the people whose job it is to create money out of thin air. The theologians of the money-religion we call economists. The money-religion is what rules our world right now, but it is no more than a religion. It is based upon equally spurious myths.

Other people are lead by ambition, or sex, or by hatred. Some people are lead by fear. Other people are lead by beauty, by love, by poetry. Some people are lead by football. Synchronicity is just what you choose to follow in the grand cascade of events that make up your life. You can choose the good, or you can choose otherwise. You can choose to be lead by what is helpful to your world, or you can choose to be lead by something else. Sometimes you can choose to do nothing but sit on your haunches and ruminate.

Some people – most of us these days – are lead by what we see on the TV. There's a whole world of constructed reality there on that screen which keeps us distracted from ourselves and our purpose. If there's a war going on but we don't see the bodies, maybe it doesn't really seem like a war. We don't hear the screams of pain, or the horror, or the wails of grief. We're not there inside the traumatised child's mind when his parents are splattered like wet mud all over the walls of his home. We don't know the hell of it. So we buy all of these constructed arguments about peace and democracy and protecting our way of life. We buy all of the calm reassurances that justify the madness: that we're fighting this war for the sake of peace, that war is the route to peace, that only war can bring us peace, instead of more and more and more war.

The TV screen is an instrument of hypnosis. It flickers at you in a certain rhythm, constant and unrelenting. It spirals into your unconscious. It makes you think you know what's going on. Meanwhile it saps you of imagination. It saps you of empathy. It saps you of intelligence. It saps you of your soul.

So you can choose. You can choose to turn your telly off and go and watch the sunset instead.

My friend King Arthur Pendragon – who believes himself to be the reincarnation of the historical Arthur – refers to synchronicity as "Magic". Magic is an affirming event, a confirmation, as when he went to Stonehenge and asked for a sign, and a black and white bird flew out of the stones and hit him in the face. This was at the time when he was asking the universe for confirmation of his identity. Arthur took that bird as the sign and called it magic. He's been dressed in a white nightie with a circlet ever since.

The dictionary definition of the word "magic" is the use of charms, rites, incantations or spells to influence events; an extraordinary power or influence producing surprising results and defying explanation; the art of influencing events and producing marvels. From the Old French, magique, from the Latin, magice, from the Greek magike, from magos, one of the members of the learned or priestly class, from the Persian magush, possibly from the proto Indo-European magh, to be able, to have power, related to the word machine. Magic as a machine of power.

Traditionally magicians would invoke forces in order to control events. They would claim to whip up rain, or bring the clouds, or make the winds blow, by the force of their magical will. It's the first step on the road to science, as no wise magician would attempt to invoke forces he didn't fully comprehend. Often the magician would work by knowing the event in advance. By knowing the stars he would understand time. By understanding time he would know what would happen. This is what Stonehenge is for. It tells you in advance what will happen and when. It tells you the times of the solstices and the equinoxes with astonishing accuracy. It is a Neolithic sun temple, over 5,000 years old, and yet its measure of time is more accurate than will be achieved again for another 4,500 years at least. That, surely, is a form of magic.

If the magician, understanding the workings of the universe, were to predict an eclipse, say, what power he would have. He could tell the people it was he who had ordained that the sun should go out and make the people bow down before him in fear and awe and wonder. Knowledge is power, and power is an addictive drug. That is why we should never trust magicians.

In our use of the word it works both ways. It's more like a conversation than a controlling mechanism. It involves listening to the world as well as telling it what to do. Magic involves signs, portents, auguries as well as spells and enchantments. It's an exchange with nature, a two-way process. It is reading the universe and then asking the universe for support. It is trusting to fate. Perhaps it is trusting to randomness. It is trusting to the randomness of the universe and then living according to its signs. It is a way of short-circuiting the fatalism of social conditioning by following other rules. It is making up your own rules instead.

Magic is imagination. It is imagining a world into existence. William Blake said, "What is now proved was once only imagined." David Widgery said, "the most revolutionary force is the power of the imagination."

By following the thread of synchronicity we release the magic of the imagination to create new possibilities in a new world.

3. A Midsummer Night's Awakening

There's something about Stonehenge. It's buried in the soil around here. It's carved into the stones. It's marked out in the landscape. It's in the air you breathe.

You look at it from some angles and its just a jumble of useless old stones littering the earth, but from another – from behind one of the triathlons, say, looking out over the sunrise above the heel stone on solstice morning – it is grand, it is epic, it is iconic, it is unique. It is cosmic, in fact. You take a photograph of that and you show it to any one, anywhere in the world, and they will know where it is.

But it's not just the stones: the whole landscape is scattered with forms: with burial mounds and processional avenues, and standing stones, and other great circles. Durrington Walls is nearby, as is Woodhenge. They are all part of the same grand complex. There were houses here too, thousands of them. And every year, maybe two times a year, people would descend upon this place from all over the country and from abroad, bringing their animals with them, their whole families, from every direction, to hold some kind of a celebration.

You can sense this in the landscape. You can feel that this was once a thriving community, full of life, full of action. The humps of the burial mounds lined up in rows, the shapes carved into the landscape, the wide, high plain stretching out all around, all speak of a sacredness and a presence, a purpose. And one thing is clear. One thing we can be sure of. Whatever other purpose this structure in stone is designed for, whatever other activities might have gone on around here, its main purpose was time.

Stonehenge is a clock. It's a great calendrical-clock. It measures out the days. It tells you what part of the year you are in. It is very precise. It tells you the exact moment of the Summer Solstice, and the exact moment of the Winter Solstice, the longest day and the shortest day. It tells you the exact moment of the Equinoxes, the days when night and day are of equal length. The people who built it were very sophisticated. This monument, this temple, this timekeeper, this clock, was raised here, at this specific point on the Earth's crust, to give you a precise reading. Nowhere else would do.

It is an observatory. From here you can view the stars and take a measure of them. You can see the movement of the stars across the night sky, but you can also measure the movement between the stones. This gives you a reading of time. Time is space. It is movement. It is distance. As time moves, so the Earth moves, so the stars move, and by sitting in the centre of the circle here at Stonehenge, you can take an exact measure of all of this. From here, perhaps, in this centre of time, came the standardisation of measure which brought the world together.

The houses they have found around here conform to a type which existed throughout the British Isles. They had built in beds and cupboards, a hearth in the centre, a pounded chalk floor. They were built of wood and thatch here in Stonehenge, but of stone in the Orkneys, where wood was unavailable, but they are clearly the same design. Thus you can say that the civilisation which built this great monument to time was one which stretched throughout these Isles. The stone circles which litter the landscape of Britain are evidence of a unified culture. The pigs they brought to the great pig-feast which took place at the winter solstice in Durrington walls came from many miles away. Thus we can see people travelling across the land, using the ancient track-ways and trade routes, to gather together in this place, to celebrate a common time and a common purpose recognised by all the people of their time.

People gathered here. All of the ancients track ways point towards it. It is too great an enterprise to have been undertaken by only one tribe. All of the tribes must have taken part. Perhaps they sent their brightest and best here to learn the art of the stars and the meaning of time. Their artists, their poets, their priests, and their magicians. Their scientists. Their musicians. Their engineers. Their workers in stone and wood.

Perhaps it was the University of Time and Mind for a great civilisation which embraced the whole known world.

There was a city nearby. The city housed the workers. Perhaps, too, it housed the magicians and the intellectuals, the ones who had devised this great scheme, who had worked out in precise detail how the whole thing was to be done. The bluestones came from 150 miles away, from the Preceli Mountains in West Wales. They must have been dragged overland, or brought by rafts along the coast and up the rivers. Why the bluestones were chosen and how they were brought here isn't known. Perhaps it will never be known. But it is a feat of engineering, of organisation, of almost unimaginable grandeur and, once more, it links the country together into a whole.

Later the sarsen stones were brought. These are much larger, though the distances are less. They were probably brought from Salisbury Plain itself, or from the Marlborough Downs.

They are a type of sandstone, created by sand bound with silica cement, very hard, very dense. It was a huge undertaking to move them. The sarsens weigh up to 30 tons. They had to have been dragged overland, perhaps by means of rollers. Then they had to be carved and raised into the upright position and the lintels lifted to sit on top of them. The joints between the lintels and the upright stones were mortise and tenon joints. The tenons were cut into the upright stones and the mortises into the lintels. The joints must have been precisely measured to fit. And then the lintels are carved to make a neat circle, like the circle of the horizon. The whole thing must have taken decades perhaps centuries, to finish, using only stone tools, stone to cut stone. There must have been a dedicated team working on the structure year in, year out. Once erected, with the sarsens hefted into holes in the ground, and then linked together by the lintels, with all that huge weight bearing down, it would have made a very solid structure indeed, which nothing less than an earthquake would have moved.

The use of mortise and tenon joints makes something else clear too. These joints are normally associated with wood-working, so the people who built Stonehenge were clearly craftsmen in wood before they were craftsmen in stone. Perhaps, then, we can imagine other great structures in the landscape, but built of wood rather than of stone. Certainly Woodhenge, which is part of the wider Stonehenge complex, about a mile away, overlooking Durrington Walls, was one of these. Now it just consists of a collection of concrete posts laid out to mark out where the wooden posts were once buried. There are 168 posts altogether, laid out very close together in concentric circles inside a bank and a ditch. The post holes are sizeable, meaning that the original posts could have been fairly substantial too: perhaps even whole tree trunks weighing up to 5 tons each. Like Stonehenge it is orientated to the midsummer sunrise but, unlike Stonehenge, the closeness of the posts would have made it impossible to have held a gathering within its confines.

So what was it for, exactly? We do not know. But we can imagine. Was it decorated? Was it painted? Was it carved? Was it roofed? How tall was it? Did it, too, have mortise and tenon joints connecting one level with another? Perhaps there was more than one storey. Perhaps it towered up above the landscape like an ancient pagoda, tier on tier, like an observation platform from which to view the landscape.

The whole vast complex, consisting of stone circles and wood circles and standing stones and avenues, took hundreds of years to evolve. There are several phases of building, and several sites where work was going on. Indeed, there is evidence of activity here over 10,000 years ago. Possibly it was a sacred site long before any of the major structures were begun. Possibly observations of the movement of the sun and stars from this vantage point go back many thousands of years.

And there were great feasts here too, great carnivals of indulgence, where huge quantities of pig meat were consumed at the mid-winter festival. It was the Old Stone Age version of Christmas. Possibly it was Christmas. It represented the death and the rebirth of the sun. The sun is stuck on the horizon. It stands still for three days. That is the meaning of the word "solstice": standing-still sun. Maybe it feels like all of the energy of the sun is gone. The sun is dying. The light is at its weakest and the dark is at its strongest. The people mourn the passing of the sun and give encouragement for its return. They light huge fires which burn incessantly, day and night.

The three kings of the belt of Orion follow the brightest star Sirius, in a line, pointing towards the exact place on the horizon where the new sun will be reborn. And then it is born: a new sun. A new king. A new year. A new beginning. Thus time is circular and the old always gives way to the new, which always grows old again, forever and ever, Amen.

And then, on this day, the day of the new sun, in the thirteen month of the year, perhaps the people celebrated. Perhaps they drank. They were known as "the Beaker People" because of the vessels they used. The beakers were of decorated clay. We can only imagine what they were filled with. With cider, perhaps, which is easy to make. You put apples in a pot and leave them, and they start fermenting themselves, from wind-blown yeasts. Press the juices out of these pots and there you have it: cider. Possibly they put other things in the pots too: like psychedelic mushrooms which would have aided in communication with the gods of the place. The psychedelic mushrooms would have been gathered at the autumn equinox.

Certainly they ate. They ate huge quantities of pig meat. The bones of the pigs are piled up in that place, from centuries of seasonal celebration. Perhaps the pig bones were thrown on the fire, so that the hidden fat spluttered and burned, and the bones exploded from the heat, sending sprays of sparks into the air, to make a firework display. Perhaps they were the original "bone-fires". And then, later maybe, they dragged the bones from the fire and interpreted the blackened cracks that were formed as a way reading the future. Was this going to be a good year or a bad year? What do the auguries proclaim? Perhaps it was from "reading" the cracks in the bones that the art of writing was developed. Thus reading the future became a way of holding the past, and time became circular once more.

But then, these people didn't only have one Christmas, they had two. They had one for the mid-winter, and one for the mid-summer. That too is the time of the standing-still sun, when the victory of light over darkness is complete. But in this moment the seed of winter lies, and the darkness begins to creep back. It is the birth of the dark-god, a time of fruitfulness, but also of decay. The people will stay up all night to watch the rising of the sun on the morning of the longest day, to watch it flash its fire above the heel stone, as it does now, bringing its impregnating light into the centre of the circle.

And perhaps that is the meaning of Stonehenge, because if you look, all around the landscape there are burial mounds. Lines and lines of burial mounds, circling the monument like planets in the solar system. So Stonehenge is the land of the dead, the place where the dead are buried, where the most important figures from all the tribes are brought at the end of their lives. Perhaps this is another example of its unifying purpose: that all the different tribes brought their heroes here to be buried, their priest-kings and oracles, their magicians and their poets, their warriors and their queens.

So then maybe the stones represent the dead, and the light of the sun represents life. The stones are in a circle, like a womb. A womb of cold stones, the womb of the dead. So the light of the rising sun pierces the womb to bring life to the dead. Light that quickens, that brings the dead back to life. Perhaps that is the meaning. The ancient people believed in reincarnation, in the circle of life. Perhaps they brought their dead here to be reborn. See the red fire of the sun creeping over the stones, blushing them with its sexual energy. Feel the warmth of the sun pulsating into the dark earth, bringing forth its buds of life. Out of the darkness comes life, and life proclaims life, and no one ever dies.

Perhaps.

This is the Christmas that people forgot, the other Christmas, celebrated from time immemorial, in ages past. Even in Medieval times it was still celebrated, as the feast of the Nativity of St. John: the John in question being John the Baptist. It was second only to the birth of Christ in its importance. Shakespeare knew about it, and populated the festival with Fairy Queens and dunces, with high art and mummer plays, with spells and enchantments, with Oberon and Puck. It is clear from Shakespeare's writing that the mid-summer festival was deeply significant to the popular mind of the early 17th century, and that it incorporated a veritable riot of folk-lore themes in which hidden elemental forces were portrayed.

The term "heel stone" - referring to the specific stone which lies outside the circle, and above which the sun rises on the Solstice morning – might refer to the fact that it "heels" at an angle. Or it might be that it should really be spelled "Hele stone": Helios being Greek for the sun. Stonehenge is a temple of the sun. It measures the sun's journey through the year. It is dedicated to the sun, the great life-giver of our world. It is built to celebrate a sunrise. And in this it reminds us of something else. In some ways a sunrise can seem like a mundane event, maybe. Certainly it is an everyday event. But it is also a cosmic event, meaning that it takes place in the cosmos. It links the sun and the earth into an interlocking embrace of cosmic proportions. We tend to see it only from our own perspective. But did the builders of Stonehenge know more than this? Did they understand the complex interrelationship of the sun to the planets, and of the planets to the earth? It is tempting to believe that they did.

What is true is that they made precise observations of what was going on in the sky and that they could make predictions about it. Stonehenge is a prediction. It is a prediction in stone. It knows beforehand where the sun will be at a certain time of the year. This is the significance of Stonehenge, then as now, that it places us within the cosmos. It links us to the sky. We are made whole by it. We are earth beings, but we are sky beings too. This is what Stonehenge was built to celebrate. This is why people came here. This is why people come here still.

So the people gathered. They gathered at the mid-winter, and they gathered at the mid-summer, to celebrate the turning of the year. They did this for hundreds, possibly thousands of years. They came from all directions, from all parts of the land. Stonehenge linked them, as it links us now. It is the very heart of these Isles.

Psychedelics

1. LSD Refugees

I'm in the toilet, sitting on the closed lid. It's dark, though not completely. The orange glow of the streetlight outside is making a bubble-effect pattern through the frosted glass, and there's a splash of light under the door from the hall. And there's my own internal light too, of course, those geometric flashes of colour that tend to dance before your eyes whenever external light is dimmed or diminished.

I'm in the toilet because I've just had an anxiety attack. There's a knot of tension in my stomach. It's like that feeling you have when they've finished cranking you up to the top of the roller coaster and you look down at the sheer drop in front. A lurching sensation, a real physical pang which, if it were to be verbalised, would come out something like: "Oh my God! Oh Jesus! Oh Lord! What the hell am I doing here?"

Except that a roller coaster ride is over in a minute or two, and the ride I'm about to embark on will last all night.

I've just taken LSD. For the first time in 25 years. That little brown drop of liquid, placed on the end of my finger and ingested some 30 minutes ago, is about to play havoc with my sense of my self.

Suddenly there's a kind of humming noise. This low-down, deep-bass growl sound, like the boom of an organ in an empty Cathedral, like the lowest, low-down bass note on a massive pipe-organ going in and out of phase. Reverberating. In and out. Hum. In and out. Hum. Like that. Slowly and deliberately. With a sort of rhythmic insistence.

It's hard to say where, exactly, the sound is coming from. It's not in the room, as such. It's not in my head. It's just there, at some deep level. It's like I'm hearing the sub-atomic pulse of the Universe in the very fabric of matter, so low it's thrumming in my guts. And then it's as if an invisible pair of hands had taken space itself and was squeezing it like a concertina. In and out. In and out. The Universe is pulsing to a living heart beat.

Now the colours in front of my eyes are circling, shifting, swirling, weaving, shaping, changing to make an endlessly morphing, moving mandala, the colours coming in from all sides now, streaming at me, taking on dimension and form, creating a sort of tunnel down which my all too mortal eyes are staring in fear and awe and wonder.

In and out. In and out.

That's my breathing.

Where am I?

Oh yes, I'm in the toilet.

That's when I decide I have to leave. Not just the toilet. This house.

Downstairs they are playing the *Ace of Spades* by *Motörhead*

> *The ace of spades, the ace of spades,*
> *I don't want to live forever,*
> *The ace of spades...*

I pop my head around the door. Back in control, momentarily.

There's a bunch of people in there, sitting around on the soft chairs and settees ranged around the room. Posters on the wall (including one of Che Guevara). Lamp to one side, draped in a red, translucent scarf, giving off a soft, silky light. Low table in the middle of the room, scattered with bottles from our earlier drinking. No one's drinking now. One person is rolling spliffs. This is the person who'd given me the acid. He's hunched up over the table, concentrating, looking like a big, friendly devil. He turns to me slowly with this arch look, out of the corner of his eye. It's like he knows what's been going on in the toilet.

The rest of the room are chattering in what seems, at first sight, to be a perfectly normal manner. There's a lot of laughter. But, you realise, this is nervous laughter. There's kind of hum in the air. The trip is coming on. You look people in the eye and you can see it: a sort of swirling depth of colour with a startled spark in the middle.

I must admit I'm panicking. I'm afraid that if I stay I'll not be able to get out again. The room wants to suck me in and hold me there forever. It looks like a bordello dungeon in the mansion-halls of hell. All I want to do it to get out of the front door.

There's one man sitting near the door. This is my charge, my guest for the evening. A man who calls himself Arthur Pendragon.

I say, "Um, I'm off. I'm off. I'm going home."

"What about him? Aren't you going to take him with you?" says Polly, indicating Arthur.

She's in her early 50's, an old friend of mine. She says it like he's some sort of a package I've got to deliver.

"Oh yes. Are you coming Arthur?"

"Yeah, yeah."

And he gets up, and we go out together saying our goodbyes, closing the door behind us. Who knows what will happen next? Who knows what demons of hell or angelic apparitions are lying in wait for us on our strange journey home?

In the late sixties, of course, LSD was on everyone's mind. That was my era. I was in my teens at the time. I'd been interested in acid ever since I'd first seen Timothy Leary in a news item on TV, since seeing a picture of the *Grateful Dead* in a Sunday newspaper (they looked so cool, with their granny glasses and long hair), since hearing *Lucy In The Sky With Diamonds* from the Sergeant Pepper album down at Robert Russell's place. *Lucy In The Sky With Diamonds* was, I was reliably informed by Robert Russell - who was an expert on such things - an elliptical reference to the LSD experience.

"See, Lucy in the Sky with Diamonds," Robert Russell said, pointing out the letters as he went along, "It spells LSD."

> *"Picture yourself on a boat on a river,*
> *With tangerine trees and marmalade skies."*

I pictured myself doing just that.

I used to go to a large municipal library about four or five stops on the bus from where I lived. I loved that library. I loved the sense of hushed reverence that seemed to pervade the place, the smell of the books, the air of musty restraint. There was one particular corner I used to frequent. It was full of peculiar tomes about psychic phenomena and the like. I guess it was the parapsychology section. There was a book about LSD. I got it out. It was a case-studies book, full of people's first hand experiences of the drug. They were describing all sorts of weird events, like tasting colours and smelling sounds. Synaesthesia. Visions. Nightmares. Surrealistic dream phantasms. Hallucinations. I guess I thought it must be like a picture show, a bit like Disney's *Fantasia*, perhaps, with cartoony colours swirling and dancing about. I imagined the tripper would lie back and just watch the entertainment as it unfolded on the TV screen of his mind. I had no idea.

I'd taken a few drugs up till now. I'd smoked cannabis at a festival once, and it felt like my body was melting into the ground. I'd drunk some beer and laughed loudly in the evening and then been woken up by a raging thirst and a head full of concrete. I'd taken some cough medicine containing Morphine and watched grey, night-time visions in a detached, headless sort of way. I'd sniffed some glue and disappeared down a funnel in my brain. Drugs did all sorts of things to you, but they always still left you feeling like you were yourself. Not so acid, although I didn't know it yet. Acid is like eating of the fruit of the Tree of the Knowledge of Good and Evil. Once you've taken it, nothing ever looks the same again.

I finally managed to get some in the summer of 1971. It was California Sunshine, pretty well the last of the strong, pure Owsley acid coming out of the West Coast hippie scene at the time. It was a big, orange tab, like a flat square, about the size of my fingernail. I say "big" because acid after that got smaller and smaller, till it came in tiny pillules, the size of pinheads. They were called microdots, and they were always black. That was the only kind of acid in the 70s.

I was with Colin, a friend of mine at school. We got the acid from an older head. "Head" was a word we used to describe each other back then. We were either heads or freaks. This guy seemed so sophisticated at the time, although, thinking back on it, he was only about 20 years old. A child like us. He had bright red, bushy hair and a beard. I can't remember his name. Graham maybe. We took the acid and went out to the park. I was wearing my new skin-tight loon-pants, made of fine-weave corduroy. Straight black hair, parted in the middle, just grown over my ears. Colin was little and blonde, with a similar hairstyle. He was wearing his trippy tee shirt.

We were walking through the park when it hit. When I say "hit" I mean that literally. It was like a blow to the temple, and then, there I was, catapulted into a different world. It was so disorientating I felt I'd lost my balance. We were walking up a slight incline through some clumps of grass. Only now the clumps seemed like vast tracts of untamed jungle, and I was trying to make my way through them. The rise was suddenly mountainous. I think I actually did lose my balance, and had to grab hold of Colin's arm for support, only he was as unbalanced as me. We were holding onto each other, wobbling. And there was a strange feeling in my body. It was like my body had become lighter. It was made of cork, light enough to float on water. And when I lifted my legs to get over these epic jungles of deliriously knotted grasses, my legs came right up. Right up. It was like my eyes and my legs had become disengaged from each other. Like my eye didn't know what my legs were doing. Everything loomed and lurched as if the whole world was made of elastic.

I said, "wah!" Words were coming out of my mouth, only they didn't have any meaning. I was still holding onto Colin. I looked him in the eye. He didn't say anything. He was silent, in some other place. Words were tumbling from my lips in a torrent of nonsense, like someone had opened the sluice-gates of my mind, and all of this dammed up verbiage was being released. I was trying to find Colin. He was there, but he was somewhere else at the same time. Where had Colin got to?

Graham was looking at us, worried. He was standing about three feet away. He'd come on like this oh so cool head, but I don't think he had any idea what was happening. Now he had these two raving lunatics on his hands, one of them gabbling incoherently, the other in stunned catalepsy. Time had hit a brick wall. It had come to a sudden catastrophic end at this exact moment, like a train hitting the buffers. Colin and I were stuck here in this moment of foreverness, on a slope in the middle of a park in suburban Birmingham, boomed into oblivion.

How long did this go on for? Well, forever, of course. Or for a few minutes. In the end some sort of sense floated in through the forests of time. It became obvious that Graham was panicking and wanted to get rid of us. We started walking home and eventually came to the parting of the ways.

Then I was on my own, walking down long streets lined with restless confusion. Colours were everywhere, in every branch of every tree, in the pavement, in the hedges. The colours conveyed strange messages. It wasn't clear whether the messages were in my head, or out there, in the world.

I got home and braced myself for normality before knocking the door. My mum answered it. As the door opened I was assailed by this scent. Pungent, sweet, like slightly gone-off meat. It was obviously the smell of all those human animals nesting in there. The smell of human. My smell. Immediately I was back up there amidst flying lights, reeling. I went into the living room and the rest of the family were watching TV. I tried watching TV too - this little black and white flickering thing in the corner - only I couldn't make any sense out of it. The room was streaming with viscous colour, bending, looming. It was all too distracting. I got up and went to bed.

Later my mum popped in to see how I was.

"Are you all right?" she asked.

"Yes," I lied. "I'm a bit tired. I want to go to sleep."

But there were too many colours for me to sleep.

I took LSD, on and off, for a number of years after that. I learned how to cope with it. Sometimes it was an ecstatic experience, sometimes less so. I was always searching for something, some meaning in my life. I guess I thought acid might help me to find it. The earlier hippies had told us that acid was going to change the world. By the mid-seventies this had become Holy Writ. Acid was the sacrament that would bring on the New Age. It was a new evolutionary step. And - young and naive as we were - some of us believed it.

No one is completely sure how LSD does what it does. One of the explanations is that it works on the Hypothalamus, the emotional centres of the brain, blocking the regulators that censor the flow of information. Normally information is carefully ordered into what is important for survival and what is not. What you're getting with acid is sensory overload. Everything assumes an equal importance. The brain just seizes up, trying to make sense of it all. In this sense, what you are experiencing is not hallucination, a kind of unreality, but MORE reality. It is this, maybe, that makes acid so disorientating, the sense that this isn't some living cartoon to be observed from a safe distance, but more real than the real world; something to be lived not commented upon.

I used to get my acid from Colin, the same man who I'd taken that first trip with. I'd hitch over to Colchester where he was living, and he'd sell me about 20 at a time, most of which I'd sell on. Always black microdots. There was a whole industry in the 70s. A bunch of crazy hippies trying to sell the stuff as cheap as possible. It was 50p a tab for nigh on ten years or more. Less if you bought in bulk.

I never quite lost my mind on a trip as I had that first time, but I was never entirely comfortable with it either. Some people love it. Some people don't. It depends on your personality. I wasn't what you would call a happy hippy. There's something about acid that's just not like other drugs. There's a part of the experience that the mind simply cannot accept. It messes about with time and it messes about with language. I'm a punctilious linguaphile by nature. It really didn't suit me.

But - well - I believed the hype, didn't I? Timothy Leary had spoken to us from on high, as the High Priest of the High Church of the Holy Sacrament. He'd said, "this will change your life."

And - Lo and Behold! - nothing much happened.

I'd thought it would help me with my writing. I was writing science fiction short stories at the time. After the acid I became self-obsessed. My stories became a form of emotional naval-gazing, almost always exclusively about myself. In the end I gave up writing for several years.

The last time I took LSD I was in my mid-20s. This was in 1977, the beginning of the punk era. We took the acid and went to look at the sea. I wasn't all that impressed. I'd been doing this, "being a freak", surfing the impossible realms, roaming in these weird wildernesses of alienated thought-forms for too damn long now. I'd also just come through a crippling depression. What was I doing with my life? Endless days overly focussed on internal processes. I wasn't making anything. I wasn't doing anything. I'd stopped functioning as a person at all. Didn't know who my friends were. Wasn't even sure I had any friends. Stuck in this out-of-the-way seaside town bringing myself down.

Not that that last trip had been bad in any way. It was comfortable enough. Pleasant. But I realised then that it wasn't going to change the world. It wasn't going to change my life. Only I could change my life. I vowed never to take it again.

So why have I taken it, all these years later?

That's difficult to say. I was drunk for a start. I remember it being offered and looking around the room, asking everyone if they were going to take it too? Everyone said yes. Someone bought out the bottle. It was about the size of a salt cellar, with a dropper on the top. He squeezed the bottle while I held out my finger. I remember the little blob of brown liquid glinting on my finger like a polished jewel. It looked so innocuous, so harmless. I'd just drunk gallons of another kind of liquid and the most that would do would be to have me babbling nonsensically before sending me to sleep. I looked at the acid, weighing it up, for maybe half a second. Should I? Maybe? Yes? And then it was just: "oh fuck it! Why not?" And it was in my mouth. Gone, but not forgotten.

I guess I thought I could handle it, and I wasn't expecting it to change the world this time. I'm fifty-something years old. I'm an adult. It's easy to forget just how warping the LSD experience can be. The intervening years had formed a sort of cushion against the sharper edges of memory.

And I was right, to some degree. Being older does help. Once we were out of the door, it was lovely. Acid is usually much better in the open air. The world of nature is a safe, kind place, full of presences. You sense the life-force rustling through everything like a wind. So I was walking home with Arthur, and he's all dressed in white and his hair is white and floating like a mad magician, and he's talking about his mum and dad, and I'm listening.... listening to him, listening to the breeze, listening to our footsteps echoing down the empty streets, hearing colours and seeing sounds, being at one with myself and my surroundings. I'm guiding us home. This is my town. I'm in my element.

It was after we got back to my place that things began to go wrong. Arthur went to bed, and I did a conditioned thing. I did what I always do when I get home. I switched on the TV. This was late at night, perhaps 3 or 4 in the morning, and the only thing on TV was BBC News 24. So there were these images of mothers and children being driven by unnamed soldiers, running screaming from the guns. You could see all the pain and fear etched into their faces: the pain of mothers in fear for their children, the pain of children in fear of their lives. And now that was the world. That was what the world was like. It was utterly, unspeakably evil.

I can't say now where the film was from. It could have been from any one of a number of places. Such scenes are the norm these days. No one is immune from the horror of war any longer. Even children are targets.

Acid works well with the imagination. It works well when you can project your child-like senses into something neutral and safe. Music is nice. Trees are nice. Soft breezes and lyrical sunsets are nice. But heavy reality is like a grinding chainsaw to your heightened sensitivities. Those images on the news were a reminder of how ugly and vicious the world is becoming. I came down with a jolt.

After that I was stuck with this caustic chemical pumping inexorably through my veins, that wouldn't let me relax, wouldn't let me sleep, wouldn't let me be, but which had absolutely nothing to offer. All the visionary colours were gone. It was just grim reality out there. Bleak and drained. I guess I was creaking through the house moaning to myself, waiting for the dawn.

The following day I just sat around. What else can you do? I felt like my brain had been put in the blender and liquefied. All I could say to myself was, "I'll feel better in the morning, I'll feel better in the morning."

And I was right. A good night's sleep did me the world of good. But I'm left with a puzzle, whether to take it again or not. Elements of the trip were a healthy reminder that the world is not quite as we perceive it. It was good to be made aware of the sheer beauty of the natural world again, the way the trees shivered with a kind of innocence, how everything seemed to glow with its own internal light, the sense of personality in every discrete object, as if the whole world were alive, and not some dead thing to be administered and then forgotten.

I remember from my early readings in that case-histories book, that often people who had taken acid would claim to have encountered God. But that's not what it is at all. What you encounter are the gods in the old sense, the spirits of wood and stone and water, the feeling that places are alive with their own presence. There's also the reminder that imagination - that long-forgotten childhood thing - is real and substantial, and that it has a place in this world.

On the down side, you are so over-sensitised that it's as easy to get sucked into another person's unconscious cycles as it is to get trapped in your own. The barriers are down, both between different people, and between various parts of yourself. That's what had happened with the news item on TV. That snippet of horror had sucked me into a depressive portion of myself which then would not let me go.

That's the problem with acid, you're not even in control of your own mind.

So - on balance, and for the time being at least - the answer has to be no. No I will not take acid again. Not until the world is a better place, that is.

2. John Lilly: psychedelic scientist

There's an interesting video on YouTube. It's called "The Scientist: John C. Lilly."

It is the recording of a TV programme which must have come out some time in the late 80s. The programme is called "Thinking Allowed." It has a very simple format. A psychologist/ interviewer called Jeffrey Mishlove is sitting face-to-face with his subject - in this case, Dr. Lilly, the "Scientist" of the title – and asking him questions.

Dr. Lilly presents an odd spectacle. He is dressed in a wide-collared safari suit of some brown, shiny material, and has a coonskin cap on his head, of the kind that Davy Crocket wore. He has sharp, angular features and a little beard and is wearing an earring in each ear. It's hard to say how old he is in the video. He is sprightly and perceptive-looking with a warm, sceptical smile. He could be anywhere from his 50s to his 80s. In fact, he is 73.

You wonder if the costume is deliberately chosen. Dr. Lilly has often been described as a pioneer. You can see him as a sort of psychic frontiersman. Like Davy Crocket, he set out to explore the outer reaches of a brand new continent. His writings are like the reports-back of an adventurer in the New World. He is describing new flora and fauna, mapping new territories, meeting new cultures, learning new languages, facing new dangers, crossing new barriers, in a pioneering effort to give us some glimpses of what this strange new continent is like.

The programme is hard to follow as Dr. Lilly speaks in a barely comprehensible drawl.

Fortunately there is a transcript available, so you can watch the programme, and read the words at the same time. It is worth doing this as it makes for a good introduction to Dr. Lilly's world view.

His most famous statement – which he repeats in the interview, and throughout his writings – is as follows:

"In the province of the mind what one believes to be true, either is true or becomes true within certain limits. These limits are to be found experimentally and experientially. When so found these limits turn out to be further beliefs to be transcended. In the province of the mind there are no limits. However, in the province of the body there are definite limits not to be transcended."

So that is the place that Dr. Lilly is exploring: the inner continent he refers to as "the province of the mind".

Of course he isn't the only person ever to have crossed over into this realm, nor the only person to have returned with reports of what he found there. What makes him a little different is that he is a very rare breed indeed: a man who combines scientific rigour, scientific objectivity, with a deep-seeking mysticism, and a willingness to go as far as it is humanly possible in the exploration of the furthest reaches of human consciousness.

It is worth keeping the statement in mind as we begin to explore his work. Beliefs are working tools for Dr. Lilly, and he adopts them and then discards them as necessary. This is a radical form of scepticism in which even the most basic assumptions about the human condition are questioned. But the strangest thing of all is not so much what the statement says, as the context in which it was originally made.

The first time the public would have heard it was in a book which appeared in 1972 called *Programming and Metaprogramming in the Human Biocomputer*. The book is still available in its original form as a downloadable text on the internet, and, in a revised (but inferior) form, as a book.

It is very dense and difficult to read. This is deliberate. Its first appearance was as a scientific report on research carried out on behalf of the National Institute of Mental Health in the period from 1964 to 1966. In fact Dr. Lilly was the head of a major research programme with American government funding. He had a large department working for him. He was looking into the relationship between the brain and the mind. As part of his research he had developed a very thin electrode which could be inserted into the brain, and had discovered an electrical waveform, known as the Lilly Wave, which, when sent down the electrode, could be used to stimulate the brain without causing physical damage. He was experimenting on monkeys and dolphins. By this means he had shown that by stimulating various parts of the brain he could elicit particular responses, such as fear, anxiety, pleasure, sexual arousal etc.

There is a memorable scene in his autobiography where he is brought before a panel consisting of the various United States intelligence agencies who show a rather unhealthy interest in his work. Later he finds out that they are planning to develop it as a form of weaponry, stimulating the brains of captive dolphins in order to control them remotely to use as living torpedoes, a scenario which is played upon in one of the two films which are based upon his life, The Day of the Dolphin (the second is Altered States). But actually, by the time of the report, he had long since abandoned this area of research and had launched into other, much more unconventional pursuits.

The reason he had abandoned the research is that he had had a revelation. He now believed that dolphins were an ancient form of intelligence on this planet, equal to human beings - "more advanced, but in a different way" - and had begun work in interspecies communication: that is in talking to dolphins. He described dolphins as ETs from Earth. He said, "when one considers that these beings have had brains as developed and more so than humans, and had them for perhaps 50-100 million years longer, they merit the highest regard by us."

It is a measure of how serious this research was taken by the scientific establishment at the time that in the early 60s Dr Lilly was invited to a conference supported by the National Academy of Sciences and the National Research Council. The conference was about the possibility of contact with extraterrestrial life-forms. Dr Lilly's work was considered important because he was already attempting to communicate with non-human life-forms on this planet. It was understood that some of the problems he encountered would be of use when considering the possibility of communication with beings from other planets too.

At the same time he was also undertaking another, parallel, research programme.

In 1954 Dr Lilly had invented the flotation tank – also known as the isolation tank - in order to experiment with aspects of sensory deprivation. He had continued with this particular research throughout the 50s and into the early 60s, immersing himself in the floatation tank in his laboratory for extended periods of time.

Also, by this time, there was an explosion of research into the effects of the molecule lysergic acid diethylamide tartrate, LSD-25, on the human mind. At a certain point Dr. Lilly had decided to begin experiments with this too.

In those days there was a very pure pharmaceutical form of LSD available from the Sandoz corporation, and Dr. Lilly applied to get hold of some of this. His request was granted. One wonders, now, what the American government and the Sandoz corporation thought he was doing with the substance. Probably they thought he was giving it to his dolphins. In fact he was taking it himself.

The first two times he tried it, it was in the recognised way, as it was practiced at the time, with a trusted guide on hand to help him, in safe surroundings, but the third time he used it, it was in the isolation tank back at his lab.

This is where Dr. Lilly's research begins to stray into the seriously unconventional.

In the two years from 1964 to 1966 Dr. Lilly, under the auspices of a National Institute of Mental Health research programme, entered an isolation tank some 20 times, having taken very large doses of pure, unadulterated LSD-25 intravenously, where he conducted thought experiments upon himself. It was the results of these experiments which he wrote up in the form of *Programming and Metaprogramming in the Human Biocomputer* and presented as a monograph to his bosses at the institute.

The basic theory is presented in the title. We are human biocomputers, programmed beings. As he says in the book, "each of us may be our programs, nothing more, nothing less."

It's a radical concept, and in a single imaginative leap it resolves the mind-brain dichotomy. If the brain is the hardware, then the mind is the software, of a sophisticated, complex, ancient biocomputer. There are layers of programmes, from the lowest, to the highest: from the genetic, to the instinctive, to the subconscious, to the conscious, to the supra-conscious and beyond. The "Metapogramming" of the title refers to these higher levels of consciousness. At the heart of the biocomputer is the self, which Dr. Lilly refers to as the Self-Metaprogrammer.

In a later book, *The Centre of the Cyclone: Looking into Inner Space* he is much more straightforward about what he was actually experiencing in the isolation tank. In particular he explains what he meant by the line "beings other than himself, not human, in whom he existed and who control him and other human beings", which is one of the basic belief systems he was testing with his thought experiments.

These are his "guides" which he talks about having met at several points in his life, either under threat of death, or in the isolation tank.

He describes them as follows:

"These two guides may be two aspects of my own functioning at the supraself level. They may be entities in other spaces, other universes than our consensus reality. They may be helpful constructs, helpful concepts that I use for my own future evolution. They may be representatives of an esoteric hidden school. They may be concepts functioning in my own human biocomputer at the supraspecies level. They may be members of a civilisation a hundred thousand years or so ahead of ours. They may be a tuning in on two networks of communication of a civilisation way beyond ours, which is radiating information throughout the galaxy."

It is a measure of Dr. Lilly's radical scepticism that he doesn't attempt to impose his interpretations on them. The guides are always presented as "maybes". Are they angels? Maybe. Are they extraterrestrial beings? Maybe. Or are they just "helpful concepts"? And the answer to this is maybe too.

There are several encounters with these beings throughout his work. In some of the books he refers to the meetings as "The Conference of Three Beings." The third being is himself, of course: or rather he is the "controller" of the "earthside agent" called John Lilly.

In *The Centre of the Cyclone* he describes one particular trip he undertook, with the guides nearby as unseen presences. "I am out beyond our galaxy, beyond galaxies as we know them. Time has apparently speeded up 100 billion times. The whole universe collapses into a point. There is a tremendous explosion and out of the point on one side comes positive matter and positive energies, streaking into the cosmos at fantastic velocities. Out of the opposite side comes antimatter streaking off into the opposite direction. The universe expands to its maximum extent, recollapses, and expands three times. During each expansion the guides say, 'Man appears here and disappears there.' All I can see is a thin slice for man. I ask, 'Where does man go when he disappears until he is ready to appear again?' They say, 'That is us.'"

Later he gives the guides a name. He calls them ECCO. This stands for Earth Coincidence Control Office. It is also Italian for "This is it". Later again he developed a whole complex scenario around them.

In his later years he began experimenting with ketamine. It seems he became addicted to it. He was injecting ketamine on an hourly basis for months on end.

The reason he started taking it in the first place is that he was subject to regular migraine attacks. When he was first given the drug it relieved the migraine. Gradually, by the use of ketamine, he was able to rid himself of the migraine attacks altogether. The price he paid for this were several close brushes with death and his rejection by the scientific community.

He used ketamine on an almost non-stop basis for 13 months altogether, during which time he entered a strange, paranoid world. In this world, ECCO were seen as "good" agents, but they were opposed by an evil opposite, called the solid-state entity (SSE).

The story is very similar to the Terminator films.

Computers were taking over the world. At some point in the future they had developed into a single, conglomerate entity. Their needs were different than the human. The human needs warmth and water, whereas the solid-state entity needs coldness and dryness. By the end of the 21st century Man was confined to domed enclosures controlled by the entity. By the end of the 23rd century the entity had removed the entire atmosphere from planet Earth. By the end of the 26th century the entity was in contact with other such entities, and was using the planet earth, now devoid of carbon based life, to travel throughout the galaxy.

So convinced was Dr. Lilly by this scenario that at one point he resolved to tell the government about it. He rang the White House asking to speak to the president. The person on the other end asked what he wanted to speak about?

"I wish to speak to him about a danger to the human race involving atomic energy and computers."

Needless to say, he didn't get to speak to the president.

These later experiments with ketamine are unfortunate, as they diminish his reputation as a scientific observer. He was several times hospitalised during the period of intensive use of the drug and only stopped taking it in the end after a near-fatal accident, which he attributed to the intervention of his guides at ECCO.

These days Dr. Lilly is an almost forgotten figure. There is something quaint and dated about his writing. For instance, he uses the term "far out" a lot. In fact, it might reasonably be assumed that the expression originates with Dr. Lilly. In his case it can be taken quite literally. He is certainly travelling to some "far out" places, on the edge of consciousness, as well as the edge of the universe.

But we can also see him as a sort of precursor to the New Age. His work with dolphins (which continues to this day), his in-depth explorations of consciousness, his invention, and persistent use, of the floatation tank, his communication with his guides and with other extraterrestrial entities, his encounters with various therapies, all of this makes him the original cosmic psychonaut.

As one of his collaborators on the dolphin project, Jennifer Yankee Caulfield, said of him:

"There were those who thought he was brilliant, and there were those who thought he was insane. I, of course, thought he was a little bit of both."

He died on September 30th 2001 aged 86.

Drugs

1. Drug Problem or Drug Solutions?

- **Reclassification**

On the 29th of October 2003 cannabis was reclassified as a class C drug in the United Kingdom. This doesn't mean that it is became legal. It simply means that, as a consequence, possession of small amounts of cannabis are now less likely to result in a prison sentence; but it is still up to the discretion of the individual Police Authority to determine the exact policy.

In other words, whether you go to prison or not is dependent on which part of the country you happen to live.

At the same time, Michael Howard was refusing to say whether he ever smoked it or not, which implies (to my mind at least) that he probably did. Otherwise, why not simply say "no"?

You may wonder what all the fuss is about. There can't be all that many people under a certain age who haven't tried it. And while for people of my generation there was a degree of deliberate rebellion in the act, for younger people it is merely an everyday part of growing up, like going into a pub for the first time, or taking your first driving lessons.

It seems there is a certain amount of confusion around the subject. Is it dangerous? Well, yes. Excessive use has been known to cause a form of psychosis amongst those with a tendency to mental illness. But then again, excessive drinking and smoking is dangerous too. So is excessive eating or excessive speed while driving. No one is suggesting making driving a crime because some people have a tendency to go over the speed limit are they? For that matter, excessive home-decoration is a known killer, more people dying from domestic accidents than all the drug related deaths put together.

Maybe we should make DIY illegal then? There are probably countless hen-pecked husbands out there who are already relishing the prospect.

Mind you, there may be other, much more compelling reasons to keep cannabis illegal. In my experience it has a tendency to make you dumb. Anyone who has sat in a room full of dope smokers will know what I'm talking about. All those meaningless sentences: "Yeah man, yeah, far out, too much, yeah." The inane giggling at nothing in particular. The long periods of dopey silence. That's why they call it "dope": it turns you into one.

Also dope smokers have a problem with short-term memory loss. They tend to forget what they were talking about half way through a sentence. As for making practical arrangements: well forget it. They live in another time dimension than the rest of us, always at least two hours late, too entranced by the cosmic imminence of the moment to notice what time it actually is.

Well I'm being facetious here. And the fact is that there are serious political and social implications to the continued prohibition of what is, in all other respects, a very useful crop, not least to third-world farmers. Just to give you one glaring example: Afghanistan, once the source of a particularly prized and almost insanely strong black resin, is now the source of a large percentage of the world's heroin instead.

I use the word "prohibition" deliberately, just to remind you of one particular legal experiment back in the thirties. And the fact is, that reclassification of cannabis does nothing to take it out of the hands of the same criminal gangs who, in that earlier era, made huge profits from their control of illegal alcohol.

It's called "supply and demand." Where there is a demand, there will always be a supply. What matters is who controls that supply, and for what purposes.

- **Human rights**

As it happens I never touch the stuff myself, having had my own vaguely psychotic experiences back in the seventies. I decided I didn't like it any more and gave it up overnight. This was after three years of smoking it all day, every day, from morning till night, and I didn't miss it in the slightest, and have never missed it since.

My sincere belief that cannabis ought to be made legal has nothing to do with the intoxicating effects, however. It has to do with the arrogance and absurdity of legislating against anything that grows out of the ground. It would be like making parsley illegal.

There are also human rights implications, to do with the criminalisation of such large numbers of otherwise law-abiding citizens.

Ask yourself this: why is there more crime on this planet now than there used to be? Part of the reason, surely, is that we have made more things illegal.

Most of the arguments for the continued prohibition of cannabis are, in my view, actually arguments for its legalisation.

The fact that cannabis may harm teenage boys, for instance, is an argument for an age limit to be set on its use and, by definition, you cannot put legislative constraints on something that is beyond the law.

Prohibition of cannabis has had the same effect that prohibition of alcohol had in an earlier era, that is it has brought vast revenues to the gangsters, while, at the same time, hugely inflating prices.

I cannot imagine that those who argue for prohibition are intending to encourage gangsterism, and yet that is precisely the effect. Gangsters thrive wherever there is a profit to be made from illegal substances.

This is made worse by the fact that cannabis is so much more than just an intoxicant. It is also a food, a medicine, a building resource, a source of fibre for paper and cloth, a source for biomass and oil, a source for biodegradable packaging, good for the soil, good for the air, good for the planet.

It has a recorded history going back over two thousand years, and has probably been used, in one form or another, ever since human beings first began to work and to build.

It grows in almost every climate and almost every condition, on mountains and in deserts, in the tropics and in the temperate zones, all over the Earth.

Wherever human beings have migrated, there you will find cannabis.

What I find most intolerable is the arrogance of certain people in power, who think they know better than the rest of us what is good for us and what is not.

Legislation against cannabis is actually legislation against nature and against history.

It is legislation against farmers.

It is legislation against our future survival on this planet.

Me: I'm just fed up with being told what to do by people who really don't know all that much.

- **Diamorphine**

Currently there is a shortage of diamorphine in the UK. Diamorphine is the world's most powerful painkiller, used in the treatment of people dying of cancer and other dreadful diseases. The current shortage means that many people may be suffering undue pain and indignity in the final stages of their lives.

Diamorphine is the clinical name for heroin. As diamorphine it is legal on prescription. As heroin it is a Class A controlled substance. Anyone caught possessing heroin can get up to a seven year prison sentence. Our prisons are overcrowded with heroin addicts and awash with heroin.

Meanwhile the British army are fighting and dying in Helmand province in Afghanistan in order, apparently, to eliminate opium production. About 87% of the world's opium is grown in Afghanistan.

Diamorphine is a semi-synthetic derivative of opium. In other words the British army are in Helmand province in order to eradicate something that we are short of in the UK.

This is only one of the many contradictions inherent in the drug trade. Here is another.

Wars are about the control of commodities. The war in Columbia is about control of cocaine. The war in Afghanistan is about control of opium. By limiting the supply we increase the value. In other words, by attempting to eradicate heroin production we actually encourage it.

So - you have to ask - who's purpose does this serve? Who has most to gain from the restriction in the amount of heroin available?

In case you can't work it out: it is drug dealers who gain, the warlords and drug barons. It is drug dealers who reap the huge profits that are generated by turning an abundant and cheap commodity into a rare and expensive one.

What you probably don't know is that for many years the CIA were also directly implicated in the world heroin trade, as shown by Dr Alfred McCoy in his book, The Politics of Heroin in Southeast Asia.

In other words the supply of heroin has been historically facilitated by the very organisation charged with its destruction.

Due to its controlled status, diamorphine is also becoming increasingly expensive to produce legally. This is because there are obvious security issues around its production.

You can't just set up a heroin factory like you can a sweet factory. You have to have a large security force to protect it. So, although the NHS is spending about the same amount on diamorphine as it spent two years ago, the drug companies are actually providing it with about a third less.

So we have a resurgent Taliban in Afghanistan. We have poor farmers fighting to prevent the loss of their only cash crop. We have warlords and drug barons. We have a shortage of expensive-to-produce diamorphine. We have large profits being made by drug companies and security companies. We have people dying in unimaginable pain. And we have junkies on our streets and breaking into our homes in order to get the money to pay for what is, in fact, an abundant substance in nature.

Hasn't anybody noticed yet? Current drug policies aren't working.

- **White Lightning**

So this is my view. I think that cannabis should be legal, and that heroin should be treated as a medical rather than a criminal problem. Different drugs have their different purposes, and most of them are the by-products of nature in any case. The idea that we should spend our time legislating against what grows from the earth seems to me to be the height of insanity.

But there's one other drug that I want to talk about: alcohol.

Now I'm an old drinker myself. I've spent more hours in pubs than I care to remember, and most evenings I will have a can or two cooling in the fridge, ready to open should the occasion arise. Which it usually does: around ten-past-ten, just as I'm starting to get irritated with the inanities of the Ten O'clock News, while waiting for Newsnight to start.

I've also taken, or watched the consequences of, almost every drug, legal or otherwise, that the world has to offer. And what I have to say now is: that alcohol is as dangerous, as addictive, and as life-destroying as any of them.

The reason I'm saying this is that I have just had a direct experience of someone whose problems with alcohol bear comparison with the worst excesses of heroin addiction.

I won't name any names. I'm sure most of you have known people like this. As for the rest, what I'm about to describe can be understood as a particular example of what I take to be a general malaise: the problem of a whole generation of lost and disillusioned youth who, for lack of any other stimulant, have turned to alcohol as a cheap, mindless and meaningless thrill.

I say "cheap" and I mean it. The joy of alcohol is the joy of the old-fashioned pub, with its atmosphere, and its company, with its camaraderie and its banter. But pubs are expensive, and there's a lot of very cheap and very nasty alcohol out there. Specifically there are those white ciders, like White Lighting or Diamond White, usually around £3 for three litres: seven and a half percent proof. That's about 50p a pint and twice as strong as anything you would find in a pub.

Actually to call them "cider" is almost a breach of the Trade's Descriptions Act. If these brews have ever even been close to a cider-apple, it was probably very early in the process. Since then, who knows what other ingredients they've added, what other peculiar chemicals they've mixed in to make the hit even stronger?

This is the stuff that the kids are drinking; and not in the pub, where social pressure can usually keep the lid on the worst excesses of alcohol. No: they're drinking it in the street, or at home, and in vast quantities, and this is real trouble in the making, a real danger to our community.

So you think that a few dope-smokers lolling about in their front-room listening to Jimi Hendrix is a problem? Or a few people dancing the night away to juddering rave-music and being all lovey-dovey on Ecstasy? You ain't seen nothing yet.

So I watch a nice, mild-mannered, middle-class lad from a good background turn into a ravening monster overnight; I watch a young man (hardly older than my son) with good prospects, with a job, a girlfriend and a flat, lose everything in the space of less than six weeks because he can't even look at alcohol without it turning into a life-threatening bender, and I think that if there's a case for regulation of drugs then this is it.

White Lighting should be available on prescription only.

- **Binge drinking**

Meanwhile alcohol prices went up by 6% above the rate inflation in the budget, supposedly to combat binge drinking.

That's 4p on a pint of beer, 14p on a bottle of wine, and 55p on a bottle of spirits. So, now, I can already hear the binge drinkers thinking to themselves. "Fourteen pence on a bottle of Chardonnay. Clearly I will have to drink more responsibly from now on."

Anyone who imagines that this is the way that drinkers think is either self-delusional or stupid or both.

The price of alcohol is NOT the cause of binge drinking. The cause of binge drinking is the discrepancy between the price of drink in the supermarket and the price in the pub.

Alcohol from the supermarket is still very, very cheap.

I went up to Tesco to check. There was a special offer on Carlsburg: an 18-pack for £6.49. That's 18 cans of medium strength lager for the price of two pints down the pub. If that's not an encouragement to drink at home then I don't know what is. Even assuming you were planning to go out, you'd be likely to down a few cans of lager before you stepped out of your front door. Most binge drinkers are tanked up long before they hit the pub.

And Carlsburg is at the sophisticated end of binge drinking culture. If you are really interested in experimenting with the lifestyle then I would suggest cider: preferably one of those white varieties like White Lightning, 7.5 proof, strong enough to turn your brains into noodle soup.

The problem is in the quality of the alcohol, not the price.

The French get cheap alcohol, but you don't see many of them falling over on the High Street, waving their legs in the air and showing their knickers.

Wine in France is relatively cheap, but consumed with a certain savour and intelligence. The French drink from childhood, and have never felt the need to introduce licensing hours or limitations on their drinking.

If price was the cause of binge drinking then the British would already be the most responsible drinkers in Europe.

This is also one more nail in the coffin of the traditional British pub. This from a government led by Gordon Brown, the man who wants to promote "Britishness" and who would have us all taking an oath of allegiance to the Queen whether we want to or not.

The joke here is that these exhortations to patriotism come from a man who, under Tony Blair, presided over the transformation of the British Armed Forces into a mercenary army ready to serve the interests of a handful of foreign corporations in their quest to grab the Earth's resources.

How patriotic is that?

He was also - as Chancellor of the Exchequer - responsible for the on-going sell-off of our public services, most of which have been knocked out at bargain basement prices in the corporate takeover of these Isles.

It's no wonder young people want to get drunk. They've had their future sold from under them. There's been a "For Sale" sign on the door of the nation for nearly thirty years now.

Britain. Sold to the highest bidder. Too drunk to care.

2. Dancing With The Demons: the deadly romance of heroin

> "Restlessness within its very self, dissolved and self-dissolving
> private property..."
>
> **Karl Marx**, The Communist Manifesto.

Kodan is dead. Who was he? He was a man who died before his time, of an overdose of heroin. He thought he could have one last blow-out before going into rehab. It was a blow-out all right. It blew out his life.

It's an old story this. Anyone who has ever had dealings with junkies knows a version of this story. The junkie tries to go clean. Six months off, a year, but that old niggling urge is still there, like the voice of absolution whispering in his ear. And then one day there it is in front of him, for real, in the hands and eyes of another junkie, and he thinks, "well it can't do any harm. Just one last time, for old time's sake." And the deed is done, the dose is too strong, the heart gives way and - bang! - he's dead.

Life is cheap, they say. For a junkie it's worth precisely ten pounds a wrap, with all the inevitable consequences: the degradation, the lies, the hurt, the betrayal of love, of friends and family, the manipulation, the theft, because to a junkie nothing really matters but junk.

It hurts to have to say this of my friend, but it's true. In the end the person he betrayed the most was himself.

I first met him some time in the early nineties. He wasn't really a junkie then. He was just practicing. It was late summer and the poppies were out, nodding on their stalks like little green sages with a secret message to convey. You'd be walking along with him and his neck would rise. "Pop, pop, pop," he'd say: like that, turning his head left and right like a radar dish. "Pop, pop, pop." And he'd leap a fence into someone's garden and come back with all these poppy heads. And then later he would boil them up to make this awful, greeny-yellowy slop. I tried it myself once. I was sick for two days.

But I never saw any harm in Kodan's obsession then. He was the most down-to-earth, yet the most cultured man I ever met.

We were good friends. We talked a lot, about anything and everything, about philosophy and art, about politics and religion, in the pub or at home, as we skedaddled here and there, from the far south of England, to Scotland, his home. We talked to save the world. And Kodan could listen too as well as talk. He could absorb your thoughts and play them back to you. He made you feel as if no one could understand you like he could. He was comfortable with intellectual intimacy.

So we had a bond, Kodan and I. It was only later that I discovered he had the much same bond with everyone else.

I said, "Kodan, there's a fine line between being merely a charming person, and being a con-merchant, and sometimes you come quite close to that line."

He said, "ah, but at least I know where the line is."

It was also later that I discovered that that's all the talk ever was to him: just talk.

Who knows what forces drive us this way or that: why Kodan chose to be a junkie, while I chose to be a writer? And he did choose. He worked at it, over a number of years. From poppy tea to codeine tabs, from cough linctus to "chasing the dragon", from skin popping to, finally, the whole junkie works, the needle, the spoon and the tourniquet. To him this was all the height of romance, like dancing with the demons, like a love affair with death. It was his version of poetry.

There's something else about junkiedom: the lure of the inevitable decline. Because all junkies follow a certain trajectory. Sooner or later, it happens to them all. They even have their own expressions for it. "I'm a scum-bag junkie." "I'm a rob-yer-grannie junkie." In the end the call of chemical absolution is too strong and the bonds of mere loyalty too weak. That's the game every junkie is playing, sliding ever closer to the moment when he will betray every decent thought he ever had, every hope and every dream. Every chance of redemption.

One day Kodan was paying me a visit. I used the word "junkie".

"We don't use the 'J' word," he said. "It's like calling a black man a nigger or a gay man a queer. There's as many types of heroin addict as there are people using it. We don't all mug old ladies for their pension books you know."

He was wrong about that. In the end that's exactly what he ended up doing.

I was also noticing something particular about his habit. It was pure self-indulgence. He didn't score drugs to share them, like other drug users share spliffs or pints, or a line of this or that. He wasn't concerned about how you were feeling. It was a ritual played out with himself alone. He was an S.S.S., a member of the Secret Society of Swallowers, engaged in an experiment with his own body-chemistry, in the laboratory of his blood.

I said, "there'll come a time Kodan, when I'll stop being your friend. You'll think it's about money or something, but it won't be."

He said, "but you don't care about money, Chris. It's not important to you."

I said, "that's where you're wrong, Kodan. Money isn't all that important, sure, except when it's a matter of trust. It's your word I care about."

And I was right. I fell out with him in the end. He paid me a visit and he was lying to me again, from the second he walked through the door. Claiming he'd been mugged and he'd lost all his money; claiming he'd "accidentally" bumped into a friend on the way down, a dealer, and that was why he was late, and could he borrow some money, till next week? And I knew there was no accident involved and exactly where his money had gone. I asked him to leave, and I've never seen him since. That was last year.

When I heard he'd died I was angry with him. I was marching up and down in my living room shouting at him in my head. "You stupid big lunk," I was saying, "you stupid bloody twat." I was still angry at the funeral. I couldn't believe that that was his body in there, in that coffin, lying like a 37 year old lump of meat in its box. Angry because he'd made me be there. Angry at the stupid bloody church music and the stupid bloody prayers.

It was the following day when I realised what I was really angry about. Someone showed me a picture of him from when I'd first known him, when he still had something to give. He was fresh-raced and alive. I burst into tears. I thought, "I've come to say goodbye to my friend." And I knew that I was angry because I'd never see him again, because he'd died before I'd had the chance to forgive.

In the end I don't care if he was a junkie. He was my friend and I loved him.

3. Requiem for a Dreamer

It was in the woods on Tankerton Slopes that I bumped into him, this skinny old tramp with a beard. He was carrying a plastic bag with all his things in it. He sat down on the bench and started rolling a cigarette, clearly puffed out with the effort of getting up the hill. I said, "that cigarette won't help." And he said, "I know, I was just wondering if I needed one or not."

Well he must have decided he didn't need one after all, as he put his rolled up cigarette into his tobacco pouch and carried on his way.

"See you later Chris," he said, and waved me goodbye.

That startled me. How did he know my name? He was this dirty old tramp, almost on his last legs by the looks of it. I couldn't remember ever having met him before.

And then something began to register. I watched him as he laboured his way up the rest of the hill, looking frail and old and already half drunk, though it was early in the day yet. There was something familiar about him. I couldn't quite put my finger on it. I kept looking and looking hoping that my gaze might begin to unlock the mystery. There was like the ghost of another person in his features, someone younger and more vigorous, someone I might have known in a past life.

It took a while for it to click. It was some weeks later, and I was delivering letters. I delivered one to a house which until recently had been empty, but was now in the process of being renovated. The letter was for an ex-resident of the house, someone I knew from my drinking days. That's when it registered who the tramp had been. It was Iain Gremo, a drinking buddy from the old days. That's who the letter had been for.

Well I say, "the old days" and that makes it sound like it was halfway back to the Middle Ages or something, but the last time I saw Iain Gremo was only about five years ago. And he wasn't that old: in his early fifties maybe. Certainly a lot younger than me.

The last time I'd seen him had been in the Labour Club. I'd cut down on my drinking by then and rarely went out any more, but this was a special occasion. I went to meet a friend of mine who I knew always went out for a drink after work. I guess I was looking for company. And Iain was there, and he joined us at our table. I can't remember what we talked about. Talking with Iain was always a bit of a tussle. There was a kind of edge to his banter, as if he was privy to some source of knowledge I had no access to. That was the tone behind his words, as if he knew something I didn't.

I can remember one occasion. I don't know whether it was then or some other time. I was talking about politics: about the exploitation of one part of humanity by another, about the social breakdown in our world. And Iain said, "what about the animals? We are destroying the animal kingdom. Maybe the world would be better off without us human beings."

That registered with me. He was talking from some other point of view than mine, though it made sense. But what I hadn't realised at the time was the note of fatalism in his words. Maybe he was already planning on taking out the human race one at a time, starting with himself.

He could be quite funny and quite annoying at the same time. He talked about sex a lot, with a kind of visceral relish, licking his lips as he did so. And there was one occasion on one of the Friday night jam sessions down the Club when he dominated the proceedings by singing this impromptu song. He was making the words up as he went along and, while it was funny for the first few minutes, it soon began to wear. There were other musicians than Iain waiting to play: musicians who knew how to get along with other people, who knew how to blend in, who weren't trying to dominate the evening. It was a joke, but not a particularly funny one. He was laughing, but he didn't care if you were laughing with him or not. He was very drunk.

But the point about this Iain was that he was still full of life. The old tramp I'd met on Tankerton Slopes seemed to have no life left. He'd aged at least forty years in less than five. He was the living embodiment of Einstein's theory, that time is relative. He was like a man at the end of his life, a man for whom time had already run out.

I only saw him once more after that. This was near the level crossing on Glebe Way. He walked right past me but didn't recognise me this time. It must have been about mid morning, when I was at work. Again he was carrying a plastic bag, which I imagined had alcohol in it by the way he was staggering, but he was stopping to drink milk from a carton. He stood on Glebe Way, on the approach to the level crossing, and he was pouring milk down his throat. After that he went on his way, through the gate and over the level crossing. For some reason I stood staring at him, watching him go on his way. It was like I'd had a premonition. I wanted to call out to him, but didn't. He was even dirtier and more decrepit looking than before. I imagined he must have been sleeping under one of the beach huts over on West Beach.

That was the last time I saw him.

Afterwards I kept thinking about him. What had happened? He was so skinny, the thought of AIDS popped into my mind. I couldn't think what else might have enervated him so much. Later I rang up a friend and asked him.

It wasn't AIDS, my friend told me, it was alcohol. He was drinking a bottle of vodka a day. After that he'd stopped paying the mortgage and had lost his house. So now he was homeless and alcohol dependent too. The descent had happened really quickly after that. Within the space of little more than a couple of months he'd turned himself into that broken down old man I'd met on Tankerton Slopes. It was really startling how quick it had been. From a man with a life, to a man with just the remnants of a life. He'd become a ghost, a walking ghost: a shadow walker in the realm between life and death.

I decided I needed to talk to him and went looking for him, but by the time I did that he was already dead.

I can't tell you when he died exactly. It was last week, about the same time that I was talking to my friend on the phone about him. Maybe even at the exact same moment. Someone must have found the body. The police came and picked him up and took the body away.

I'd like to blame someone, to say that something more should have been done, but from what I hear everything that could have been done, had been done. The social services had been alerted and he'd spent time in a homeless shelter, but he'd upped and left there of his own accord. No doubt there were drinking restrictions and he wanted to drink. His friends had tried to help him, but he was so out of control in the end no one could do anything. The drink had him. He'd given his life over entirely to drink.

I've just remembered something. This was a few weeks back. There was what looked like a dead body sprawled on the pavement just off Canterbury Road. It was curled up on the curb in a half foetus position. It was only when I went up to him that I realised he was breathing and fast asleep, dead drunk in the middle of the day. I was delivering letters and had to get on with my round, but I spoke to one of the residents and suggested they ring the police. I don't know if they did. We exchanged a few words about drunkenness and what leads people to get into such states. It's only now that I recognise that it was Iain Gremo.

And that's it. What more can you say? A man has died. He clearly chose his own end. People offered him help, but he didn't want help. The drink had become more precious to him than life.

People need to remember this when they think about drugs. Drink is a drug too. Drink can kill a man as surely as heroin can. More surely, in fact. The heroin death is a relatively peaceful death. It's like you are going to sleep, like your lungs simply can't be bothered to breath any more. It's actually very hard to overdose on heroin. But drink is like poison. It shuts down the body one organ at a time. It eats at the liver and it eats at the brain. It eats at the heart and it eats at the limbs. Your blood vessels begin to explode from the inside and you die very slowly over a period of months.

Iain Gremo had begun to die more than a year ago. Perhaps he'd decided to die. It's hard to imagine what must have been going on in his mind. It was like a Faustian pact in reverse. Instead of selling his soul for power and prestige, he'd sold his life for a measly drink. It's kind of sad, but he can't be any worse off now than he was those last few times I saw him, utterly drained of purpose or direction, utterly drained of meaning, just looking for the next drink.

Well I say that, but what do I know? Maybe he decided he preferred living out of doors, and it was the sudden cold snap which got to him.

Who knows what was going on?

But the skies have been crystalline of late and the sunsets have been wild.

So I hope his last sight on earth was of one those epic skies. I hope he gave his heart up to the vastness of the sunset, that he took his last breath as the stars began to sparkle over the darkening estuary, and that his soul was carried out into the channel by the off-shore breeze.

Written in Stone

Columns from *Prediction* magazine

1. Elvis has left the haunted building.

When people ask me about my belief system, I always say that I am a sceptic. By which I mean: I neither believe nor disbelieve, but rather choose to reserve my judgement on most things.

Take the subject of ghosts, for instance. I've never seen one myself, but other people say they have. So I can't believe in ghosts, but I can't disbelieve either. I guess it depends on who is telling you the story and what you think they might be getting out of it.

My friend Jude, who lives in Glastonbury, quite often has ghostly experiences. She told me that one day, walking along Chilkwell Street, she was greeted by an old lady on a doorstep.

"Hello," the old lady said, brightly.

"Hello," said Jude, and then walked on, not thinking any more about it. It was only later that she heard that the old lady had died the day before she met her.

It's the sheer mundaneness of the encounter that makes this particular story at least plausible. There's no histrionics here, no ghoulish ghastliness, just a little old lady hanging around in the world a little longer than is normally expected of dead people, saying hello to any passing person with the extra-sensory equipment to notice her.

You may wonder why she was hanging around. Who knows? Maybe it was a nice day, and she didn't feel up to the journey just yet. Maybe she liked saying hello to people. (She was probably a nice person in life, why not in death too?) Maybe Charon was on strike, and the heavenly ferry hadn't arrived. Maybe she was just whiling away the time of day, being far too interested in the local comings and goings to let a little thing like death distract her.

Anyway, she did her small bit of polite domestic haunting for a day or two, and was on her way, never to be seen again.

Another friend of mine, Steve, stayed in a haunted house once. This was in Gabalfa in Cardiff, a few years back. The story of the haunted house had been in the local papers, which were offering a challenge for people to stay in it overnight. So Steve and a friend took up the challenge, got the keys, and spent the night there.

There was some dispute over who, exactly, this ghost was supposed to be. Some said a headless soldier, others the spirit of Elvis Presley (although quite why Elvis Presley would want to visit Gabalfa in Cardiff escapes me: perhaps he'd been recommended it by the spirit of Richard Burton, who might, at least, have heard of the place). Anyway, whoever it was, Steve and his friend nabbed a couple of bottles of wine, and let themselves in.

It was a quite ordinary house, still furnished. Nothing unusual at all. Except that, at certain times, the room would go deadly cold, and there would be this strange smell, like lavender. This is known in the profession as a cold spot, and is quite common, apparently.

Steve is the sensitive type. He knows about these things. Me, I'm far too worldly for that. I probably wouldn't even have noticed the cold spot, being far more likely to be interested in the wine.

Well I'm sorry. My ghost stories seem to lack punch. Steve went to bed, and had a really nice night's sleep. And that's all there is. He says he had a better night's sleep than he normally does.

There was a bit of a kafuffle the following day, however. Steve went out to the nearby shop to get some stuff in for breakfast, and was instantly surrounded by the local kids, wittering on enthusiastically about the house and its haunted status. Later the previous tenants turned up (these were the ones who had declared the house to be haunted) and then the tenants before them. It was this last family who had been the source of all the rumours. The grandmother was reputed as a medium, and used to dabble in the occult occasionally. It was she who would channel the spirit of Elvis and who claimed to see the headless soldier.

So maybe now we know what this was all about. A dispute between tenants. The previous tenants and the ones before them hated each other, and there was a good deal of taunting between the two families, the former calling the latter "evil".

Later again the press turned up, and Steve invited the reporter in, but he refused. He stood on the doorstep and asked Steve some questions. Had Steve noticed anything?

"A little bit of astral disturbance," said Steve, and he saw the reporter write it down - "astral disturbance" - very carefully, in his notebook. And what was it like to sleep there?

"Very nice," said Steve. "I had my best sleep ever."

2. Predictions vs. the pub.

I expect we will be hearing a lot about Nostradamus in the next few months, this being the 500th anniversary of his birth. No doubt the copy of Prediction magazine you are holding in your hands right now contains at least one article on the famous prophet, and probably several more references to boot, this being one of them.

There you are. That makes me a prophet too, having written these words on a sprightly morning in early September, nearly two months before you will actually be reading them. I can make several more predictions as well. I'm fairly certain, for instance, that on the morning you went to buy your copy of the magazine, the sun came up. It will be either sunny or cloudy. Later that same day you will speak to someone in a shop... or it could be on the phone, or on the street, or in your home. You will have the overwhelming urge to drink liquid in some form, and to ingest food. Several cars will pass along your street. Politicians will squabble meaninglessly on the news tonight and within a day or two EastEnders will be on the telly.

This, of course, is the stuff of prophesy. Keep it vague and generalised enough and you're sure to hit the mark. I always laugh, for instance, when the astrology column in my local paper predicts that I will be going shopping just before Christmas, or that, during the summer holidays, I may be contemplating a journey. My take on astrology columns is that - amidst all of that news of faraway events and things you have no control over - the astrologer seems, on the surface at least, to be talking directly to you. It's a comfort to imagine that, out there, there is someone thinking about you; albeit that the person doesn't actually know you, has never heard of you, and doesn't care in the slightest whether his predictions apply to you or not. Let's face it: there are worse ways of making a living. Sometimes the predictions will mirror something you will later have experience of... sometimes not.

The danger lies in taking any of it too seriously.

There's something I refer to as the "Macbeth Syndrome": the temptation one always has to set about fulfilling a prophesy.

Macbeth, if you remember, is hailed by the mysterious witches on the heath as Thane of Glamis, Thane of Cawdor, and king thereafter. He is already Thane of Glamis, and soon learns he has become the Thane of Cawdor, and so sets about to make the third prediction come true; and in this lies his downfall, his tragedy. You want to take him to one side and, putting your arms solicitously around his shoulders, say, "hang on a minute there Macca, my old mate, why don't you just lie back and let it happen? If it's going to happen, it's going to happen, and there's no point in getting yourself all worked up about it. Just make sure you keep your missus away from the knives."

I remember hearing someone on the radio in August 1999 who, convinced that the forthcoming eclipse was the one predicted in Revelations that presaged the onset of the dreaded apocalypse, was on his way home to commit suicide. He had the saddest voice, full of tremulous despair and quiet resignation. I can only hope the poor man had a few friends who could dissuade him from his awful plan and take him down the pub instead. One apocalyptic prophesy is much the same as another, and we may as well be enjoying ourselves if one of them does, finally, come true.

If you remember, there was also a lot of fuss about a rogue comet that Nostradamus had predicted would hit the Earth in the July of that year. When the comet never actually happened, all the Nostradamus apologists were saying that he wasn't actually predicting a comet at all: he was predicting the release of the film, Deep Impact, having presciently mistaken the special effects for reality (naturally enough for a sixteenth century seer, unused to the filmic arts). This is called being wise after the event and is one of the reasons I can't forgive the man for coddling together such a grim array of irritatingly fuzzy verses. I mean, most of them are so vague and indecipherable, you could make them fit any event you like.

He is also constantly predicting Muslim invasions of Europe, when any reading of history will quickly point out that it is almost invariably the other way round. I think the people of Iraq and Afghanistan might have a thing or two to say about that.

As for me, I seem to be suffering from a dose of the Macbeth Syndrome myself right now, having just had my stars read by a friend of mine. I like to hedge my bets, you see. One of the things he told me was that, around September time, I would be - to use his phrase - "stepping into danger", and that the experience would be the making of me. I would be given the choice between a bright and successful future, or remaining a mangy dog. Well, I'm not sure if the mangy dog epithet suits me all that well. In fact it is such a dismal image I can only hope that it is an entirely temporary phenomenon. So I'd best step into danger then.

And that's the whole problem, of course: how much the predictive arts are a real keyhole into the future, and how much we feel compelled to make them come true.

Maybe I should start to listen to my own advice and, wrapping my arms metaphorically around my own shoulders, take myself down the pub, where I will drink a toast to Nostradamus, Macbeth, and to all mangy dogs everywhere.

And that's one prediction, at least, that I won't mind fulfilling.

3. Bed and Breakfast Philosopher.

You probably realise by now that I am slightly down on the New Age and some of its pretensions. It's not that I object to New Age people as such: it's just that some of the philosophy seems inherently self-reverential and smug.

This was illustrated for me when I stayed at a New Age bed and breakfast establishment once.

You may wonder what difference there is between a New Age B'n'B and the ordinary kind. Well this one had muesli for breakfast, was entered through a courtyard with tinkling windchimes hanging from the trees, smelt of joss sticks and patchouli oil, had printed homilies all over the kitchen walls (like: "arms are for hugging" and "dogs are angels with paws") and defined itself very specifically as a "bed and breakfast with a sacred space".

Not that I ever found what the sacred space was for, exactly, or even where it was.

The proprietors also had a habit of addressing you in a kind of meaningful whisper, with an air of knowingness in their tone, as if they were privy to some great secret that us ordinary mortals were too stupid or too undeveloped to ever hope to understand. There were two of them: a middle aged woman (obviously the boss) and a younger man, probably in his thirties, with a shaven head and a medallion around his neck. The house was large, well-decorated, with a huge TV and sound system in the living room, and a Range Rover parked up in the drive.

So we were all sitting in the living room, myself, the proprietors, and all the guests - about half a dozen of them: earnest, sincere people taking a well-earned rest from their spiritual exertions - and the conversation was circulating amiably and politely, as it does when a bunch of strangers find themselves sharing the same room. It was also immediately obvious that the proprietors saw themselves less as landlady and landlord of a bed and breakfast establishment, and more as spiritual guides, or higher beings, with a profound message to convey. This was evident, not only in their tone, but also in the words they spoke.

For instance, at one point the landlady started talking about angels. "Watch out," she said jocularly, "my wings are starting to show." She thought this was very funny, and tittered at her own wit. Meanwhile I was starting to get seriously irritated with the air of self-satisfaction that seemed to be wafting about the room like incense smoke.

At the same time, the landlord was talking to one of the other guests, a very attractive American woman in her early twenties. She was clearly troubled, and was talking about herself, her life and her confusions. It seemed she was engaged to be married, but that she was having second thoughts. Which is why she was here in this sacred B'n'B, no doubt: in the hope of finding some answers.

The landlord was nodding sagely with a look of studied sincerity in his eyes.

"Hmmm," he mused, lightly tapping his fingers to his lips in an attitude of prayer, like a deep thinker contemplating the mysteries of the Universe. He paused and looked her straight in the eye.

We were obviously due for a moment of enlightenment, for words of startling profundity and wisdom.

"Life is what you make it," he said.

Pardon? Did I hear that right? I had to bite my lip to stop myself from screaming.

This was at the time that the massacres were happening in Rwanda, when all of those tens of thousands of people were being butchered by deranged tribesmen with machetes. So - you have to ask - was life what they made it? This is not to speak of the rest of the world: of all the victims of terror and oppression, the poor, the hungry, the ill-housed, the sick, the dispossessed, the exploited, the grieving mothers and fathers of all the dead children of the world. Is life what they make it too?

See what I mean about smugness? Not just smug, but bland and virtually meaningless.

So here we are, in this comfortable living room, in the comfortable west, with a comfortable TV in the corner, and a comfortable Range Rover parked up in the drive, with a comfortable bed to look forward to, and a comfortable breakfast in the morning, with our comfortable thoughts to hold on to, like a cosy hot water bottle in a fluffy cover in the shape of a teddy bear. "Life is what you make it." As if we deserve all our comforts. "Life is what you make it." As if the rest of the world deserves its pain.

People say things like this all the time, of course. It's the sort of thing my Gran used to chortle, while blanching onions ready to pickle for the autumn. But then, my Gran never charged people for her advice, nor would she have delivered it with such an air of portentous gravity.

It wasn't even much use to the American woman, still puzzling over her prospective marriage. Mind you, I had the impression that our New Age bed and breakfast guru was offering himself as a possible alternative for an enlightening session of horizontal yoga, an impression that was confirmed the following day when the abused fiancé rang up leaving a message on the answer phone. It was not very polite, and it accused the proprietor of all the things I had suspected, threatening to arrive that very day and offering to "pull his head off", amongst other equally ripe and colourful phrases.

So I was beginning to believe those wise words in the end. Maybe life IS what you make it after all.

4. Death and Pain.

There's a great line in *Donny Darko*, the movie from which the 2003 Xmas number one, *Mad World*, came. At some point an old lady whispers in the hero's ear. Later he reveals what she had said. "Every living creature dies alone."

That line had haunted me ever since, not least because I know that it is true. Whatever else you do in your life, whoever you share it with, at the moment of death you are utterly alone. Beyond that I think we cannot know.

But there's one thing in life, too, that can serve to remind you of that sense that you are ultimately alone in this world. The experience of pain.

I had toothache: a terrible, grinding, gnawing toothache. It came in waves, rising up from the depths of my chest and engulfing my whole being till I was no more than a receptacle for pain: an empty bag-of-bones whose only purpose, it seemed, was to act as host for this alien monster wracking my head and my chest and my jaw and consuming my very existence. Pain. Just pain, pain, pain, pain, pain.

There are no words to describe it. When I spoke to my flatmate about it, he looked at me sympathetically, and made all the right consoling noises, but it made no difference. I was here, alone in this exclusive bubble of pain, and there he was, outside, in the normal pain-free world, and there was absolutely no way we could make contact with each other, no way we could communicate. We were literally in different worlds.

Eventually I called a taxi and went to the Dental Hospital. I told the taxi driver about the pain, and he smiled and nodded and made the same kind of noises my flatmate had made earlier, and it made no difference either. It was the only thing that I could talk about at that moment: the only thing that existed in my world.

Finally I was sitting in the dentist's chair and he was asking me what the problem was, and I was moaning and pointing and making incoherent gurgling, groaning sounds with my mouth wide open.

"I can see you're in pain," he said, and gave me a shot of anaesthetic. That dentist was the only man in the entire world who could make any sense out of my predicament at that moment. He was the only person with the answer to the inarticulate question that my mouth throbbed to ask. He told me to go outside and wait until the anaesthetic had started to take effect. He was my saviour, my saint, my redeemer.

And now the pain was gone. Bliss is not only the presence of something new in your life. It can also be the absence of something too. The absence of pain. Sitting there in that Dental Hospital waiting room, on a dreary Monday morning, surrounded by hospital staff and patients, all busy with their personal concerns, all locked into their own separate worlds, I felt a wave of bliss like a warm liquid embrace washing over me, releasing me from that terrible pain.

It was then that a strange thing happened.

I'd been sitting there for a few minutes, enjoying the relief of my new pain-free existence, when I noticed someone across the room looking at me. He was maybe twenty feet away, but his eyes were searing into mine with a sizzling jolt like electricity. It was as if he was trying to communicate with me across the room: something very, very deep, something very, very personal. I had no idea why he would want to do this, and I looked away.

After that he got up. He started walking across the room. And then it was as if he was a puppet whose strings had been snapped, and he fell, crumpled, to the floor, while several of the nurses rushed over to help

That was when I understood what his look had meant. It was the same look I'd given my flatmate the night before, the same look I'd given the taxi driver and then the dentist. The look of pain. So deep that there are no words for it: so personal that it speaks from a void of utter aloneness. And I'd been so engrossed in my state of self-centred bliss that I had simply not been able to recognise it.

Not that I would have been able to do anything about it even if I had understood. And it was clear that the dramatic act of falling on the floor in front of everyone was the only coherent way he had of expressing his pain at that moment. He was taken into the dentist where, I presume, he was given a shot of anaesthetic, after which, no doubt, he became as blissfully ignorant as I.

I won't go on about this story. I saw the dentist, who found the source of the pain, and who did whatever he did to resolve it for me, and since then I have been relatively free of pain in my life, barring the odd headache and the occasional bout of nagging self-pity. I've never experienced real pain since.

Well I started off talking about death, and then went on to tell you about my toothache. Not that I think that death and toothaches are alike in anyway. I can't presume to know. And, in fact, death could be considered a relief from some sorts of chronic pain, so I won't question it on that level. But the thing I feel that unites them is this sense of aloneness: this sense that words are not enough.

And that is something we all need reminding of occasionally.

5. Common Belonging.

> He who binds to himself joy
> Doth the winged life destroy;
> But he who kisses the joy as it flies
> Lives in eternity's sunrise.

Wm. Blake 1793.

You'll have to excuse me this month. This is a very wordy piece. It's all about words. I've been puzzling about us human beings and our relationship to the planet.

It started a few nights back. I have a tendency to insomnia. So it was one of those nights, just sitting there, nothing on the TV, too tired to read, but too agitated in my mind to go to sleep.

I was thinking about our relationship to private property. It's one of the central issues in my philosophy. What do we mean when we say we "own" something? And how does this sense of personal property or belonging relate to our broader sense of being human and to the values we share?

It was that word "belonging" that stopped me short. Think about it. It's a classic Anglo-saxon combination: two words telescoped into one meaning. To "be" and to "long". To be-long.

The word, "long", of course, has several meanings. Principally it represents a measure of extent or duration. Long as opposed to short. A long time as opposed to a short time. But you already know this.

A be-longing is a "being" that "longs" over time, that endures over time. An object or being that "belongs" to us does so by the power of be-longing, of longing over time. Even if it is new, to say that it "belongs" to us is to state our intention to keep it, to hold on to it, to endure with it, to give it time.

But there is another sense of the word "belonging", as when we say that we belong to something or someone outside of ourselves - to a club, to a community, to love, to society at large - when we express our yearning to be a part of something greater than ourselves, not to belong to any particular organisation or thing, but to our shared sense of time and value. When we say we wish to belong.

Whereas the first sense of the word, as an object we own, is exclusive - "that which belongs to you, this which belongs to me" - the second is inclusive: "those which belong together." To belong, in this sense, is to want to share, while at the same time it also means to long for, to yearn for, to desire. To long is to yearn for a long time, longingly - lovingly - with all our hearts. To "be-long" is to endure in this sense of shared longing, with all the people we care about and love.

That dual sense of meaning inherent in one simple word - between the objects we hold exclusively, and the subjects we value inclusively - is what lies at the heart of our human dilemma.

Actually, when I say I started by thinking about property or ownership, that's not quite true. What I started with was the word "common".

It's a very important word in the English language and in English culture. Common as in our House of Commons, who once took the head off a king. Common, as in the Commonwealth, first spoken of during the English Civil War: meant literally, at the time, as the wealth we held in common. Common as in the common people, the commoners, the likes of you and I. Common, as in crude and slightly dirty - which is the sense my mother always used it to describe people who are too obvious in their feelings. Common as in our common culture, as in the bawdy songs and dances that would accompany us at our festivals, in our feasts of common sharing. Common as in our common law, our common right, our common sense, our common customs and the common lands that once belonged to us all. Common as in community. Common as in communication. Common, dare I say it, as in comrade, the common greeting of friends; as in camaraderie, the pleasure of friends in their mutual company. To commune is to share, both in our worlds and in our needs.

And it is here that we draw a line between our public and our private sense of ourselves, between our public and our private property. We all need both of course. We need our public and our private selves. We need the sense of what belongs to us and our sense of self-belonging. The problem right now is that all the emphasis is on what belongs to us privately, and very little on what belongs to all of us publicly. In fact the very notion of common property is an anathema. We may have a few public services and public spaces left, but either they are already privately owned, or they soon will be. Meanwhile, for those who can afford it - a minority of the world's population - there is a wealth of diversion in the form of gadgetry and personal entertainment to enjoy behind the drawn-out curtains of our own home towns.

All of this - what the merchants of privacy offer to us to consume at our private tables in our private feasts - only serves to communicate our sense of longing in the broader sense of ourselves, our sense of ourselves as communal as well as private beings. In our sense of ourselves as a World Community.

This is the deeply spiritual question that lies at the heart of our hopes for common humanity. How we answer to it will determine the future of life on this planet. Or of human life at least.

6. Reality Is What You Make It or The Gorilla in the Room

Do not adjust your mind
It is reality that is malfunctioning

What's a tree? How do you see it? Is it the same tree when it is in bloom on a sunny spring morning as when it appears in silhouette against a stormy sky in the depths of winter?

A tree consists of many things: of leaves, of shoots, of twigs, of bark, of buds, blossoms and branches. There are unseen parts too, a network of roots reaching deep into the earth and whole worlds of fungal growth which nuzzle through its fibres.

There's not one tree, but many. Each tree is different depending on your mood, on the day, on which part you focus, on how you view it and from what angle. Which tree is the "real" tree? Is the tree you can't see any less real than the tree you can?

If our perception of such a simple thing as a tree can change so dramatically, then our view of reality itself must shift and change at least as much.

There's the famous story about the blind men and the elephant, as told in a number of different cultures. It goes something like this: Several blind men are led into a room and asked to touch an elephant and then describe it. One man touches the leg and says it is like a pillar. Another man touches the tail and says it is like a rope. The next man touches the ear and says it is like a fan. The fifth man touches the shoulder and says it is like a wall, while the last man touches the tusk and says it is like a pipe.

You could tell a similar story about a tree. It's a parable about the way we understand the world. We are all constrained by our individual perceptions.

You might say that these men were limited by their disability, and that is why they couldn't take in the whole elephant, but there's a famous experiment by Dan Simons and Christopher Chabris, first carried out in 1999, which demonstrates that we are all capable of not seeing.

The experiment involves a video of two teams passing basket balls back and forth. One team is dressed in black, the other team is dressed in white. The video lasts about a minute, and the viewer is asked to count how many times the white team passes the ball.

The teams are darting about, dodging in and out, circling and weaving, passing the balls between themselves. It's hard to keep a track on the action, but you count the passes and confirm the result, which is then displayed on the screen at the end. After this you are asked to watch the film again, only this time you are told not to count the passes.

It is only on the second viewing that you realise that in the midst of the action a man in a gorilla suit had walked determinedly across the basket ball court, stood still for a few seconds, beat his chest vigorously, and then walked off again.

You were too busy counting the passes to notice the gorilla in the room.

I've seen this film myself, and it is startling. The first time you watch there's no one there. The next time you watch, there he is, a man dressed up like a gorilla, too obvious to miss. The process is called "inattentional blindness".

What this shows is that sometimes we see only what we are told to see. It is this mechanism that magicians use for their sleight of hand tricks. They divert our attention from the important action by focussing our brains on irrelevant details.

So it is with the news these days and with the war on terror. It's not a real war since there is no discernable enemy as such. There's no army. No generals. No troops. No chain of command. No political leadership. No spokesmen. No one to negotiate terms with.

It's a catch-all phrase by which a diverse set of people with varying outlooks from different parts of the world can be lumped together to give the impression that they are all part of the same conspiracy, united in their common hatred of our values.

It is by this process that an Afghan tribesman, an Iraqi insurgent, a Pakistani militant, a Lebanese patriot and a dentist from Forest Gate can be made to appear as all part of the same movement. The only thing they have in common is that they are all Muslims.

The irony is, of course, that by declaring this a war, and by acting upon it in ways that rip real people's lives apart - by torture and imprisonment and the indiscriminate use of force - we have made it come true. We have created the conditions in which terrorism can thrive.

And meanwhile, behind this smoke-and-mirrors facade, this noisy game of death and distraction, some people are doing very nicely thank you.

One man's loss is another man's gain. One man's crisis is another man's business-opportunity. The gorilla in the room is checking his share options. He made ten million dollars while you were reading this.

7. Memory.

As you know, I am fairly sceptical by nature and not usually given to the vagaries of mystical speculation, preferring to think about the things I can actually do something about. However, I believe I was visited by a ghost the other night and think that this needs some consideration.

Well, when I say "ghost", this isn't quite the right word. A ghost implies something insubstantial, like a wisp of smoke, something drifty and wraith-like and slightly scary, whereas what I experienced was more like a kindly presence, as if there was someone in the room with me, looking over my shoulder and commenting on what I was doing.

This happened on the night of Monday 29th March 2004 at about 11.00 pm, and, just to get things clear, I was in the process of smoking a very strong spliff of Moroccan pollen at the time, something I am not normally accustomed to doing on a regular basis. The reason I was smoking a spliff is that I'd just heard that a friend of mine had died and – out of respect for her, and the fact that I knew she liked a smoke herself – I'd decided to make an exception to my normal rule. Well, that's my excuse anyway.

So that probably explains it then. I was stoned, that's all, and thinking about someone who had just died. And it was, in fact, this person who came to visit me, nestling intimately about seven inches behind my right ear, and whispering kindly thoughts to me about the nature of the world and of life and death.

Her name was Jacqueline Memory Paterson, who some of you will know as the author of a unique and wonderfully evocative book called *Tree Wisdom*, about the ancient knowledge of trees. And, the truth is, I didn't really know Jacqui Paterson all that well, having only met her twice in my life, when she was already dying of the terrible disease that finally claimed her life. And yet I did know her. Friendship is something a lot more than mere duration, and Jacqui and I clicked from the moment we laid eyes on each other, assuming an intimacy and a knowledge of each other that only normally comes with experience.

Anyway, she came to visit me. Or I started to think about her, and by some strange mechanism of the mind, I allowed those thoughts to be conveyed in her voice. However I put it, the impression was that I had been graced by her presence.

I had the curtains open. Across the road from me there is a small park full of trees. I was thinking about Jacqui and feeling sad at her passing. And then it came to me, this quiet, intimate voice just behind my right ear. "Don't feel sad," she said. "Look at the trees. It's spring. The trees are full of blossom, the earth is bursting with life. This is the time of Life. Enjoy this time, for me."

Well I know you're not supposed to laugh when a person dies, but I did. I laughed out loud at that, a full, round, hearty belly-laugh full of poignancy and hope, full of memory.

That's the word: memory. It was a word that Jacqui had chosen to name herself with. And I knew how meaningful it was then, as I looked across at the parkland trees sparkling in the lamplight, as I felt all those intimate stirrings of nature, both in the world and in me, and I knew that this is the great human gift, memory, the thing that we are entrusted with.

And that's precisely what Jacqui did with her life. She drank in the world with her eyes and her soul and she committed it to her memory and to her heart, forever. And the question now is: is that memory gone because she has gone? I think not.

The sense of her presence in the room with me that night told me very clearly to trust the world and to trust our presence in it. To trust ourselves. That we are gifted with memory for a purpose, and that God, or Spirit, or Nature - or however you want to name the Ground from whom we derive our being – experiences the world through us, and that we have a duty, therefore, to ourselves and to our humanity – to all of humanity – to do our best to make it good, and to commit it to memory, because in the end memory does not die.

She was a very earthy woman was Jacqui, a creature of the earth, who took delight in the earth and all its startling forms, in its abundance and its splendour. She loved life. She loved life with a fierce loyalty, like she loved her children. And she told me something else, too, while I was sitting there in my shadowy room, with my note book and pen, late at night. She said, "recognise your own children as all children and all children as your own children." She said, "there is no justification on the planet – ever! – for killing a child."

And I thought about my own child then – introducing him to her, as it were. I thought about how he'd come to me in a dream even before he was born. How he'd handed me a silver dollar, and had shown me the glories of nature with an all-encompassing gesture of faith, and how, when he was born, I had thought that he was like Christ: that the whole world had changed because of his presence in it. And then I thought that all children are this: that they are all Christ when they are born, beings from another realm with a message of love for us all.

It was the following day before I took down a copy of her book from my shelves, and read the following dedication:

For Becky and Jody and all the children of the world.

Ghosts

1. Vlad the Impaler

I guess most of you will have heard of Vlad III, Prince of Walachia, also known as Vlad Tepes. One of his titles was Dracula, and he was probably the original for the central character in Bram Stoker's novel of the same name. He must have been one of the most evil people ever to have existed.

He is Romania's most famous historical figure.

"Tepes" means "Impaler". He got his name because impaling was his preferred method of execution. This is how it was done. The victim had his legs yanked apart, by horses attached to ropes, and then a sharpened stake about the size of a fist was inserted between the buttocks, up the anus. The stake was greased with pig-fat to allow ease of inserting, and to stop the body shock that might cause the victim to die too quickly. It was then pushed carefully through the body parallel with the spine so as not to puncture or damage any of the major organs. The impaled person was then lifted above the ground and staked into position where he would die slowly, probably over several days. Sometimes the stake was only partially inserted so that the force of gravity could be allowed to do its work, driving the stake through the body millimetre by millimetre, as the body slowly grazed its way down the stake, until it emerged out of the body, through the mouth or the upper chest cavity, and the victim died in writhing agony.

That "pig-fat" detail is particularly telling. It shows the care that Vlad took not to damage anything too much at first, so as to prolong the process. Greasing up the stake obviously eased the insertion somewhat, allowing for a more leisurely death.

This must be the most horrific death ever devised by anybody, worse than crucifixion even. It's not only that the person dies slowly, in great agony. What is worse is the idea that the person has this alien object, this stake with its rough bark and splinters, running through their body, which they can feel from the inside, and that they will drift in and out of consciousness, always returning to this awful sensation, always awakening to the full horror of their predicament, with death as the only solace.

Imagine it, to wake from the restful state of sleep, emerging from that blissful unconsciousness, into this: this knowledge, this terror, this pain, this stench, this awful realisation, with this alien object rubbing up against your inner organs, your heart and lungs and liver, knowing that you must soon be dead, that these will be the only sensations left to you before you exit this world.

The peculiar thing is that the Romanian people are proud of him. He is seen as a great patriot in that he defeated the Ottoman Turks, and attained a brief independence for Wallachia, where he ruled. It probably helps that his main victims were Turks, Saxons and Hungarians, but he was not averse to staking up a few Romanians too, when he was in the mood. And indeed, there is a weird kind of moral certainty about him, an insistence on fair trade and honesty and an imposition, by these gruesome punishments, of a strict moral and legal code. Not many people were willing to break the law under Vlad's watchful regime.

There is one story which perhaps gives you the psychology of all of this. It is that Vlad left a golden cup in the central square of Tirgoviste, the capital, and so feared was he, so far did his rule extend, that that cup remained untouched throughout his reign. No one dared steal it. And you can imagine this, too: the extent of Vlad's all-encompassing control, reaching into every home, every heart, every mind, in the form of a golden cup, symbol of his reign, which no one dares to touch. This, it seems to me, is true psychopathic terror. You can imagine the satisfaction he would feel, even in the confines of his remote castle, to know that this cup was there, accessible, but unmolested, in a public place. That cup would have been like an eye in every citizen's heart. Every time people passed it, they would know. Vlad is there. He is watching. He knows what we think.

The name "Dracula" is from "Drac" meaning dragon; "ul" is the definite article, and the "a" ending means "son of". So Dracula means, "the son of the dragon". The Dragon is a reference to membership of the Order of the Dragon, to which his father belonged, and Vlad's coinage had a dragon on the reverse.

It is also a Romanian vernacular term meaning devil or demon, which is appropriate enough too for Vlad.

As to whether he was ever a vampire as such, this is a matter of speculation. What is true, certainly, is that he drew special pleasure from the suffering of his victims, that he would happily dine amongst fields of the dead and dying and that, perhaps, this was a source of psychic strength to him. Is it possible to drink the suffering of the dying, to suck up the agony of their souls, knowing you are the creator of their torture, their unbelievable pain? Maybe. Maybe Vlad was some form of a psychic vampire.

But here is the story that most betrays the full horror of Vlad's peculiar form of vampirism. It was not only that he liked to eat amongst the dead and the dying, or that he appeared to enjoy the suffering of his victims. There is one other detail which brings to light the full extent of Vlad's ripe insanity. You see he didn't like to eat alone. He liked to have someone to talk to as he ate. Maybe he distrusted his ministers. Maybe he knew that they were afraid of him and that he was unlikely to hear the truth from their lips. He had no friends. Thus he was in the habit of having someone impaled directly in front of his dinner table, so that he could talk to them as he ate and they were dying.

SO THAT HE COULD TALK TO THEM!

AS THEY WERE DYING!

Imagine that.

And you have to wonder, also, what those conversations must have been like. Vlad there, at table, tucking into his meat and drink, pulling the flesh from the bone with greasy fingers, while his helpless victim is perched in front of him, impaled like a kebab on a stick, moaning in grief and pain: what possible conversations could they have had?

So many were his victims that it was doubtful he would know immediately who it was in front of him. Or perhaps, being a precise sort of a ruler, he would have asked his henchmen to find out the name of the person beforehand. Perhaps he would also know the crime. So he could begin the conversation either by asking the name of the victim, or by addressing him by name. Either way, there would be a grim kind of intimacy in his tone, almost a note of concern.

Maybe he would enquire after the person's health?

"I hope you have learned your lesson," he might say, as if the whole gruesome business was really just the equivalent of a smart smack across the thighs: as if impaling people had a purpose beyond the sense of power it gave him.

He might ask after the victim's wife and children. What were their names? What were their hobbies? Did they enjoy sports?

Perhaps he would philosophise with his unwilling guest, pondering the meaning of life.

"You know, I was just thinking the other day how short life is really. You live, you die, and then it's all over. I wonder what it all can mean?"

Of course the beauty of such conversation is that the other person wouldn't really be able to answer back. He might give out the occasional groan, the odd croak. Certainly little more than animal noises. But then, I imagine, Vlad would have to acknowledge such sounds. After all, what's the point of a one-sided conversation?

"Good point," he might say after one guttural bellow of anguish. "Yes, I too believe that life has some meaning, some purpose. As for myself," he might add, while picking his teeth after his meal, "I think that my purpose is to bring moral certainty to the world. Yes it is a harsh punishment I have inflicted upon you, but think of it this way: you are acting as a lesson for the whole country, and by your death I have brought honesty and moral integrity back into our small state of Wallachia, for who, now, will do as you have done? Who, now will cheat the foreign merchant of his gold or beg or take money from the widow-woman? Who will be slack or lazy in his work, or shirk his duty? You see what good you have done by your death? You have made our world a better place."

And on and on like this, expounding his philosophy at great length, before, finally, wiping his hands on a cloth and taking his leave.

"Yes, thank you for an interesting and stimulating debate. There is much to ponder here, I think. And now I will leave you to your death. God have mercy upon your soul!"

Actually, on reflection, I think that Vlad would know precisely who his victim was. He would have the details of their crimes before him, on parchment, to be read out to them, to remind them of why they were there. He demanded that his people be honest and hard working. Merchants who cheated their customers sometimes found themselves mounted on a stake besides members of the lower orders.

As I say, Romanians regard Vlad as a culture hero. They have a sort of admiration for the character, for his decisiveness, and for his energy in action. Talk to a Romanian about Vlad and you will often hear the phrase, "yes, but in the context of the time": meaning that the age in which he lived was brutal. And yet it is a measure of Vlad's extreme brutality that, even in the context of the time, when violence and murder abounded, and where vicious punishments were the norm, the particular horror of Vlad the Impaler was recognised by everyone.

It was the late 1400s, and the printing press had just been invented. The story of Vlad appeared shortly after his death almost simultaneously in Germany and in Russia as a popular chapbook, and was read throughout Europe for the next sixty years or so. In this sense, Vlad was the original horror-comic character. The printed story was published with suitable woodcuts of people with oddly serene faces staked up in fields while butchers with knives and axes chopped up human remains and Vlad ate his lunch.

So it was in the beautiful mountains of Transylvania that Vlad's victims had been staked, sometimes in their thousands, in huge displays of mass torture referred to as "the forests of the impaled." Whole cities had been impaled just to teach some moral lesson.

And there were nice comic-horror touches too, to all this grim nastiness. Like the famous story of the guest at one of his mass stake-outs, who showed a certain prim disgust at having to eat amongst all the stench of decaying flesh. Vlad felt such sympathy for his sensitivities that he had him staked a little higher than all the rest - once he had been impaled for his impudence - so as not to offend the man's delicate nose.

He clearly had a sense of humour.

When I first heard about Vlad I had a genuine feeling of horror and revulsion. I think it was the addition of the detail about the pig-fat that did it for me. I couldn't help imagining the greased up stake entering my own nether regions, pushing up into my innards, being driven through my own body, and being lodged there amongst my own vital organs.

History, though, has a way of filtering out its own worst excesses. So Vlad's tale comes to us via medieval chapbooks - popular horror stories of their day - through arcane vampire lore and 18th century vampire tales, to Bram Stoker, who used the name for his character and the location as a setting for his most famous book. And after this we have vampire films with Bela Lugosi and Christopher Lee in the starring role, or other famous actors playing the part, starting off as horror and ending as camp theatrics. And then we have all sorts of popular cultural accretions, vampire masks and vampire teeth and vampire cloaks as a bit of fun for Halloween. And then somehow, by some strange circular historical and cultural logic, all of this returns to the home of Vlad the Impaler himself, to Bran Castle in Transylvania, where there is a picturesque medieval castle which had little to do with Vlad when he was alive, but which was the location for the film Bram Stoker's Dracula, starring Gary Oldman (one of the better excursions into the genre) and where there is a market selling all this Halloween tat, witch's hats and devil's horns, along with all the vampire gear, including two spectacularly badly translated pamphlets on Vlad, from which I got most of the previous information.

I mean: how do you account for this?

Poor Vlad must be turning in his grave (assuming he has a grave and isn't actually one of the undead) to have his monstrous sadism turned into a parlour game for children.

2. We're Here Because We're Here, A soldier's death in Vieille-Chapelle, September 1915

> It was the song they sang as they marched to the trenches. "We're Here Because We're Here." It was sung to the tune of Auld Lang Syne, a sardonic joke sung in full-throated defiance of death. "We're here because we're here because we're here because we're here."
>
> But underlying that song there is a question: a question to which the song gives no answer, stark in its simplicity. "Why are we here?"

• **Ivor Coles**

There's a grainy old sepia photograph of him standing in front of a shop. He's maybe 12 or 13 years old, wearing a flat cap and a donkey jacket with leather patches on the shoulders, with knee-length breeches and woollen socks, with these huge shiny black leather clod-hoppers on his feet. They are far too big for him, clogs rather than shoes, with wooden soles turned up at the toe. The clothes are functional and sturdy, heavy duty work-clothes. A Miner's uniform. Perhaps they are his new work clothes. Perhaps he's just about to start his first job, down the pit. He was the right age.

He's got one hand in front of him, the thumb hovering around his waistcoat pocket as if he's about to hook it in; the other hand is tucked into his jacket as if he's about to take something out. He's leaning on the windowsill, one leg cocked forward, totally at his ease, with this cheeky look on his face, grinning broadly at the camera from under the brim of his cap, which is pulled down tight over his ears. It's obviously the fashion. A young boy with a cheeky-monkey grin on the threshold of his future with everything to look forward to. Within six years he would be dead.

His name is Ivor Coles, and the picture was taken sometime in the early 1900s - 1908 or 1909 - and he died of wounds sometime in September 1915 near a town called Vieille-Chapelle in France on the Western Front. Killed in action.

He had an older brother, Richard Coles. Richard was also stationed on the Western Front, but survived. He later married, Lily May. Lily May lived on till she was over a hundred. It is Lily May who is the thread who holds this story together.

As it turns out, if you look at the dates, Ivor must have been underage when he joined up. He was born on the 24th June 1897. He was less than three months into his eighteenth year when he died so he must have joined the army before the proper age of recruitment at 18. Also, according to Richard - who would tell the story in later years - Ivor was only a few days away from moving to Richard's regiment, on compassionate grounds. The British Army usually allowed members of the same family to serve together. But then the big push came, the move never happened, and Ivor Coles died as a private in the 9th Battalion of the Welch Regiment (sic).

There's not a lot more you can say about him. He died anonymously, another anonymous death in a war where death was the norm, routine and unavoidable. A conveyor belt of death. A death factory in full-production.

- **The Crown Jewels**

Years later Richard went back to find him. He scoured the cemeteries of the Western Front looking for his name, but it wasn't there. He thought he saw it on the Menim Gate, where all the missing are listed. The ones without bodies. The ones whose bodies had been blown to bits, smashed and pulped into a goulash soup and absorbed into the Earth. There was one name there which resembled his brother's. Ivan Coles rather than Ivor. Maybe they just got the spelling wrong. Anyhow, it was enough to satisfy Richard, enough for him to say to himself, "well I've found my brother now," to pay his respects and then to leave. And that's how the story stood. An old story. As old as time. As old as history. One of those stories that most families are familiar with, like a thread from the past left dangling in the present. A story without an end or without resolution, like a detective novel with the last pages missing.

Later again Richard's granddaughter, Vanessa, went to the Menim gate to check the story out, scanning the thousands of names to find the one that her grandfather had seen. It wasn't there. There was no I. Coles listed on the Menim Gate.

So the mystery deepened. Ivor Coles had just sort of disappeared from history, lost without a trace. He had no grave, no memorial, nothing to mark his passing in the great river of time, nothing to show that he had ever been here, that he had ever mattered. Nothing but an old grainy photograph tucked away in a biscuit tin in someone's bottom drawer, all-but forgotten.

Except for Lily May, that is. Lily May who had married Ivor's brother. Richard sometimes spoke about him, about his lost brother, and Lily May always remembered this, even after Richard had died.

That's how the thread of history is kept alive. It's in the minds of the living. In the minds of the people who remember. Lily May never met Ivor Coles, but she shared his surname, and she remembered the stories her beloved husband had told her about their childhood together in South Wales, remembered even when she was a hundred years old and had great-great grandchildren who would play around her ankles while she snoozed away her last few months, delicate and brittle like an old clock.

And who was Ivor Coles anyway? His life was so short it could hardly have impacted on this Earth. He was here, and then he was gone, along with a whole generation of young men. He left no progeny. He left no mark. He added little to the world's store. Had he lived he would have gone back to being a Miner, feeding the power industry with his sweat and his muscle, digging the coal deep underground. But he never went back. And who's to say? Maybe he never even fired a shot while he was on the frontline. Maybe his only contribution to the factory of death was his own body, swallowed by the mud in the mangled Earth.

But Lily May had a secret. All those years she kept it. It was a tightly wrapped bundle which went everywhere with her. From the South Wales Valleys where she started out, to the Wealds of Kent, where the family eventually settled, Miner following Miner across the landscape of Britain in the search for work, Miner's families following on behind. And that's how Lily May got here with her bundle.

It was a simple brown paper bundle, tightly wrapped in Sellotape, wrapped and wrapped, tighter than a Nun's wimple and containing just as many secrets. She called it the Crown Jewels. "Don't open it till something happens to me," she'd say, in her broad South Wales accent. "That there's very precious." And she'd brandish it about with a flourish, with a twinkle, enjoying the mystery. Everyone thought it must contain diamonds at least. Or pearls. Gold and silver. Ancient artefacts from the mysterious East.

It turned out to be mainly paper. Little more. Nothing of obvious value. So it was passed on to Warren, Vanessa's brother, as the family historian after Lily May died. "Here," they said. "You might like this."

And it was in here that Warren found the clues that lead us back to Ivor: to finding him again.

- ### How to lose a human being

The bundle was full of paper. Old faded sheets of time, folded, brown and musty with age. The usual things. Birth certificates. Death certificates. Marriage certificates. People's wills. Most of it was hardly surprising. But there were a couple of new things in there: one a verification notice, sent to Richard and Ivor's parents, John and Rhoda, by the War Graves Commission. It contained the name of a cemetery, with a plot number, a row and a grave number, plus an army number, only it was made out in the name of T. Coles giving the date of his death as the 25th of September 1915.

T rather than I.

A simple clerical error, a typing error. You take the bottom off an I and it looks like a T.

That's all it takes to lose a human being. A typing error.

It was a printed form part filled in in pencil. You were supposed to correct the details and send them back. Only no one ever did.

Later Warren checked the army number against an identity disc which they'd found behind the glass in a picture frame tucked behind a wardrobe in Lily May's house. The picture was of Lily May's husband, but the identity disc was Ivor's.

The number on the verification document and the number on the disc matched. They'd found the whereabouts of Ivor's grave at last. All the information was on the document.

And there was something else in the bundle too, something even more precious.
The bundle didn't contained jewellery, but it contained a work of art.

It was a small package, the size of a man's outstretched hand, wrapped in brown paper. Inside the brown paper, a yellowing cotton cloth, and inside that a layer of tissue paper. And inside the tissue paper, wrapped up like a sacred relic, like Tutankhamen's remains, there lay a simple chalk cross.

It's about nine inches by seven. The cross is carved from a single lump of chalk, possibly with a penknife. The rear side of the object is a plain, smoothed surface, but on the other side the cross stands out in relief from a flat background, resting upon a plinth of steps. It is meant to be displayed in an upright position, facing forward to give the impression of a cemetery cross standing upon a platform of ascending steps.

And all across the cross, in elaborate, ornate, copperplate lettering, in ink, using a fountain pen, written so that they too form the shape of a cross, are the following words :

RIP
In
Loving Memory
Of
Pvt Ivor Coles
Killed
In
Action
At
Givenchy
FRANCE
Sept 15 1915

He Gave His
Life England's
Honour to Save
Now he Lies
in a Soldier's Grave.

It is poignant in its simplicity. This plain, simple cross made from the bones of the soil, from the very chalk landscape that had swallowed Ivor's body, that had drank his blood and consumed his flesh, maybe even from the trench in which he lay shivering, afraid, in the muck, with the stench of death in the air, just before he was sent over the top to be chewed up by the teeth of the guns in No Man's Land, snared upon a wire to die, to give up his young life for some abstract cause; this cross carved with slow care and dedication in the weeks and months following by a comrade-in-arms, by a man who had watched him die perhaps, and who had wrenched this lump of rock from the living earth and carved it in his memory, so that Ivor's name would not be forgotten. "In Loving Memory," he wrote. He meant every word of it.

- **How to find a human being**

This was the great secret that Lily May had kept all these years, wrapped up in a bundle, a memorial to her long-lost brother-in-law, a message from history.

Not that this cross or this bundle answer all of the questions. In fact they bring to light new ones.

There are discrepancies. The dates, for a start. The cross has it that he died on the 15th of September, while the verification document delays it until the 25th.

Perhaps he was wounded on the 15th and died in hospital ten days later on the 25th Except that there was a big offensive on the 25th - the so-called 2nd Battle of Loos - in which Ivor's regiment took part. Before that an uneasy stalemate had existed across the front line, an eerie peace broken only by the occasional skirmish. On the 25th thousands of men had died, mown down by the enemy guns, or gassed by their own side, or blown to smithereens by the artillery-fire while ducking for cover in No Man's Land. It was much more likely to be that day. Or perhaps he had taken part in a skirmish on the 15th, been killed by a sniper's bullet, but in the mass of deaths ten days later, in the confusion of slaughter, this one lone private's death had got muddled up.

Who knows? It's a mystery.

And then, the other great mystery. Why, when he received the verification document didn't Ivor's father return it with the amended information, the I instead of the T, and acknowledge his son's resting place?

What father wouldn't want to know the place of his son's burial?

Perhaps he couldn't read?

And why was the location of Ivor's grave kept hidden, even from his own brother?

Mysteries on mysteries, and questions to which we will probably never have answers. But it's the questions that bring Ivor to life again. It's as if, in the anonymity of his death he planted a seed. A seed in history. And in the moment of remembering Ivor Coles, so long-forgotten, we remember all the others who died in that carnage - the War to End All Wars - and in that moment, too, remember the futility of war, its meaninglessness, and by that give meaning to Ivor Coles' death.

- **Final rest**

So, after 90 years the family had finally found the burial place of Great Uncle Ivor. All of the information was on the War Graves Commission letter, and in 2006 Warren and Vanessa and their respective partners went to lay a wreath of poppies on his grave, to pay their respects.

They had solved the mystery and brought Ivor Coles back into the bosom of their family once more.

Now all that is needed is to get the grave re-carved so that it reads I. Coles instead of T. Coles, as it should. When that day comes there will be a dedication ceremony at the grave.

Lily May would be proud.

The Empire never Ended

1. Philip K Dick, Valis and the Psychopathology of War

*(Being the text of a speech delivered to an
anti-war meeting in 2004)*

*How does one fashion a book of resistance, a book of truth in
an empire of falsehood, or a book of rectitude in an empire of
vicious lies? How does one do this right in front of the enemy?*

Philip K. Dick

- ## THE EMPIRE NEVER ENDED

There was a very strange book written sometime in the late seventies by the science fiction writer Philip K Dick. It's called *Valis*, and it really is the oddest, most exasperating book I've ever read. On the one hand it is clearly autobiographical, containing details about Dick's own life, his failed marriage and his nervous breakdown; on the other there are fantastical elements in it which might be describing something that had actually happened, but might just as easily be science fiction conceits. I won't go into the plot here, except to say that there is a single line he repeats over and over again throughout the book, always in bold, **The Empire never Ended** - he says, like that - **The Empire never Ended**.

He's talking about the Roman Empire.

In some form or another, the Roman Empire has continued to flourish, long after its apparent demise, taking on various disguises. In fact, he says, the time between the era of the early Christians in their on-going spiritual war with the Roman Empire and now - the time he was writing in, the late seventies - is false time. That era and this era are beginning to coalesce. These are - the times we are living in now - literally apostolic times.

This of course may be just a science fiction conceit, a plot device to keep the novel going. Or Dick may have believed that it was true. Who knows?

I suspect the latter.

However you want to view it, there may be some truth in this assertion. It may not be literally true, but psychologically, spiritually, economically, militarily, you might say, The Empire really has never ended. Or if it ever went away for a time, it has certainly returned with a vengeance.

In fact, you only have to look at a bunch of riot police in full combat mode, with their shields and their batons, with their close formations, their phalanxes and their armour to know that Roman military techniques are still very much in evidence.

The Empire is a psychological as well as a military state. It exists as a mental construct, as a psychopathic state of mind, as a system of control. It exists in all of us. All of us are infected with this thought-form virus. It's no use hating George W Bush, as the world's most prominent psychopath. In his position we would do exactly the same. It's not a question of right versus left. It's not even a question of right versus wrong. It's a question of survival now. It's a question of finding out what we have to do to survive.

War is not just like peace but with bombs. It is a wholly different state of being. In war the psychopaths are in control. Everyone is a psychopath to some degree. A psychopath is someone who thinks of everyone else as an object, a mere source of gratification. Not every psychopath is a killer. Most psychopathologies are controlled in a state of peace, since the first concern of the psychopath is to blend in. But in the state of war the psychopath is unleashed on the world. The psychopath as ruler, as state, as war-profiteer, as war-monger, as war-addict, and in every single individual.

War is the psychopath's playground. Now all the rules are dispensed with. Now every human is an object of sensory gratification. Now power rules. Now I can take pot shots at the little objects around me pretending to be human. Nothing matters any more but my own self, my own self-gratification. Other people's bodies become playthings in the hands of the torturers in all of us. This has always been the case in a state of war. It's either self-gratification or self-sacrifice. The worst and the best. And there is a whole historical power psychology dedicated to this cause, the retention of war as a means of gratification and control. This is the true meaning of "The Empire." It's what Philip K Dick means when he says, "**The Empire never Ended.**"

- **War and Imperialism**

The following is from a 1919 essay called "The Sociology of Imperialisms" by **JOSEPH SCHUMPETER**.

He says:

> *"There was no corner of the known world where some interest was not alleged to be in danger or under actual attack. If the interests were not Roman, they were those of Rome's allies; and if Rome had no allies, then allies would be invented. When it was*

utterly impossible to contrive such an interest-why, then it was the national honour that had been insulted. The fight was always invested with an aura of legality. Rome was always being attacked by evil-minded neighbours, always fighting for a breathing-space. The whole world was pervaded by a host of enemies, and it was manifestly Rome's duty to guard against their indubitably aggressive designs ."

You only have to replace the word "Rome" with "The United States" for that statement to become perfectly true of today's situation.

The other thing about the Romans is that they regarded all other nations as barbarians. Civilisation was the unique preserve of the Roman State and Roman society. All other people, unless under the power of the Roman State, were intrinsically inferior.

There was a very funny item in the news the other day. It was on Channel Four. Some British reporter "embedded" with American Troops in some part of Iraq having to deal with the local populace. It was just weird: this American soldier, trying his darndest to be friendly for the sake of the Cameras, extolling the virtues of the American Way of Life to a room full of Iraqi men and women, while, outside, US forces were bombarding an empty vineyard. Why were they bombarding an empty vineyard? It was just in case some insurgents might be intending to use it, they said.

Apparently, in America, if you don't like your mobile phone company, you can just change the company. And if you don't like your politicians, you can just change your politicians. That's how the friendly soldier was trying to sell the invasion to the Iraqi population. Politicians and mobile phone companies are both part of the democratic way of life that the United States is bringing to Iraq.

Hooray!

The guy was sincere, by the way. He'd obviously been hand-picked for this very reason. He was clearly a nice guy who just wanted to educate these dumb Iraqis about America. He was trying to civilise them.

The Iraqis, meanwhile, were looking perplexed. They just wanted know why he was bombing their vineyard.

I mean. The Americans - the country that bought us Coca Cola and Mickey Mouse - trying to civilise the Iraqis. This is one of the most civilised nations on the planet: or at least it was until the British and the Americans took over, that is, until oil was found there.

I'm not being anti-American here, by the way. We British share as much of the blame. The empire that Philip K. Dick is talking about is currently the preserve of the American state. Previously it was the preserve of the British state. Take a look at those borders, with their straight lines and their squiggles. The Iraqis didn't draw them. The Americans didn't draw them. The British did. They drew those lines to delineate where the oil was. The Americans are only following an Imperialist design that the British had already laid down in the sand.

- **Some facts about Iraq**

Modern civilisation began in Iraq. The Iraqis invented agriculture. They invented astronomy and astrology. The entire astrological system still in use today in every Daily Newspaper was invented in Iraq over five thousand years ago. They discovered the planets, they mapped the stars. They invented the 24 hour day, the sixty minute hour and the sixty second minute. In a very real sense we still live within Iraqi time. They invented the seven day week. They invented mathematics and writing. The earliest known work of literature, the Epic of Gilgamesh, written in cuneiform script on clay tablets in about 2750 BC in the land of Sumeria, in a region of modern Iraq, talks about a place called Uruk, of which Gilgamesh is the King. This is how ancient and consistent this region is, that the name of the country still holds. The book describes one of the earliest cities ever built, which housed a population of over 50,000: its immense walls, its towering public buildings, its statues and its architecture.

Interestingly, I put the word "Uruk" into my search engine and got the website of one of the critical anti-American groups currently working in Iraq: uruknet.info. Clearly the Iraqis know their own history even if we don't.

Abraham was born in Iraq, in a city called Ur in the North. In that sense you can say that God was born in Iraq too: that the idea of God was born there. Also, according to the Bible, Eden is located in Iraq, between the Tigris and the Euphrates rivers. You can read it in Genesis 2:10-14. Iraqis living in this region agree. They believe that this was once Eden. Even as little as twenty years ago, this still was Eden, the place where the marsh Arabs lived. Before the first Gulf War, that is, before the marsh Arabs uprising, before Saddam drained the marshes and drove them all out.

Iraq has always been a place of religious tolerance. Several of the world's religions have flourished here, plus some that could not have survived anywhere else. Not only does it support Sunni and Shia Muslims, it is also home to Assyrian Christians, who still recite the Gospels in their original Aramaic, the language of Jesus; Nestorian Christians, a sect who believe that Jesus had a duel nature, one half purely human, the other half purely divine, plus the last of the Gnostic sects, the Mandaeans, followers of John the Baptist, who to this day practice daily baptism in baths they refer to as The River Jordon, and who refer to God as The Great Life. Plus, until 1948 Iraq had one of the largest populations of Jews in the Middle East, a population who were respected according to Islamic law, along with Christians and Mandaeans, as "People of the Book." There's been a Jewish population in Iraq since 791 BC.

In fact, take a note of this: pogroms against the Jews were not committed in Muslim countries at all, but in Christian countries. Until 1948 and the establishment of the State of Israel, Jews were respected throughout the Middle East. That's just a fact. Iraq had no sustained history of anti-Semitism before 1948.

This is a selective reading of the history of Iraq, as any history must be. I offer it only as an antidote to the current popular understanding of Iraq as a country of terrorists. The problem with culture is that it can be wiped out in a generation. Attack and humiliate one generation and watch what happens. Watch the lure of crime. Watch the sectarianism. Watch the terrorism. Watch the violence. Watch the kidnapping and murder. You can wipe away a thousand years of culture in the space a few years. That's exactly what has happened in Iraq.

Of course, as you know, there was talk about weapons of mass destruction and an Iraqi nuclear bomb. It was all false, of course, as we know now, but it was at least plausible at the time because, in fact, Iraqi scientists were quite capable of creating such things, not just nuclear as well as biological weapons, but advanced technology for peaceful uses too. In other words, as well as being an ancient state, Iraq was - at least until the sanctions and then the war - an advanced state, an educated state. Iraqi doctors, Iraqi scientists, Iraqi designers, Iraqi technicians are amongst the most qualified in the world. Iraqi artists, Iraqi writers, Iraqi film-makers and Iraqi musicians abound. This is a culture that encourages art, that encourages science, that encourages learning, and has always done so.

The idea that we have anything to teach the Iraqis about civilisation is absurd.

• **Boondoggle Nation**

After the invasion the occupying army sent troops to protect the oil ministry and the oil fields, and allowed the Museums to be looted. All that Sumerian, Assyrian and Babylonian art. All of that cultural treasure from the oldest civilisations on this planet. Stolen. Looted. Taken away. Where to? Into private collections, no doubt. Into the hands of those who declared this war. I'm fairly certain that some people already had their shopping lists before the invasion and that they were allowed to do this.

The point about Imperialism is that it is profitable. War is profit. Economic growth is a measure of economic activity. In fact, a pile-up on the motorway contributes to economic growth. Ambulances have to be sent out, police cars, fire engines. The emergency services. Cars have to be cleared from the road. Cars have to be replaced. Insurance has to be paid out. It's all economic. It all adds to growth. How much more so a war, then? Armaments have to be made, armies have to be trained, uniforms have to be cut and sown. Buildings have to get blown up and rebuilt. Infrastructure has to be destroyed and then remade. No mention of people note. People don't come into this equation at all except as collateral damage. People are merely seen as objects in an economic landscape.

The beauty of all of this for the United States and British elites is that the public are paying for it all. They pay private companies to build arms, and armies to use them to knock down buildings, and then private companies to rebuild the buildings again. Private companies to guard the oil fields. Private companies to fix the electricity and the water supply. Private companies to make a profit and all out of taxpayers funds, what Noam Chomsky calls The Welfare State for the Rich, what the Americans, colloquially, call a boondoggle. Maybe this is why the water and the electricity don't work so well. Why, months after the invasion, there's still times of the day without an electricity supply. Even Saddam could keep an electricity supply going.

They said that there was no alternative to the occupation, because the Iraqi security forces couldn't keep security. But there was an alternative: a United Nations mandate lead by armies from Muslim Nations.

Would the Iraqi Insurgency have been blowing up Indonesians and Jordanians? Or Syrians and Iranians? Of course not. But then again, the idea that Iraq could have been overseen by Syrian and Iranian forces is unpalatable to the oil lobby currently in control of the US government.

Also, given the high degree of technical expertise in Iraq, who should rebuild Iraq but the Iraqis? Not substandard American manufacturers like Halliburton, out to bleed the Iraqi and the American public dry. The Iraqis can rebuild their nation themselves. They have the skills. They have the intelligence. All they lack is access to their own resources.

Instead we have a state sponsored American army protecting Iraqi oil so that American private companies like Halliburton can draw the profits.

None of this bears any resemblance to what we like to call capitalism. None whatsoever. All of this is done through the agency of the state for the profit of those who control the state apparatus. Capitalism is just a euphemism. It's a cover story. This is not a capitalist system. The capitalist system died sometime in the 19th century during the South Sea bubble. Since then capitalism has been state sponsored. Maybe it always was state sponsored. All that guff about "enterprise" and "risk-takers". These people take no risks. They live in state-sponsored luxury. This is not a capitalist system, it is an imperialist system, the only difference being that instead of a single emperor you have a whole class of emperors who share the spoils between them. 2,000 Neros instead of one, and all of them just as mad, all still fiddling as the Earth burns. They control the armies. They control the government. They control the research and development. They control the economy. They control what we see on the news, and to a large degree, as a consequence, they control what we think.

We have bread and circuses. We have Oprah Winfrey and the FA cup final. We have Tescos and Sainsburys. We have Hollywood blockbusters and TV soap operas. We have wars we never asked for against nations we've never heard of. We've got threats from around the globe. If international terrorism doesn't get you then the bird flu will. We've got drug companies making ridiculous profits while our recreational drugs are in the hands of the mafia. We've got trivia and tat and then fear around the corner. We've got obscene wealth in the midst of obscene poverty. We've got lies to send us to war, and lies to keep us there. Lies, lies and more lies.

One final thing, from me to you. You can take it or leave it. You can believe it or not. I don't care either way. This is it. The revolution is both political and spiritual at the same time. Anything that is only spiritual, or only political is not revolutionary. It's like man and woman.

It's like left and right. It's like heart and soul. All things come together in this. The revolution is political and spiritual at the same time.

Not one. Not the other. Both.

As to what these terms mean, exactly, I'll leave it up to you to work it out.

2. The Opposite of Love

In memory of **Brian Haw**

"The worst sin toward our fellow creatures is not to hate them, but to be indifferent to them: that's the essence of inhumanity."

George Bernard Shaw

The opposite of love is not hate. The opposite of love is indifference.

Hate, in fact, is a form of love, since you cannot hate what you have not previously loved, or which has not hurt or wounded or threatened that which you love. Hate is love bent out of shape. Hate is love which is itself wounded. Hate is love broken or betrayed, tortured or defiled, raped or murdered, molested or mutilated. Hate is love when confronted by injustice, or by violence, or by cruelty or by hate. Hate breeds hate, just as love breeds love. Hate is love grown bitter. It is love roused to anger. It is love forced to witness the destruction of innocence. It is love in shackles. It is love enslaved. It is love deprived of hope or freedom or a say over its future. It is love humiliated, made to crawl, love whose spirit is broken. It is love's ache at the loss of a loved one. It is love's rebellion at the corrosion of liberty. It is love's stand against the darkness of repression.

Hate is love's wound.

I remember being at a demonstration a few years back. It was a Kurdish demonstration against the Turkish government, then engaged in the wholesale repression of Kurdish culture and Kurdish identity.

There were about 20 or 30 people there. It was outside a government department in Whitehall as the British government were helping the Turkish government at the time by means of financial loans. Most of the people were members of the Kurdish Diaspora, people who had fled the border areas in South Eastern Turkey where the fight for Kurdish independence was taking place. There was some drumming going on, and some of them were dancing. They had their arms linked in a line and were doing this elaborate stepped dance involving handkerchiefs being waved in the air. I remember it very clearly: the kicking and the dancing and the trills and whoops of excitement. There were a few cars lined up by the side of the road including an old VW van, onto which one of the demonstrators was attaching some posters with information about their cause.

I was there with my friend Paul, who knew some of these people personally. He introduced me to the man who was decorating the VW van. The man smiled and said hello, and shook my hand formally. He had gentle, kind eyes.

Paul said, "show my friend the pictures."

And the gentle-eyed Kurd opened a folder, and showed me the first picture. He said, "these are photographs taken by Turkish soldiers as trophies. They sell for a lot of money in Istanbul."

It was an enlarged colour photocopy of an ordinary snapshot. It showed a Turkish soldier in a snowy, mountainous landscape wearing a blue beret. He was kneeling down on one knee, grinning triumphantly, holding up a pair of objects in his hands. It was hard to make out what they were at first. They were about the size of footballs, and, indeed, that's what I took them to be. But then my eyes focused on the detail, and I saw what they really were. They were severed heads.

The Turkish soldier was holding them up by the hair as trophies. The snow was stained with patches of blood, as blood dripped down from the ripped tendons of the neck, as blood stained the soldier's hands. I had never seen anything like it before in my life. The eyes in the two heads were rolled backwards into the skulls. Open-mouthed, they seemed to be screaming some unimaginable blasphemy to the sky. I immediately began to cry. The picture was like a jolt of extreme violence, like something from a nightmare. Ordinary Londoners passed by in motorcars, blissfully unaware.

Paul was looking at me pointedly, while the quiet-eyed Kurd spoke to me in a gentle even voice.

"Yes," he said, "I have seen 23 of my family killed. My brother was killed. The Turks came to the village and called everyone out of doors. They took ten of them and shot them in the head while the others watched. The people were made to clap. If they didn't clap, they too were shot. My brother was 14 years old."

There were several more of these photographs, of soldiers holding up severed heads, sometimes one head, sometimes two. Sometimes a number of soldiers would be standing in front of the headless corpse while one of the soldiers held up the head.

Then my Kurdish friend showed me another photograph. This, too, was like a snapshot. It was even arranged like one. It showed a family ranged around in someone's living room, on their knees, posed, looking at the camera. There are family trinkets displayed on shelves, and pictures and wall-hangings on the walls. Before them is a dead body. The body is naked, and has long white gashes along the legs. You can see the bone. The family consists of a woman and several children. The woman's eyes are wild, though her face is held in a taught mask. The children just look towards the camera, eyes as deep and unfathomable as the eternal night.

My friend said, "this is the dead-man's family. They are being made to pose by the corpse. Those wounds on his legs are where he has been tortured."

I was utterly speechless. There weren't any words. In the whole universe there wasn't a single word that meant anything anymore.

I've never forgotten that moment. I remember going into a shop soon after to go to the toilet. There were all the products lined up in their various displays, looking shiny and new. But I couldn't help seeing the blood that seemed to flow from the photographs underlying this conspicuous display of opulence all around me. I couldn't help thinking of the murder of innocence.

So, now, imagine those children made to sit before the corpse of their beloved father while an enemy soldier takes a photograph. Their faces betray nothing of their feelings. But what will be seething in their hearts? What rage, what anger, will have been born there that day? What hatred? What acts of revenge? What future violence?

Hate breeds hate breeds hate breeds hate, but hate is born from love.

Now imagine that on a world scale: in Palestine, in Iraq, in Afghanistan, in Pakistan, in Yemen, in Syria, in Somalia, in Libya, in Bahrain. All over the world. Everywhere there is a war.

Thousands of corpses. Tens of thousands. Unimaginable numbers. Who knows how many corpses or how many children there are, just like these children, being tortured by the horrors of war? Who knows the scars on the heart or the heart's wounds or how much blood has accumulated in the soul of the world? How much sorrow, how much anger, how much violence, how much love seeking revenge?

And you wonder why these photographs are not seen by everyone, all of these mutilated corpses in forgotten corners of the world: why they are not allowed on our TV screens. They should be on the front page of every newspaper: the consequences of war. We should see the bodies ripped apart, the innards spilling out of the wounds like the human sweetmeats they are. We should see the Mothers screaming for their dead children. We should see into the Father's eyes, unmanned by their inability to protect their families. We should see the children's naked fear. We should see the broken bodies in the hospitals, the bloodstained sheets, the body parts. We should see the broken homes and the broken lives. We should be made to feel their pain. We should all be made to feel the consequence of our own indifference.

Because the opposite of love is not hate. The opposite of love is indifference.

3. Gaza: This Is Not A War, It's A Massacre

Published on-line 12/01/09 during the Israeli assault on Gaza.

> *"They stole my land, burnt my olive trees, destroyed my house, took my water, imprisoned my father, killed my mother, starved us all, humiliated us all. But I am to blame: I shot a rocket back. So they stole more of my land, burnt my olive trees, destroyed my house, took my water, bombed my country..."*

Anonymous placard on display London Jan 3rd 2009.

There's a story going about. It runs something like this: because Hamas have been lobbing rockets at unarmed civilians in Southern Israel, the Israeli government have been forced to attack them in Gaza. The death of ordinary Palestinians (including more than 400 children) is entirely due to Hamas, who use their own people as human shields. The Israelis use every means possible to minimise civilian casualties.

The story is told in this form in the National Post in Toronto by Lorne Gunter: "Suppose you lived in the Toronto suburb of Don Mills," he writes, "and people from the suburb of Scarborough – about 10 kilometres away – were firing as many as 100 rockets a day into your yard, your kid's school, the strip mall down the street and your dentist's office?"

Or again in this form in a letter to the Irish Times in Dublin by the Israeli Ambassador, Zion Evonry: "What would you do if Dublin were subjected to a bombardment of 8,000 rockets and mortars?"

The answer is implied in the question, of course. What would you do if you were being unjustifiably attacked in this way, by some irrational, brutal enemy, whose only purpose is to destroy you and all that you love?

This is the justification for the onslaught against Gaza which has been taking place since December 27th and which has now claimed in excess of 800 lives.

It's a story, of course. Some stories are true. Some stories are not. This particular story has the advantage that it sounds like it could be true. Indeed, you can see the proof, there, in those spiralling smoke trails swarming into the sky, and in the scenes of devastated buildings and hysterical human beings that follow.

We all tell stories.

We construct the world in narrative form so that it fits in with the image we want to create.

This is as true of nations as it is of individuals.

The trouble with this story is that it seems to have taken hold in everyone's mind, and that you hear it, in one form or another, over and over again, either implied, or openly stated, from BBC reporters and other journalists, or written between the lines of almost every newspaper article; not to speak from the mouths of your friends who, while shocked at the terrible images coming out of Gaza, at the scenes of horror and carnage that are being shown (most too horrific to be aired) nevertheless shrug with sadness and resignation at the end of their sentence and mention those rockets.

It always ends up with those rockets.

Almost no one asks the opposing question: what would you do as a captive and dispossessed people living in the 21st century equivalent of the Warsaw ghetto, whose border points and crossings were controlled by armed soldiers, living under a blockade with barely the minimum food and fuel to subsist upon, who are regularly subject to targeted assassination, to arbitrary arrest and violent attack, and now, it seems, to a full-scale military assault terrorising a whole population, slaughtering women and children and whole families in their beds?

How do a few home-made rockets compare to that?

Indeed there is a grotesque imbalance in the reporting of this on-going brutality, where scenes of dismembered Palestinian children held by blood-splattered parents screaming with horror and grief are shown next to scenes of an Israeli women crying because a rocket has landed nearby and disturbed her sleep.
So far, at the time of writing, 10 Israelis have been killed. Five of those were Israeli soldiers killed by their own side.

This in not a "conflict" in any recognisable sense of the word. It is not a battle. The language of war does not apply in this case. The fourth largest and second best equipped army in the world are facing a rag-tag militia armed with home-made rockets welded together in workshops usually reserved for car repairs.

It is often said that Hamas are targeting civilians. This is a philosophical absurdity. You cannot target those rockets. They are the equivalent of tin cans full of weed killer. Hamas are targeting no one. The most they can do is to point the rockets over the wall that imprisons them in the vague hope that they might hit something. We see pictures of scenes where a rocket has hit a car or a house or a yard. How many more of those rockets are landing harmlessly in fields? They make a big noise and they make people jump. They bring attention to the Palestinian cause. Occasionally they kill people. This is always to be regretted. But the degree of murder and mayhem, of terror, of violence, of bloodshed and carnage, of psychological trauma, on the one side, is entirely disproportionate to the level of provocation on the other.

The Israelis, on the other hand, say they do not target civilians. However, they know perfectly well that civilians will be killed, are being killed. They also know in what numbers they will continue to be killed. If a gang intending to commit a robbery take weapons with them and then "accidentally" kill the guards, they are not only guilty of the lesser crime of robbery, they are also guilty of murder. Committing a crime while in pursuit of some other goal is no less of a crime.

We've heard the story: now here are some facts. Hamas are the legitimate government of Gaza, having been elected in free and fair elections in 2006, making them the only democratic government in the Arab world. Many of the buildings destroyed in the first wave of Israeli attacks were government buildings, the necessary infrastructure of a nation. By destroying those buildings the Israelis are making it impossible for the people of Gaza to govern themselves, regardless of which party they choose. Also, many of the so-called legitimate targets killed in the first wave of bombings – those ones not counted amongst the civilian dead – were unarmed policemen and government bureaucrats, mere functionaries of government, not Hamas operatives or terrorist targets at all, just men and women employed to do a job. Again, it is clear that Israel are targeting the civilian infrastructure in order to make Gaza ungovernable.

So, having backed a coup against the elected government of Gaza, which was vigorously defeated by Hamas, the Israeli government then imposed a blockade, depriving the population of food and fuel and clean water. This is a form of collective punishment and is a crime under International Law. By sealing Gaza off from the rest of the world, by limiting its access to the basic necessities of life, Israel has turned this overpopulated land of refugees into a ghetto, the exact equivalent of the Warsaw ghetto of the earlier 20th century, a place where a whole population is imprisoned and punished merely because of their race.

But, you say, they should still not be firing those rockets. True. There was a ceasefire. It went into effect on June 19th 2008, and despite the fact that Israel never fully abided by the terms of the agreement, continuing to maintain a partial blockade despite international pressure, rocket fire from Gaza had virtually stopped, it being recognised by independent observers that Hamas was doing everything within its power to discipline and control other groups, such as Islamic Jihad, with access to weapons.

The ceasefire was broken on the 4th November 2008, not by Hamas, but by the Israeli Defence Force in an attack against a house in Gaza in which six members of Hamas' military wing were killed, including two commanders.

This is the background to the renewal of rocket attacks after this date, a fact that the Israeli government know full well, but which their spokesmen omit to mention whenever they talk about rocket attacks as the excuse for the current invasion.

Try looking at it the other way around, once more. Imagine if Hamas had managed to kill several high-ranking members of the Israeli Defence Force in a raid. Imagine what Israeli propagandists would have made of that, what news headlines there would be throughout the world. And it's a measure of the blatant and unapologetic bias of our media industry that not only was this hardly noticed at the time, but it has been completely forgotten in all subsequent reports, which continue to proclaim, along with Israeli spokesmen and women, that the "cause" of the current conflict is Hamas rocket attacks on Israeli citizens, not Israeli attacks upon Hamas.

Since then, of course, it has been a horrifying tale of atrocity and murder. UN schools full of women and children targeted. Whole families slaughtered. Cousins, uncles, fathers, mothers, brothers, sisters, sons and daughters killed. There is probably not a single family in Gaza now who hasn't lost at least one member of their extended family. Ambulances and aid workers being shot at. Over 800 dead[*] and several thousand wounded, a large percentage of them women and children. Dismembered bodies lying in the streets. Corpses tangled in the dust and rubble of collapsed buildings. Hospitals overwhelmed, the corridors running with blood. Children starving while their parents' bodies rot. Shortages of food and medicine. Days without fuel. Nowhere to run, nowhere to hide. No shelters. No route out of the carnage. All the border crossings shut tight, penning in the entire population. Death in the streets and houses. People waving white flags being shot at. People shivering in their houses with all the windows open in the depths of winter because otherwise the boom of nearby shells would blow out the glass. The daily fear, the daily trauma, the living nightmare of existence, a whole generation of children who have only ever known this horror, this fear, the death that comes screaming from the sky. Imagine what this must do to a child's mind.

Is there such a thing as hell? Of course there is. Hell is man-made. It is a war-zone, and it exists in Gaza right now.

So there are stories and there are stories. 1.5 million stories in Gaza. Stories of fear and injustice, of mutilation and dismemberment, of pain and grief and horror. But here is one story that sums it all up for me. It is the story of the extended Samouni family, sheltering in an building owned by one of their relatives, 70 people in all, who were directed into the building by the IDF, which was then subsequently attacked, killing 25 or more relatives, most of them children, and leaving many more wounded. One shell after another after another hit the building, the doors and the roof. Fathers and mothers gazing helplessly on at the sight of their children, brains lying splattered on the floor.

The Samouni family are not Hamas. They are farmers. They have taken no part in the resistance, and, indeed, are critical of Hamas. But the collective punishment of the Palestinian people includes the Samouni family too it seems. No Palestinian is innocent.

So, now, ask yourself does this make Israel more secure or less?

And if in five months or a year or five year's time one member of the Samouni family, driven mad with grief, straps an explosive corset around their waist and walks into an Israeli mall and blows themselves up along with a number of innocent Israelis, will the news reports ever refer to what happened on the day an entire family were targeted?

---

* The final figure was between 1,166 and 1,417 Palestinian deaths, the majority of those civilians.

Will they say, "It is a member of the Samouni clan, he saw his daughter's brains being splattered onto the concrete, that is why he is mad, why his heart is so full of hate"?

Of course not.

It will be made another excuse for the collective punishment of the whole Palestinian nation. And so the violence will continue.

Witnesses to a Massacre *15/01/09*

- **Wael Samouni**, 32, vegetable stall holder: "We were sitting and suddenly there was bombing on our house and everyone started to run. There were three rockets. I have no idea where they came from. I looked to my side, took hold of my boy Mohammad and I started to run. As I ran I looked back and saw on the floor my mother, two cousins and three of my children. All dead. It's a massacre. I'm 32 years old and I've never seen such things as this. I couldn't help myself or any of those around me. We just want to live in peace."
- **Nael Samouni**, 36. His wife and daughter had been in Wael's house at the time of the shelling. Both were killed: "I wanted to go and join them the night before, but it was too dangerous to go out. If anyone moved he would be shot. Then when I heard the bombing this morning I saw people running. I saw an injured man fall to the ground. I ran to help, but there was an Israeli sniper in the house next door who shouted: 'Leave him alone.' We couldn't rescue anyone."
- **Ahmed Samouni**, 16: "It was the third missile I remember. The other ones had killed my elder brother and injured people, they kept bleeding. But the third missile, that killed them all. My brother was bleeding so much and right in front of my eyes he died. My other brother Ismail, he also bled to death. My mum and my youngest brother, they are gone. Four brothers and my mother, dead. May God give them peace."
- **Mohamed el-Halby**, a paramedic: "On the day we got permission to rescue them, the army told us to leave the ambulances around two kilometres from the house. So we walked and all around us we could see they had bulldozed the area. The houses we passed had Israeli soldiers standing on the roofs. We went inside and heard screams coming from one room. There were about 15 people inside, two were dead, the rest sitting around them. That was just one room."
- **Raed el-Heleky**, paramedic: "We saw people lying dead on the streets. More than nine along the way before we got to the houses. We only went into five homes, there are other homes in the area and I am sure there are more dead in these houses. But the Israeli army stopped us from going any further."
- **Mohammed Shaheen**, a volunteer with Palestinian Red Crescent: "Inside the Samouni house I saw about ten bodies and outside another sixty. I was not able to count them accurately because there was not much time and we were looking for wounded people. We found fifteen people still alive but injured so we took them in the ambulances. I could see an Israeli army bulldozer knocking down houses nearby but we ran out of

time and the Israeli soldiers started shooting at us. We had to leave about eight injured people behind because we could not get to them and it was no longer safe for us to stay."

- **Ahmed Samouni**: "We were put in an ambulance, but there were still people inside the house, dead and injured. For days we all bled. We were so hungry; I remember giving my brother Isaac a tomato to eat before he died."
- **Ahmed Ibrahim Samouni**, 13, who was wounded in the leg: "Abu Salah died, his wife died. Abu Tawfiq died, his son died, his wife also died. Mohammed Ibrahim died, and his mother died. Ishaq died and Nasar died. The wife of Nael Samouni died. Many people died. There were maybe more than 25 people killed."
- **Ahmad al-Samouni**, 23, religious studies teacher: "One shell hit the door, killing my cousin Muhammad immediately. One shell, I believe it was from an Apache, hit the ceiling. Then another shell and another. I could only recognise my mother Rahmeh from her clothes and earrings because part of her head was gone." One of the infants was the five-year-old daughter of his cousin **Salah**. "Her last words were 'Baba, Baba' and she died. She was hit in the head."
- **Maysaa**, 19, a mother: "When the smoke began to clear, I looked around and saw between 20 and 30 bodies, and 20 wounded. The dead included my husband Tawfiq and my father-in-law Rashed, who was hit in the head and whose brain was on the floor, and a five-month-old baby whose whole brain was outside his body."

Maysaa says she escaped with her daughter and brother-in-law to the house of an uncle. There she found at least 40 Israeli soldiers and about 30 Palestinians. Some of them were blindfolded. The soldiers administered first aid to Maysaa and her daughter before releasing them, but, she says, said they would keep Musa and his uncle "in case Hamas came". She adds: "I understood that they intended to use them as human shields."

- **Wael Samouni**, later, in the hospital, talking about his 6 year old son, Abdullah, who survived. Wael had thought he was dead: "I didn't know what to do, I still don't…look at him he is so ill, they are all terrified. He cries all the time. His shoulder is hurt and it has infection but he can't stand the smell, he cries when he looks and smells his wounds. And his leg, look. I want to take him out of Gaza for treatment and I want to be able to go back to the house and get the rest of my family so that I can bury them."

The Israeli military denies targeting any buildings in the area and says it never forcibly gathers civilians in a specific building. It is continuing to investigate the incident.

Compiled from interviews conducted by *The Guardian, the Telegraph, the Independent* and *Al Jazeera*.

Money

1. We do the work. Someone else takes the wealth.

- **Economics is easy to understand**

During the 2010 election campaign I heard the columnist Kelvin Mackenzie talking about economics.

"Economics is very complicated," he said. "You have to be a genius to understand economics."

This is not true. Economics is easy to understand. Wealth comes from human beings. It's as simple as that. It comes from human beings engaging with nature in an intelligent and productive way in order to make all of the things we want and need. It is work that makes wealth.

This is so obvious an observation that it hardly needs commenting upon. All of the classical economists understood it: Adam Smith and John Stuart Mill, as well as Karl Marx.

The reason that modern economics has become so complex is that it has attempted to obscure this simple fact behind a fog of distraction in order to hide the processes by which a very few people have become more and more obscenely wealthy, while the rest of us are being squeezed to the point of desperation.

We do the work. Someone else takes the wealth.

We've been living under an illusion for the last 30 years or so. The illusion goes under the collective name of "Monetarism". It is also sometimes known as "Thatcherism" or "Neoliberalism". In the US it went under the name "Reaganomics".

It is the idea that the market knows best, that everything in the public sector is bad, and everything in the private sector is good, that the private sector only needs to be deregulated for it to provide wealth for everyone. Take away the fetters and wealth will expand, it says. If the rich get rich, we all get rich as a consequence.

The idea was that the rich are "wealth creators" and the wealth they generate will eventually "trickle down" to the masses.

Do you remember being told that?

Actually it turns out that none of this is true. The rich aren't "wealth creators" at all, they are wealth extractors. The world hasn't been becoming richer, it has been becoming poorer. The wealth hasn't "trickled down", it has been siphoned up. The rich have accumulated even more wealth while the poor have been shafted.

Do you ever get the feeling that we've been ever-so slightly conned?

- **Confidence**

I was listening to the Secretary-General of the Organisation for Economic Co-operation and Development on the radio. He was here to meet the Chancellor of the Exchequer to discuss Britain's economic future.

"The market has confidence in Britain," he said.

That is actually a very revealing statement. What it tells us first of all is that he thinks he knows what the market thinks. You wonder how he is privy to such information? Does the market talk? Or has the Secretary-General learned to read its collective mind?

Secondly it tells us that the market has human responses. It can have confidence in things - or not, depending on the circumstances.

Thirdly it tells us that Britain is one of the "good guys" in market terms, that is, it is doing things that the market likes; whereas other countries presumably are the "bad guys", doing things of which the market does not approve.

The question that arises from this is what we think this thing called "the market" actually is.

It doesn't take all that much thinking about to realise that the question itself is wrong. It's not "what", it is "who".

The market is not like the weather – some natural force which shifts according to laws over which we have no control - it is a bunch of people who, through their control and manipulation of various financial levers, are able to tell us what to do. It is not a law of nature, it is the mechanism by which we are ruled.

The "confidence" we are talking about is a kind of collective pat on the back for the British government for doing as it is told.

What we are seeing is a coup d'état against our public services. Public services are being cut in order to serve the interests of the markets.

Our choice in the general election was between a government which said it would cut public services immediately, and one which promised to do so at a later date. The choice we didn't get was for a government which would put the interests of the public first.

- **Cuts**

So that's what we chose: a government intent upon making cuts. It's cuts across the economy. Almost £2 billion in cuts immediately, and then another £8.4 billion in "reviews". Reviews refer to cuts that haven't happened yet, but which will happen in the future.

There are plans to cut a scheme that would extend free school dinners to primary school children, plus one that would have seen 7,000 new homes built. There are plans to cut over £1 billion from council budgets, to scrap free swimming for children and pensioners, and to cancel a hospital being built in Hartlepool, amongst other things. Cuts, cuts, cuts.

We were promised no cuts to front-line services. You can't get more "front-line" than a hospital.

The cuts are being implemented in order pay off the deficit.

The deficit represents the difference between what we are earning as a country, and what we are paying out. We are paying out more than we are bringing in. In order to cover the difference we have to borrow. Last year we borrowed £170.8 billion. This year we are set to borrow £167.9 billion.

We do this by issuing bonds, known as gilts. These are essentially promissory notes: IOUs. In other words, we hand out a big pile of paper, and we get a big pile of paper in return.

Actually, we don't even get paper in return. We get credit on a computer screen. They just add a few more noughts onto the end of the noughts we already owe.

Now here's the question: who exactly do we owe all this money to? That's when things start to get really murky. It's not at all clear.

Mainly, it seems, we owe money to "financial institutions" in the UK. Banks, in other words. We also owe 35% of our national debt to "overseas investors". We can assume these are banks, too, in some form. They lend money, so they must be banks.

In other words, we are cutting public services in order to service interest on debts owed to foreign banks.

Tell me: at what point did we vote to give our sovereignty away?

2. The Market has a Name. It is Goldman Sachs

"Money is a new form of slavery, and distinguishable from the old simply by the fact that it is impersonal - that there is no human relation between master and slave."

Leo Tolstoy. From *What Shall We Say?* in the Complete Works of Leo Tolstoy

- **Corporatocracy**

A few months ago Ken Clarke, the justice secretary and former chancellor, said that it would take two to three years for Britain to get out of the recession.

"People have got to understand it is going to be a long haul," he said. "We have got ourselves into a real mess."

Meanwhile Mervyn King, the governor of the Bank of England, has warned that UK take-home pay will continue to be squeezed.

You get the feeling we may be being softened up by statements such as these: that we are being prepared for a permanent reduction in our living standards rather than a temporary one.

A pay freeze alongside rising inflation means an effective pay-cut. We are seeing massive cuts in our public services and large scale redundancies. Restructuring of the NHS means privatisation by the back door. Libraries are closing. The lift on the cap on council house rents will lead to a form of social cleansing, as poorer people in wealthy areas are forced to leave.

Bankers bonuses, on the other hand, continue to rise. CEOs of large corporations continue to receive the kind of pay and benefits that would keep whole nations afloat.

The narrative being used to justify all of this is one of economic competence. There is a massive black hole in our budget which needs to be filled. At the same time, the government's economic advisors - the ones who are prescribing these austerity measures - are also the same people who entirely failed to predict the financial crisis in the first place.

Worse: they are the very people whose economic theories brought the financial system to the brink of collapse. Remember, it was these same "experts" who argued for bank deregulation and a liberalisation of the markets. Wherever these policies have been instituted they have lead to financial chaos and a break down in the social order, as wealth flows upward, from the poor to the rich.

Is this deliberate? Are we seeing the creation of a form of corporate feudalism in which a capitalist aristocracy – a corporatocracy - lords it over the rest of us, with democracy as a convenient front?

Look around you folks: it is already here.

- **The Market**

In an interview on BBC News 24 on the 26th of September 2011, Alessio Rastani, an independent trader, made certain predictions about the economy.

He said that the euro will crash. "Markets are ruled by fear," he said. "The big funds don't buy this rescue plan. They know the market is toast. The stock market is finished. They're moving their money away to other, safer, assets."

The interviewer asked him if there's anything that governments can do to prevent it?

"I don't care," he said. "If I see an opportunity to make money, I go with that. People don't remember, but the 30s depression wasn't just about the market crash. There were some people who were prepared to make money off that crash. It's not a time right now for wishful thinking hoping that the government is going to sort things out. Governments don't rule the world. Goldman Sachs rules the world."

Goldman Sachs, in case you don't know, is the world's most powerful investment bank.

Some of you may remember an interview in the Times with Lloyd Blankfein, the CEO of Goldman Sachs. In it he said that he was "doing God's work." That interview came out as a response to an article in Rolling Stone magazine by Matt Taibbi, which accused Goldman Sachs of being like "a great vampire squid wrapped around the face of humanity."

The article was called The Great American Bubble Machine. I recommend you read it.

Taibbi was very clear. Not only did Goldman Sachs make money from the depression, but it engineered it as well. In fact Taibbi goes on to list a whole series of economic crises that Goldman Sachs specifically engineered in order to make money from them, including the sub-prime crisis which brought about the financial collapse of 2008. It's a measure of the veracity of the information in the article that Goldman Sachs never sued him over it.

So the next time you hear someone on the TV telling you what "the market" demands, you should remember this.

The market has a name. It is Goldman Sachs.

- **Debt**

So our nation is in debt. It is so horribly in debt that it will take several generations to pay it off. It doesn't matter what party is in power, the end result is the same. It's job cuts and pay cuts and austerity measures for the foreseeable future.

All nations throughout the western world are in debt. There is so much debt, according to financial experts, that there isn't enough money in the entire world to pay it off.

Stop and think about that for a second. The human race is in debt to itself for more money than there actually is in existence. Even if we all tightened all of our belts and starved ourselves to death to pay off the debt, we still couldn't succeed. There just isn't enough money to do it.

You wonder how this came about. One branch of the human family is in debt to the other. A very few people have so much money they couldn't spend it in a thousand lifetimes, while large numbers are so poor they can't even afford the basic necessities of life.

Here's the problem. Money is created as debt. Banks issue money, but they charge interest on it, so in order to pay the money back the economy as a whole is forced to borrow even more money. It's a vicious cycle which will go on forever. There can never be enough money to pay off all the accumulated debts.

As a consequence money is always depreciating in value. The term "pound sterling" arises from the fact that originally a pound in money represented a pound weight in silver. At the current rate a pound of silver is worth £316 in sterling. That's how far the value of our money has depreciated. Where has all this value gone?

Why has gold gone up recently? Actually it hasn't: it is paper money that has gone down.

Something has gone horribly wrong with our financial system. Since when did we give control of our money supply to a handful of private corporations? The banking system is a parasite on the real economy, and the cause of, not the solution to, the financial crisis.

3. The Spirit of '45

I went to see the premiere of Ken Loach's new film, *The Spirit of '45* at the Gulbenkian Theatre in Canterbury. Half of Whitstable was there.

In case you haven't heard about it, it's a celebration of the achievements of the 1945 Labour government, done as a series of interviews with people who had seen the pre-war world and knew what the alternative would be. It has taken me a couple of weeks to absorb its message.

This was a very different Labour government than those we have seen in recent times. In six dizzying, triumphant years the Labour Party laid the foundations of the welfare state. It nationalised the coal mining and the steel industries. It created the National Health Service and British Rail. It began the process of decolonisation. It oversaw the return to full employment – finding jobs for all those demobbed soldiers – while rebuilding and improving our national infrastructure, building tens of thousands of council homes, and reconstructing whole cities and whole industries in the process.

Talk about austerity. This was a nation completely exhausted by war. It was broke. It was in pieces. And yet we managed to achieve all this, by sheer will and determination, in the spirit of hope, that we could build a better world than the one that had existed before.

That was the world that I grew up in. It was an optimistic world. It was a world in which we truly believed that each new generation would be better off - more secure, better educated, in better health - than the one before.

This was what was known as the post-war consensus. So all-pervasive was it that even Tory governments participated. In those days governments vied with each other, not about how much to cut our public services, as they do today, but over how many houses they had built, about how many jobs they had created, about how much they had spent on improving the quality of life for all sectors of the population.

All of this was done by government intervention, not by private industry. The glorification of the market began in 1979, with Thatcher.

It was Thatcher who sold off our nationalised industries, who attacked the trade unions, who deregulated the financial industry, who privatised our utilities, who sold off our housing stock. After that successive governments have vied with each other over who will be more ruthlessly neo-liberal than the next. As Peter Mandelson said in 2002, "We are all Thatcherites now."

And now look. The post-war consensus is broken, and private enterprise rules. The rich are getting richer and the poor are getting poorer. Our bills are going up while our wages are going down. State funding is no longer used to build houses, or to improve the quality of life for the population, but to bail out the banks and make sure that bankers keep their bonuses. Even the NHS is being made subject to "marketisation", which is a euphemism for privatisation: people's health being thrown out onto the mad lottery that is the world Capitalist system.

The Spirit of '45 has been criticised for being a propaganda film, for glorifying the 1945 Labour government, while demonising Thatcher. And it's true: it leaps boldly from 1945 to 1979 as if there was nothing in between.

But this makes sense to me. These were two markers on the page of history: two turning points that defined what went before, and what happened after.

The world after 1945 was a better world than the one that went before. The world after 1979 started to get worse again.

I know which of the two I prefer.

4. The Empire of Things

They hang the man and flog the woman,
Who steals the goose from off the common,
Yet let the greater villain loose,
That steals the common from the goose.

Seventeenth Century English protest rhyme

- **Riots**

It was Margaret Thatcher who said there was no such thing as society. "There are individual men and women, and there are families... It's our duty to look after ourselves and then... to look after our neighbour," she said. "People have got the entitlements too much in mind, without the obligations. There's no such thing as entitlement, unless someone has first met an obligation."

She said this in an interview with *Women's Own* magazine published in October 1987. Six years before that, in 1981, riots had ripped through Britain's inner cities. There were riots in Brixton in London, in Toxteth in Liverpool, in Handsworth in Birmingham and Chapeltown in Leeds. There were further riots throughout the 80s, including Broadwater Farm in 1985, and Peckham that same year.

On coming to power in 1979, on the steps of Downing Street, Margaret Thatcher had quoted from St Francis of Assisi: "Where there is discord, may we bring harmony. Where there is error, may we bring truth. Where there is doubt, may we bring faith. And where there is despair, may we bring hope."

Never have a set of words proved to be less appropriate, or more vain, or less honest, or more ignorant of the truth.

The central idea behind Thatcherite policy was an economic theory known as Monetarism. The aim of Monetarism was to break the post war consensus which had given working people unprecedented wealth - a welfare state, a national health service, free education, participatory democracy - and to redistribute that wealth to where its proponents believed it should go: back to the very rich. It did this by deregulating the banks, by breaking the trade unions, by selling off public assets, and by a form of social engineering in which traditional Labour voters were lured into property ownership by selling their council houses to them at drastically reduced rates, and in this way, getting them into debt. Debt became the driving force of the new economy.

Within one year of this we had the first riot: in St Pauls in Bristol.

- **The Enemy Within**

> *Yes, as through this world I've wandered*
> *I've seen lots of funny men;*
> *Some will rob you with a six gun,*
> *And some with a fountain pen.*
> *And as through your life you travel,*
> *Yes, as through your life you roam,*
> *You won't never see an outlaw*
> *Drive a family from their home.*

Pretty Boy Floyd by **Woody Guthrie.**

In 1984 Thatcher took on and defeated the Miners. She called the Miners "The Enemy Within". They were the bastion of working class solidarity in the United Kingdom, fiercely socialist in their outlook. This came directly from their work. Mining is a dangerous job. People who work underground have to watch each other's backs. This creates a form of solidarity which they then bring back to the surface with them, into the over ground world. Anyone who doubts this should consider the Chilean Miners. During their first 17 days underground - before they were contacted, when they were nearly starving, and fearful that the probes might not find them – they had instituted a form of democracy, a form of socialism, which many of them say saved them from a descent into barbarity.

It is out of adversity that socialism arises. It is out of love. Solidarity is another word for love.

The National Union of Mineworkers was an organisation of love. You listen to any old Miner talking about their union, and you will hear it. You will hear it in the tone of their voice and in the words they use. It was their organisation, forged out of their solidarity, out of the bonds created in the terrible conditions they encountered in their work, out of their history of struggle, out of loyalty to their class and their fierce independence. The NUM actively stood against the kind of world that Thatcher was promoting. It had to be destroyed.

We had love, and they had greed, and greed won. The defeat of the Miners led directly to the kind of world we live in now.

There was an irony here. Thatcher appealed to a form of cod patriotism. She promoted patriotic values, waving her rhetorical flag for the assembled audience. And yet she helped destroy this most British of institutions, the National Union of Mineworkers, and to undermine trade unionism as a whole – a British invention – while encouraging an invasion of international corporations in the service industry, such as McDonalds, in which trade unionism was actively banned.

Waving the patriotic flag while inviting a foreign invasion. There's a word we normally use for this. Under other circumstances we would call it "treason".

- **McWages**

*If the young are not initiated into the village,
they will burn it down just to feel its warmth.*

African proverb.

Roll on 30 years, to a new Tory government, to a new Monetarism, to a new austerity, a new Thatcherism.

And don't be in any doubt that this is exactly what it is. When George Osborne told MPs that his deficit-cutting plan had made Britain a "safe haven in the global debt storm", what he meant was that the financial institutions, to which he is obligated, have approved of his policies. They don't have to loot the British economy, because Osborne is already handing the loot to them.

It's a form of protection racket. The world has already seen what a financial mugging looks like. They've already broken the backs of governments in Ireland and Portugal and Greece. Give us your wealth, they say, or this is the fate that lies in store for you too. Give us your public property. Privatise, privatise, privatise, and no institution – not even the Health Service – is sacred.

That is what deficit reduction means. It means privatisation: not by the back door, but by the front door. Financial looting. It means taking British capital, currently held by the British state, and handing it over to financial institutions at a reduced rate. "Waving the patriotic flag while inviting a foreign invasion" again.

We are in the midst of an age of unprecedented structural change in our world, a return to feudalism. Feudalism arose out of the collapse of the Roman Empire. It involved a robber class living off the back of a servant class, using rent as its means. The new Feudal Lords use financial rent – indebtedness – in the same way. What we are watching is the collapse of the New Roman Empire into a new Dark Age of institutionalised plunder, a takeover by the banks.

The austerity measures are already being implemented, and it is the young who are being targeted. So tuition fees are going up to £9,000 a year, while the Education Maintenance Allowance for 16-19 year old has been scrapped. Inflation is rampant, while real wages are declining. There is no future for the young. No jobs, no education, no skills, no apprenticeships. These were mostly scrapped by Thatcher 30 years ago. A nation built on skill has been reduced to a service economy, to McJobs and McWages in a McSociety.

You can call it "muck" if you like.

- **As Above So Below**

*"When your most elite, most powerful members of society adopt a
strategy of plundering.... they will develop a morality that doesn't
simply permit plundering, but valorises it. When that happens the*

moral structures of a society will inevitably deteriorate. In the upper classes that leads to polite looting. In the underclass it leads to street looting."

Bill Black on the Keiser Report, 16/08/2011

The illusion that's been created is that we are separate beings. We are not. We are social beings. Margaret Thatcher was entirely wrong when she said there was no such thing as society. Society is the very essence of who we are. We are tied together by bonds of language, by bonds of morality, by bonds of loyalty, by bonds of family, by bonds of society, by bonds of love. You break those bonds and the social world begins to fall apart.

Society is the individual writ large. The individual is society in microcosm. As above, so below. The unconscious is not underneath us, it is around us. It is not inside of us, it is outside of us. The unconscious is that part of ourselves that lies in other people. It is in the obligations we owe to the people around us, in our human interactions, only barely recognised, as we negotiate our way around our social world.

In the individual personality, rampant, out-of-control egotism is a form of mental illness. Commonly called psychopathy, it is a mental state in which the individual only concerns himself with his own gratification. So if a psychopath gets pleasure from murder, then he will murder, free from conscience, because personal gratification is his only concern. Not every psychopath is a murderer, though. There are psychopaths all around us, and everyone is capable of psychopathic behaviour. Everyone who seeks personal gratification at the expense of his fellow creatures is a psychopath to some degree.

In the social sphere, the financial sector is a kind of collective psychopath, destroying the health of the economy for its private gratification. We honour the psychopath in our current world. It is the world of private gratification through private power. We give power to the psychopath, while denuding and deriding the common good that arises from our common world.

All private wealth is won at the expense of the commons. What we are witnessing right now are the new enclosure acts, the new clearances. We are beings born of the commons and not only our economic, but also our mental and emotional health, is measured by how much we bring to the common good.

- **Democracy**

"If you don't find God in the next person you meet, it is a waste of time looking for him further."

Gandhi.

I saw a BBC reporter interviewing a community activist in one of the riot areas. The activist

167

compared what was happening to the Arab Spring. "But this is a democracy," the reporter said, in a defensive tone.

Is it though?

There are four pillars to a functioning democracy. We need an effective police force, a free press, rational political institutions and an efficient financial system. All of them must be regulated and free from corruption. What we have instead is a corrupt police force in hock to a corrupt press, with corrupt politicians serving the interests of a corrupt financial elite. Corruption from top to bottom. Corruption in every avenue of our public life. Top policemen taking bribes, politicians on the make, an intrusive and bullying press, distracting us with trivia and gossip, while covering up its own illegal practices, and a City of London which is entirely out of regulatory control, and which is plundering the nation's resources for its own private gain.

And you wonder why the young riot? The kids are looting the shops. The banks are looting the nation.

Then we have the Labour Party – the Party created by the working class in the early part of the last century to institute socialist policies through democratic means – being seduced by high finance, and taking part in the financial rape of this country. Tony Blair amassing a personal fortune by taking us to war. Gordon Brown bailing out the banks and indebting the nation, borrowing money from the banks to give to the banks, imposing dangerous levels of debt on future generations. Peter Mandelson declaring: "We are all Thatcherites now." What hope for us when even our own party stands against us?

- **Things**

> *"These people are living in a financial prison, and this is a prison riot."*
> **Max Keiser**
> on the Keiser Report, 16/08/2011

We've had over 30 years of rampant individualism, of consumerism, of me-ism and the devil take the hindmost; 30 years of mortgaging our future to pay for our present consumption; 30 years of selling off our birthright for a mess of consumerist pottage; 30 years of corruption and greed, of the worship of **Things**. It is an **Empire of Things**. So we have our technology and our consumer durables, our computers and our mobile phones, our technical baubles. Well some of us have. Many of us don't have these **Things**. The young in particular, don't have these **Things**. The young from the sink estates, the second and third generation underclass.

So we've set these **Things** up in place of our values. We've substituted them for the social ties that used to bind us together, and we've told the young who can't afford these **Things**, that they are the only measure of value, that you don't count unless you can flaunt these **Things** in the faces of your peers. That only **Things** count. And then society starts to break down under the pressure of the new Feudal arrangements, in which we are becoming economic vassals paying homage to debt, and the kids take to the streets in a blind fury of acquisitive excitement. And what do they do? They steal. They loot. They plunder. They obey the rules laid down on them by the **Empire of Things**. They collect the very **Things** we told them to, declaring fealty to the **Things** that are our Lords in the new fiefdom of debt.

They do what we tell them to do and then we punish them for it.

The bankers have plundered the economy, and they have been rewarded. The politicians have plundered their expenses, and they still sit in Parliament. The Murdoch Press has corrupted our values, and yet they are still allowed to own newspapers. The police have taken bribes, and yet they talk brazenly of the criminality of the streets.

Young people are put in gaol for the theft of a bottle of water, while bankers are given bonuses for the plunder of nations. People are losing their homes because their children are suspected of rioting, while politicians, who claimed for multiple homes on their expenses, are allowed to bleat on about rioters and looters from their privileged position in the House of Commons.

It's at this point that I would like to agree with Margaret Thatcher. As she said: "People have got the entitlements too much in mind, without the obligations. There's no such thing as entitlement, unless someone has first met an obligation."

To whom do we owe the obligation? To society, of course.

5. The Irony of the Iron Lady

According to my dictionary, the word *Irony* is defined as an "incongruity between actual circumstances and the normal, appropriate, or expected result; an event or situation showing such incongruity."

Incongruity, yes. Incongruity between what is said, and what actually happens. Incongruity between the public face of an event, and what lies behind it. A kind of opposition between appearance and reality.

It is also interesting to note that it is rooted in the Greek word for *dissembling*, meaning to conceal or disguise ones true motives, to lie or to deceive.

That's exactly it. In the period following Margaret Thatcher's demise, and leading up to her funeral, the ironies have been heavy in the air, like the pall of smoke from a funeral pyre, from the many pyres of those whose lives she destroyed.

Take this, for example. Margaret Thatcher said she believed in the primacy of the free market. She closed down our public institutions in order to sell them off to the private sector, on the oft repeated assertion that the private sector was more efficient. And yet she is given a ceremonial funeral organised by the state, at the cost of £10 million to the public purse.

Really, if we were to follow the Thatcher doctrine to its logical conclusion, we should have privatised her funeral, put it out to competitive tender and accepted the cheapest bid - as Ken Loach, the filmmaker, suggested - just as she did with our public services.

Meanwhile, according to the Daily Telegraph, paupers funerals are on the increase because hard-pressed families are being turned down for funding. "Even for those who do get help, the typical sum awarded is £1,217, which is far short of the average £3,091 cost of a funeral."

In other words, tens of thousands of poor families are being short changed on their funeral costs, while one family of multi-millionaires gets state funding for their lavish £10 million public affair.

Pundits complained when spontaneous parties broke out all over the country to celebrate her death, calling them "death parties", and yet the rest of us are being subjected to a celebratory death party at our expense, regardless of our views. At least the people who assembled in Trafalgar Square on the Saturday after her death, and all over the country on the day it was announced, were paying for their own drinks.

They said that we shouldn't speak ill of the dead, and yet, when Hugo Chavez died, only a few weeks earlier, we were subjected to a torrent of abuse at his memory. Thatcher was in power for 11 years, and never won an overall majority of the vote. Chavez was in power for 14, always winning a clear majority, and yet they called him a "dictator", and her a "champion of democracy".

So in order to protest, tens of thousands of people bought a copy of *Ding Dong! The Witch is Dead*, from the 1940s musical *The Wizard of Oz*, in the hope of having it played on the Radio One chart rundown; using the free market system to emphasise their disagreement, spending their hard-earned cash to make a political point. It reached number 2, and yet, despite that, the publicly funded BBC decided not to play the track, instead inviting a journalist on to explain background to its entry in the charts, as if we were all too stupid to understand.

The rival song, *I'm In Love With Margaret Thatcher* on the other hand, was played in full.

Are we beginning to see any patterns here? When it comes to public funding, the rich get what they want. When it comes to the free market, the rest of us can go hang. It's communism for the rich, and censorship for the poor.

The reason people felt the need to disagree is that vast amounts of air time have been spent eulogising her legacy, using her death as an excuse for a barely disguised frenzy of propaganda. We've been treated to an series of rousing speeches as justification for a political philosophy which serves the interests of the few over the interests of the many. Over and over again we've been hearing lies about what Thatcherism has actually achieved and a whitewash of her multiple crimes.

They said that she promoted democracy and freedom. In fact she supported Apartheid in South

Africa and called Nelson Mandela a terrorist. She described the fascist General Pinochet of Chile as a "friend", supplied arms to Saddam Hussein, and even stood behind the murderous Khmer Rouge in Cambodia.

They said that she was a patriot. And yet she destroyed that most British of institutions, the National Union of Mineworkers in order to sell our nation to the international corporations, wiping out skilled, unionised, well paid jobs in the manufacturing industries, to replace them with unskilled, unrepresented, low-paid jobs in the service industries: selling us off to McDonalds for the minimum wage.

They said she curbed the power of the Trade Unions, and this was true. But she also unleashed the power of the City in the financial Big Bang of 1986, which lead directly to the banking crisis of 2008; replacing the power of one set of institutions, which served the majority of people in the UK, with the power of another, which only serves the interest of the very rich.

They said she broke the monopoly of the state-run utilities, which was also true; and yet she sold off our public services in job lots, turning them from state-owned monopolies into privately owned monopolies. She made the accountable, unaccountable, in other words, using public funding to subsidise profits instead of quality of service, hoiking up prices and lowering standards at the same time. Anyone who says that the rail industry is better off now than it was under public ownership needs their head examining. Anyone who thinks that we are better served by the energy companies than we were by British Gas and the electricity boards when they were publicly owned, clearly has no idea of the real state of affairs.

They said that she was against the power of the State, and yet she used state power to attack all those opposed to her, unleashing a highly paid and politicised police force in a frenzy of violent assault, firstly against the miners, and then against the New Age Travellers, and then against anyone else who stood in her way.

She destroyed mining communities, travelling communities, manufacturing communities, and wrenched the heart out of our great cities, turning them into post-industrial wastelands. She turned the South against the North, the rich against the poor, the middle class against the working class, Basildon against Barnsley. She destroyed the post-war consensus which had created a fairer and a freer Britain and killed off the hope of a generation.

No wonder so many people turned their backs at her funeral.

Therapies

1. Off the Shelf in the Spiritual Supermarket

(The Easy Way to Enlightenment)

I had this dream once. The whole of the human race was marching up the hill towards enlightenment. I was there too, elbow-to-elbow, amid the general throng. There was a sense of elation and bustling expectation.

Then, as we were nearing the top I began to notice all these little scenes. Two people were sitting in the dust by the path comparing hands and feet. "Look," one of them was saying, with child-like wonder, "we have fingers. And toes." And they giggled.

There was another couple across the way. She had on a printed, flowery dress and was sat back on her haunches, while he was leaning forward on his knees immersing himself in her eyes.

I had a sudden feeling of revulsion. There was something cloyingly saccharine - not to say, infantile - about the scene.

I looked up, and across the valley, to where I could see another hill. Over there were all these wild anarchists jumping up and down to thunderous music with their fists in the air, whooping with joy. I knew that that was where I wanted to be.

"Oh my God," I thought, "I'm on the wrong hill!"

Which only goes to show that enlightenment is a matter of taste maybe. One man's enlightenment is another man's Mills & Boon novel.

The question is: where can you buy your enlightenment these days? Can you get it off-the-shelf in the spiritual market-place, or does it have to be made-to-measure? Is it always one-off and unique, or can it be mass-produced? Can you pick it up along with the soap-powder and cat-food down the supermarket, or do you have to work at it over lifetimes of arduous mental and physical application on the top of a mountain somewhere, while living off a grain of rice a day and bathing in cold water?

Can you do it, like the knitting, while you are watching the telly, or is it more like brain-surgery: something you have to get good at before you practice?

You wouldn't let just anyone become a brain-surgeon, would you? But almost anyone can become a guru. All you have to do is write a book.

Enlightenment is big business these days. The bookshelves are groaning with self-help manuals on how to activate your auric chakras while bringing up a baby, teaching yourself divination and having ecstatic sex, all at the same time. This is multi-tasking gone exponential, and is surely designed to make us all feel inadequate.

Actually I suspect that a lot of these self-help books are more like celebrity slimming videos than true spiritual texts. They represent the author's idealised view of themselves: how the writer would like to be rather than how they really are. Why should we expect a fat celebrity to know more about slimming than we do ourselves? Why should we expect someone else's half-baked platitudes to be any more useful than our own?

Mostly these books are just a good marketing ploy for the multi-nationals, another off-the-shelf commodity item for sale down the spiritual supermarket. Special offer: two for the price of one. Buy One Get One Free. Collect enough spiritual nectar points and you can win a lifetime trip to paradise!

But then, I'm not really sure that enlightenment has to be worked out over lifetimes either. Maybe just being born is a start.

I read somewhere that we are not human beings having a spiritual experience, but spiritual beings having a human experience.

It's more about learning than it is about consuming.

Learning how to walk and talk is the first thing. After that, we have to learn to relate. Then we have to learn to work and to play, to read, to write, to enjoy each other's company, to grow up, to separate ourselves from our parents, to discover the quiet satisfaction that comes with responsibility, to reserve judgement. We have to learn honour and integrity, how to apply ourselves with diligence and care, and how to be humble about the product of our skills. After that we have to learn how to grow old without growing bitter, how not to be scared of our impending end. Finally we have to learn how to surrender our lives to the mystery beyond.

In other words, we only have to learn how to be human.

Isn't that enough?

2. Weird is the English Word for Fate

Is your glass half full, or is it half empty? Mine's neither. It's either full and being drunk, or it's empty and waiting to be refilled.

I was talking to an old friend of mine this morning. She takes an optimistic view of life. She's a half-full person. She said, "I know I get on your nerves by being optimistic all the time."

Well I thought about that. It's true I could sometimes be mildly irritated by her. She was so constantly breathlessly hopeful and enthusiastic. But it wasn't the optimism that got on my nerves. It was the platitudes.

The one I hated the most was, "it was meant to be".

Whenever anyone says that to me I want to punch them in the face. "There," I am inclined to say, "was THAT meant to be too?"

It's just such a smug phrase, that's all. "It was meant to be." It's always the statement of someone who is well-off and comfortable. No one ever says "it was meant to be" when they're down-on-their-luck and miserable. Sleeping rough tonight? Cold, hungry, tired, desperate for a kind word? It was meant to be.

Do we choose our lives? Well yes and no and maybe.

It was Robert Anton Wilson - that wisest and funniest of all the spiritual writers - who clarified the matter for me. He said that if someone is knocked down by a car, say, and hospitalised, he or she can choose what attitude they take to their misfortune. They can see it as a chance to catch up on their reading, or they can bemoan the loss of valuable time. But anyone who says they chose to have the accident is clearly talking through their proverbial parts.

Nothing is meant to be. Nothing is determined. Or rather, what is meant to be is a matter of choice. It is up to us humans to determine our lives through the decisions we make, collectively and individually. Fate is a mystery, not a resolution. When fate casts its strange shadow – as it does sometimes – over the ordinary processes of our lives, it does so with reason. Fate is the question we ask of ourselves. Fate is the choice we are given. Once we have made that choice, then our lives are determined by it. But the moment of fate itself is actually the moment of greatest freedom.

All of the previous paragraph came to me in a pub. You can call THAT fate if you like. I was walking passed the pub one afternoon, when I saw someone in there I hadn't seen in years, and joined him for a pint. One pint turned into seven (he was buying) and I ended up, several hours later, setting light to the pizza I'd popped into the oven before promptly falling asleep on the settee. It was the charred inevitable pizza of destiny.

Actually, the guy used to be my enemy. We both loved the same woman at the same time. It was like this: I'd gone out with her for a while, and then she dumped me. I went a little crazy after that, even going so far one night as to fantasise about killing her. I was reading Kabbalist texts at the time. I thought of her as the Shekhinah, as Jehovah-God's lost consort. She was the only woman in the world who ever made me want to pray.

After that he'd gone out with her, and had a child with her. And then she left him too. The night she left him she came to see me. He became wild with whiskey and jealousy, just like I had: cut off all his hair, and smashed several windows in the pub where we were drinking. She was playing both of us for a fool and – fool that I am – I had the terrible urge to follow her. This was a mistake as she wasn't really interested in me at all, merely in the effect I would have upon him.

And now, here we were, me and this guy, several years later, drinking toasts to times gone by, to fate, and to the woman we had both loved - once-upon-a-time.

It's an old story, of course. Fate often takes on that guise: two blokes chasing the same woman. It's the story of Arthur and Lancelot, and one of the constant themes of Celtic mythology. Some say the story refers to the cycles of the year, when the Oak King is displaced by the Holly King. In which case, maybe fate goes in circles too.

The English word for fate is "weird", with the secondary meaning of the uncanny or the supernatural. The weird sisters in Macbeth are weird in the sense that they represent fate, not because they are odd-looking or ugly. And that kind of tells you something else about fate too, that it carries with it an aura of otherness, as it emerges into our lives from a different vector. To think of it as a form of inevitability or determinism, therefore, is to take away its mysteriousness, to diminish its otherworldliness, to mistake the shadow for the thing, in the same way that the word "weird" has been diminished by making it merely into something strange.

It's so much more than just strange, my darlings: it is who we really are.

3. Poor Little Frankie

When my son Joe was growing up we lived next door to an illustrator of children's books and his family: his wife and their eight-year old son Frankie.

She was a Buddhist and we used to hear her chanting in the morning. It was hard to make out the words through the breakfast room wall. The tone, however, was like an hysterical vacuum-cleaner on hormone-replacement therapy, and the words sounded, to our uneducated ears, like "a-hole-in-yer-bum, a-hole-in-yer-bum, a-hole-in-yer-bum," repeated endlessly, over and over again.

They were a very right-on New Age family. Wholefood-eating vegetarians, pacifist, ecologically-minded. Little Frankie went to Steiner school.

Which is all well-and-good, you might say. Nothing wrong with child-centred education and "honouring the child", except that - deliberately or not - the whole thing was actually really cruel.

For instance, Frankie was made to wear backless clogs.

Backless clogs! On an eight-year old!

Have you ever tried to run in backless clogs? And isn't this exactly what an eight-year old is supposed to do: to run, in the sheer exuberance of his existence, for the joy of being alive? It was like he was being deliberately crippled.

Poor little Frankie.

It was the same with the wholefood diet. What child do you know who likes brown rice and lentils? Joe always got exactly what he wanted. At least that way he got food into his mouth. He liked fish-fingers and chips. He liked bacon and eggs.

One day Frankie came round to play while Joe was eating his breakfast. Bacon and eggs and beans with a round of crusty white bread smothered in butter. And you could see it in Frankie's eyes. His pupils were dilating. He couldn't keep his eyes off the food. He was just staring and staring at the food on the plate and at Joe as he was eating it. And then he was salivating, really salivating. The drool was dribbling from his mouth and over his chin. Great globules of spit dripping down over his chest, soaking into the bib-front of his multi-coloured dungarees.

Poor little Frankie. I would have loved to have given him a delicious plate of bacon and eggs too, only, of course, you cannot interfere.

He was also not allowed to play with guns. You name me a boy-child who does not like to play with guns. I won't go into the Freudian implications of this, except to say that it is perfectly healthy.

Almost anything can become a gun.

One day Frankie was round our house again, playing in the back garden. He had a stick, and he was making "dat-dat-dat" noises with his mouth, aiming the improvised "gun" at the washing pole.

"What are you shooting at Frankie?" I asked him.

"I'm shooting my mum," he said, tottering on his backless clogs. "I've tied her up to the pole and I'm killing her. Dat-dat-dat. Dat-dat-dat. Drrrrrr. Ka-pow!"

Poor little Frankie. I had to laugh though. At least he was getting his revenge.

Sometimes I wonder what became of Frankie. The family only stayed next-door to us for a year or two. I expect he's a arms-trading psychopath by now, with a passion for raw meat. I only hope he is not cruel to his own children.

But it makes you wonder, doesn't it? The things we do to our kids.

It's one of the terrible consequences of the liberal sixties, that people stopped trying to grow up. They became obsessed with their own spiritual path to personal enlightenment and refused to accept the burden of responsibility for their own children. Discipline was a dirty word. Kids were meant to develop "naturally", according to some sacred inner law of their being. Instead of which - and I've seen this - they just went feral.

I think I understood this at a relatively early point. I went to a Divine Light mission once, at the invitation of a friend of mine who had joined the sect. This was in the early '70s. It was in a large hall in Acton. Everyone was milling around with beaming smiles of bliss on their newly-enlightened faces, while the kids just ran around and played. No one was paying any attention to the kids.

One of them came up to me. He did that trick - you know: he pointed to my chest and said, "what's that", and I looked and he brought his hand sharply up to my nose, and then laughed brattishly.

Well I was a stranger. What could I do? I wanted to clip him round the ear, but it was not up to me to discipline the child. Meanwhile, his parents were somewhere else, hugging each other, no doubt, and looking lovingly into each other's eyes.

But actually kids love discipline. They need discipline. Watch a lioness with her cubs when one of them is annoying her. She will cuff it round the ear, in exactly the way I wished the parents of that child would do, just to teach him respect for his elders.

Which is how, at least, I brought my son up.

4. Light as Bone

I am writing this column in honour of a friend of mine, Frank Plott, of Renfrew in Scotland.

I've been travelling to and from Scotland a lot recently, as I'm working on a new project up there. I won't go into details here. You'll have to wait until it is finished. Suffice it to say that it involves gang warfare, sectarianism, football and God (not necessarily in that order.)

Frank just happens to be in the house I am staying in. He's a little skinny guy, as slick as a whippet, with thick, jug-bottom glasses and a nervous leg-twitch, like the piston-shot of a sleek, fast automobile.

He suffers from bi-polar disorder, what used to be called manic depression. Every fortnight the nurse comes to pick him up to take him to the hospital, where he is given an injection - or "jag" as he calls it. He doesn't know what is in the jag, though he suspects it might be Valium. Whatever it is, the consequence is that he spends most of his time asleep in his bed.

He's in his mid-forties now, and has had this illness since his late teens. He's never worked in his life.

So far this might seem a dismal little tale. What has Frank Plott got to teach any of us?

Well a lot, actually.

Because inside of Frank Plott there lives another character, someone he calls "Bone". And Bone is, by his own measure of things, The Greatest Mod In The World.

It's all etched in ink in tattoos across his body: along his arms and his chest, and all over his hands. "Bone the Mod," says the tattooed script, "Dec. '82."

That's when he took up the faith, in December 1982. He's second-generation Mod, still keeping to the ancient path.

"St. Mirran," it says, "Mod party, 1983." St. Mirran are his Scottish football team. He also supports Everton. The Mod party was his 22nd birthday.

"Scooter," it says, "1983." That was his pride-and-joy, a Honda, an essential mark of status. Then, "Dorothy 1985," it says.

Dorothy was ten years older than him, a first-generation Mod from the sixties. It was a summer romance. In the end she killed herself, by throwing herself in front of a train.

Did he know why that was?

"I don't really know why that was," he says, in his rich, melodic Scottish accent. "Depression. She was in hospital at the time, and they let her out for the day, and she walked to the train station and she flung herself in front of the train."

But those were always his girlfriends, the older women who'd seen the first wave go by. And Bone was always there, ten years later, to return them to the source.

"Mary," it says, "86." Another girlfriend, another original Mod. Then, "Brighton '87."

That was December 1987, just before Christmas. He lost all his money in the bookies. So he only had the prospect of a dismal New Year in front of him. No money. No food. Nothing but a half ounce of tobacco for comfort. And, being a Mod, he decided to go out check out the city that blazons like a beacon in the Mod mythology. He hitch-hiked all the way there, in the depths of winter, and the journey took 19 frozen hours. He'd never even been out of Scotland before.

He ended up in hospital.

"I thought I was well, but I was nay well. The police picked me up and put me in an English hospital. That's where I met Janet Willers. She looked after me in hospital."

And sure enough, there it is on his hand, the record of an accidental meeting and a passing friendship in an English hospital all those years ago. "Janet Willers," it says. Just that, and no more.

After that he was flown back to Scotland, where he spent another two days in hospital, before he was finally discharged.

And so it goes, the story of a life told in cryptic notes in pin-pricked ink upon the pages of his skin, like the notes a novelist might make for himself, as a reminder of the plot. And that's exactly what it is. Frank Plott, weaving his own plot, as the story of his life, with a central character called Bone, who is The Greatest Mod In The World.

And, well, I'm talking to him in this council flat on a housing scheme in Scotland, listening to the story of his life - asking questions, noting down the details - as he rolls up his sleeves and lifts his shirt to show me his numerous tattoos. "Isabel Blaine," it says, "1990." She was Miss Paisley in 1965, and he's still with her, to this day. Then: "Freddie and the Dreamers 1992," and "The Merseybeats."

That's when I see it. It's like a light has come on inside of him. Talking about his life in this way has made him come alive. It beams from his face and from his eyes, like an angelic presence in his life: his own story, told to a new friend, as a narrative of pure meaning.

And I think, yes we all have this. However we name it, there is always a presence in our lives: another us, in a story of our own telling, as a light that lights the way. Despite the hardship and the loss and the occasional illness - the tragedy, the poverty, the grinding senselessness of a world that devalues our very existence - we all are creatures of light in the end.

How else do we learn but by listening? And how else do we know the value of ourselves but by valuing other people?

5. Old Hippies Never Die.

"...because the revolutionaries kept overlooking the need to change themselves as well as the world, and the religious/occult kept overlooking the need to change the world as well as themselves."

Tim Corber,
Anarcho United Mystics (AUM) Newsletter, 1980

In case you haven't identified me yet, I am probably what you would call an "Old Hippie", much to my embarrassment. There's very little I can do about it now. I mean: I cut my hair a long time ago. I hardly ever go to rock concerts, I change my socks regularly, and I've long since eschewed the lure and the rhetoric of psychoactive substances; but whatever I do, those formative events of my youth are still casting their shadows over my life, like a line of poplars in the park at sunset.

I wonder if Old Teds feel the same, or Old Skinheads, or Old Punks? Probably. Except that teds and skinheads and punks had a much better wardrobe than most hippies, as I remember. You can try and imagine me in a headband if you like, or wafting about in a caftan with bells and beads around my neck and flowers in my hair, except that I'm a little too young to have indulged in quite those sartorial excesses. I did, however, wear 40 inch flared cavalry twill loon pants which dragged along the floor sucking up mud, as well as a green-and-white vertically striped school blazer, a black-and-red horizontally striped tee shirt, and red-and-white baseball boots. I must have looked like something you would find on the shelf in a sweetie shop, but I thought I was the bees-knees at the time.

I suspect that a number of my readers might also agree to accept the mantle of Old Hippie too, albeit with the usual reservations. Old hippies don't die. They change their clothes and pretend to be normal. Later on they realise that no one can ever be normal again, and they just grow increasingly dishevelled and mad about the eyes while addressing total strangers in shopping precincts and cackling uncontrollably at the unexpected Brazilian soap-opera scripts raging through their heads.

Not that I've reached that stage yet. But I'm expecting it, oh yes. Any day now.

I'm not sure why I should be telling you this. Take is as a form of therapy. You be Doctor Freud, with his notebook and his pen, taking notes behind my head, while I lie on the couch squirming with embarrassment at the revelations I feel compelled to impale you with. "Yes, Doctor, it's true, it's true. I really did spend several hours saying nothing but 'wow' while off my head on LSD and beer in a pub in Cardiff once. I think I even saw God, in the form of globular multi-coloured letters beaming covert messages into my brain, just before the bouncer threw me out onto the street."

Well we can put old hippies down if we like - we can all laugh at some of the indulgences and absurdities of the time – but the fact is that the hippies did some remarkable things. Most importantly, to my mind, they brought together two world-views or philosophies that are normally considered incompatible: namely spirituality and politics. So they protested against the Vietnam war while chanting Om in the Buddhist manner. That was Allen Ginsburg, specifically, and it was not quite so contradictory as it sounds, the Vietnamese being both Buddhist and communist at the same time.

They also recognised the importance of ancient wisdom, and practiced many of the arts celebrated in this book. Indeed, interest in occult and divinatory matters was something the hippies both recognised and celebrated, while at the same time they attempted to forge new forms of political organisation and new alliances with the old left. They were radical, spiritual, revolutionary, hedonistic, committed, anti-materialistic, environmentalist and – occasionally – wrong-headed and dangerous. But then: who isn't?

But all of this – like most things in life – was transitory. While hippie culture thrived and bloomed through the late sixties and into the seventies, by the end of that decade it had all but died, buried under an avalanche of glam-rock and New Romantic posturing, with very little of either the politics or the spirituality remaining.

Old hippies went one of several ways. They joined sects, like Divine Light or Scientology. Or they went on the road and became New Age Travellers. Some of them joined the SWP and took up revolutionary politics, while others became therapists and New Age purveyors of a variety of complicated and sometimes ludicrous practices. One or two went on to found the Green Party, while others that I know of became druids or witches. But the great sadness, to me, is not that people took up any of these things (except maybe the sects, which I never could stand) but that in the process they divorced the two original strands from each other, and began to deny the spirituality in politics, or the politics in spirituality, thus fatally weakening the two of them.

Not recognising the one is the failure to live up to the other. Because what is true politics but the recognition of the value of all human beings and their right to live fulfilling, creative and meaningful lives on this planet? And what is true spirituality but the attempt to identify in yourself the deepest source of all being, that unites and encompasses and embraces us all?

6. Holy Cornflowers.

I'm fairly uncertain about most things. I mean, I'd be an agnostic, only I can never quite make up my mind.

At the same time, I'm always willing to give things a go. As they say, you never know until you've tried. Consequently I've had extensive dealings with a variety of alternative remedies in the past. I've tried a lot of things. I've had hypnosis on a number of occasions. I've had herbal remedies, homeopathic remedies, Bach flower remedies and spiritual healing. I've tried Chinese medicine, acupuncture, acupressure, Indian head massage and reflexology. I've had aromatherapy and crystal therapy; Jungian therapy, Freudian therapy, co-counselling and transactional analysis. In fact, you name me some practice, and I'll see if I haven't engaged with it yet.

I can't say that I've ever been cured of anything. Then again, I was never very clear what the disease was in the first place.

I was going to say that I've never been harmed by alternative therapies either: but that's not quite true. There was one occasion when I had to have one therapy in order to get over another therapy.

The first therapy involved lying inside of a geometric construction made of copper piping, on a bed interwoven with crystals, holding two crystal-tipped, wand-like objects in my hands (called Vajras) listening to a tape through headphones, which on first hearing sounded like Buddhist chanting - with cymbals and gongs, bells and chimes and long-drawn-out nasal moans - and only later turned out to be something else.

It was called Soul-Therapy, and was meant to realign my auric something-or-others. Maybe my auric something-or-others needed realigning, who knows? Maybe that was the disease I'd never been quite able to put my finger on.

I said that the tape sounded like Buddhist chanting. Well it was, in a sense. Only instead of the usual patient and precise delivery of original Buddhist Sutras in Pali or Japanese, these turned out to be entirely new formulations in modern American English. This was quite disconcerting. I was just lying there on that lumpy mattress (crystals aren't soft) only half-listening to the chimes and the chants and the moaning incantations, when, all of a sudden I could make out the words.

"Holy cornflower," the voice was saying in my ear. Only not like that. Not just the words in normal English: but drawn-out like an Om, grinding on like the moan of a jack-hammer through solid concrete, straining like the sound of a vacuum cleaner with something stuck in its nozzle.

> "Hooooooooooo..... lllllllllllleeeeeeeeeeeeeeeeyyyyyyyyyyyy.....cooooooooorrrrrrrrrn-floooooooooooooooooowwwwwwwwwwwwwweeeeeeeeeeeeeeeeeeeeerrrrrrrr...."

Like that. On and on and on.

It kind of takes the mystery out of a Buddhist chant when you know what the words mean.

Well after that I was alert, as it were, listening to the words. And there were all sorts of words. Words about invoking the seven rays of the Universe, in a looping, repetitive mantra. Each ray was directed to some centre on my body, apparently. And then, words about the power of the light....

"The power of the light will banish the glamour of personal possession. The power of the light will banish the glamour of material things. The power of the light will banish the glamour of...." Over and over, the power of the light banishing the glamour of a variety of relatively harmless things. It went on for about five minutes.

Well that was all well and good. Unfortunately I have an argumentative mind. I kept disagreeing with what the voice was telling me. I couldn't see why the power of the light would want to banish the glamour of some of the things it evidently did want to banish the glamour of. For instance, the power of the light wanted to banish the glamour of this world. Why would it want to do that? Why on earth would the power of the light want to banish the glamour of this world, when it's a perfectly good world, I was thinking? And what about the birds and the trees and the animals: would it want to banish them as well? I mean, where would they go once the world had been banished? The only thing I could see that might be worth banishing was what us human beings have done to it. So maybe I could have agreed with the power of the light had it wanted to banish the cock-ups of humanity.

I'd been lying there for about ten minutes now, listening to this groaning, nasal voice invoking, banishing, calling on holy cornflowers and the rest, and I was beginning to get seriously annoyed with it. I mean, who was this person, regaling me with such patent absurdities? Were my auric something-or-others really being realigned or was I just listening to the clap-trap rigmarole of some professional monomaniac bent on showing off how elevated he had become?

There's a certain kind of mysticism whose sole purpose is to mystify. That's what I took "the power of the light" to be. Mystification to cover up the mundane workings of an otherwise shallow mind.

It was when the power of the light decided it wanted to banish the glamour of my ego that I finally found I'd had enough.

"Oh go and banish the glamour of your own ego," I thought, and leapt up from the mattress.

That's when I discovered I'd done my back in.

I'm sure there some of you who will think that I probably deserved it. Maybe my realignment was only half-done. Maybe I should have been more respectful of whoever it was on the tape. Maybe he really was a higher spiritual being with a message of fulfilment I was too undeveloped to hear yet. Or maybe it was just the lumpy crystals in that mattress, plus an excess of tension from having to listen to so much gobbledegook.

7. Down In The Dumps: or how I survived a barium enema

Like most men I know I have an eye for a pretty girl. And it's not just the obvious things which attract me. I might find myself gazing at someone's eye-lashes, or her hair, or her belly-button, or her arms. I'm particularly attracted to bellies as it happens, which is deeply frustrating for an old bachelor such as me, given the current trend for exposing large amounts of deliciously tanned belly-flesh, usually with a choice tattoo and a silvery piercing for decoration.

However, on this occasion, it wasn't the woman's belly I was looking at, it was her mouth. It was in the hospital, where I was waiting for an appointment. She was behind the reception desk. And she was very pretty, with light mousy-blonde hair, small, curved shoulders and a sly, intelligent smile. But it was not her smile I was observing. She was chewing a biscuit, and I was much more obsessed with the biscuit than I was with any other quality she might be exhibiting.

I kept glancing up from the magazine I was reading as she tucked another crunchy mouthful away. The magazine was the Observer Food Supplement and there was a wonderful recipe for a Seychelles Fish Curry which I could almost smell from the description on the page. But I kept being drawn back to that mouth. I could see her jaw working with a delicate masticating rhythm, her throat as she swallowed, her lips opening for another bite, her white teeth stained with the crumbling remains. I could taste every bite in my own mouth, as my mouth began to water.

I'd been forty two hours without food by this time. Forty two hours with nothing but sweet coffee and Bovril to sustain me.

The day before I had also taken two doses of a heavy duty laxative (one in the morning and one in the afternoon) which had had me leaping to the toilet every five minutes, while a veritable rocket-blast of liquid effluent came roaring from my rear end. I'm sure that I was raised at least two inches from the toilet seat with the force of the explosion.

I was on my way for a barium enema.

I was also very, very nervous. Not so much at the prospect of any pain (I'd been assured it wasn't too painful) as at the humiliation of bending down to the scientific rigours of the medical establishment: being slapped on a table and pinned down like a specimen in a medical experiment, while they pumped alien substances into my back-passage, no doubt with the prime intention of blowing away the last vestiges of my human dignity.

As it happens, that's exactly what it was like.

Fortunately for me and the world, bums are just inherently funny. I spent most of the ordeal laughing at the absurdity of the situation.

It was like this: first of all I had to take all of my clothes off in a cubicle, and then put on a gown with a slit up the back, with a dressing gown on top. Then I had to go and sit in the reception area again.

An old lady arrived and sat next to me. A nurse came out and offered her tea and a sandwich. The old lady looked through the selection and said, "Yes, yes. I don't normally eat meat but, yes... on this occasion. Yes please."

She opened her sandwich and began to tuck in.

I said, "is that your first food for over 40 hours?"

"Yes," she said, "it is. It was worse yesterday. I didn't know what to do with myself."

"I know," I said.

"Oh I'm sorry," she said, "you haven't eaten either. Would you like me to go somewhere else?"

"No," I said, "as long as you don't mind me drooling while I watch you."

After that I noticed that she turned her back on me and was eating her sandwich with a kind of furtive hunch, no doubt guarding herself from all that drool.

The radio was playing faintly in the background. "Sugar-sugar, oh honey-honey, you are my candy girl, and you've got me wanting you."

Then the news came on. There was a story about a doctor who had murdered one of his patients, no doubt by blowing him up from the rear end or starving him to death.

I was almost cracking up with hysteria by now. Finally it was my turn to go in. Well the doctor was very nice. He was trying to put me at my ease. He kept making jokes. Not that I found any of them funny. The joke was all on me.

So I was made to lie on a bed, with my knees bent, to one side, while the doctor took a rubber tube with a bobble on the end, and smeared it with lubricant, before inserting it into my back-passage. I was told to breath deeply while he did this. And then it kind of slipped in, with a low, slurping murmur and a satisfying schloop, like a piece of jelly slipping from a mould and slapping onto a plate.

So now I knew what it felt like to be anally retentive. My anus was gripped on this tube with a sort of fierce determination all of its own. Anything stuck up your butt makes you want to unload your bowels. Except, of course, there was nothing left in my bowels to unload.

After that the barium was pumped up into my inside, while I watched a picture on the nearby TV screen of my own insides. Barium is a radioactive material that cleaves to the walls of your bowel, thus making the soft invisible tissue visible to scanning equipment. After that the doctor blew air inside of me. This is to force the barium onto to the walls of your bowel, making it appear on the screen. Which it duly did, like magic. "That's a very nice bowel," said the doctor. "Very nice and shapely."

It was the first time I had ever been complimented on the shape of my bowel.

Having air pumped into your bowels is like the feeling you have when you follow a seven-course slap-up Indian meal with about ten pints of extra fizzy lager. It's like you want to do the longest, loudest, most explosive fart in history.
I'm only telling you all this just in case you have to have a barium enema one day. I tell you: some people I know would pay good money to have this experience.

So that's how the whole thing goes on. There you are, flat on a bed, with a tube up your nether regions, wanting to blow like crazy. The doctor tells you to turn this way. So you do. And then that way. So you do. On your back and on your side. On your stomach, on your other side, while he loads the machine and it whirs and clicks and rattles mysteriously, with this tube dangling out of your bum, stuck on with sticky tape, and trailing and getting caught under your legs. Your greatest fear as that it will catch on something and come squirting out, followed by all that barium and all that air, like a fog-horn going off in the middle of a quiet street.

Parp!

The whole thing lasts for about half an hour, after which the doctor's assistant (he wouldn't dream of doing it himself) plops the tube out of your rear-end again, and then chucks the whole lot into a bin. He's wearing rubber gloves and goggles as he peers into your nether regions, just in case.

I said, "that's a strange job you've got."

He said, "I'm not looking up back-passages all the time, you know. And I'm only here twice a week." He sounded very defensive about his job.

After that you are directed to a toilet, where, at long last, and with a huge sigh of relief, you are allowed to rid yourself of the weight of barium and air at last, with a long, satisfying vent of truly epic proportions. It was almost worth the experience just for the explosive relief at the end.

I got home at six fifteen that evening, after forty four hours and fifteen minutes without food, and ordered a Chinese meal. Well what did you expect? Did you think I was going to be bothered to cook? And then, about an hour and a half later, I ordered another one.

It was King Prawns in garlic and chilli sauce with Singapore fried noodles. Delicious. The best Chinese food I have ever eaten.

And after all that it turned out that there was really nothing wrong with me.

I'll think twice before listening to a doctor again.

Amanae

A profoundly affecting bodywork treatment is gaining popularity around the world:
CJ Stone *went to find out how Amanae works*

1. Releasing your Pain

"By starting from the invisible world the visible world was invented."

The Hypostasis of the Archons,
translated by Bentley Layton from
The Nag Hammadi Library, revised
edition. HarperCollins, San
Francisco, 1990.

The room is in the basement of a huge 19th century industrial building in a warehouse quarter in North London. The ceiling and part of one wall is covered in pipes, and there's a low humming noise, like distant machinery, thrumming away in the background.

The room has a functional air. Rooms like this are normally hidden away. They are part of the workings of the building and often neglected, full of junk and dust, old rags and disused machinery. But this room has been reclaimed. It has been cleaned up, painted white, made comfortable with seats and cushions, and lit up with the soft glow of side-lamps.

This seems apt somehow. That's what we are doing too. We are entering some old, forgotten, functional parts of the psyche, and cleaning them up to make them habitable again.

I'm lying face-down in the massage table and Eric, the practitioner, is working on the base of my skull, at the point where the skull attaches to the spinal column. Suddenly he lets out a distinct, high-toned, musical note. He's been making noises throughout the session, as have I. My noises are low-down, guttural groans and sighs, with the occasional cry of rage, while his are articulated sounds, with some semblance of words. I don't know if they are words or not. It sounds like he's speaking in tongues, or in some ancient, long-forgotten language. But this sudden high note is very unexpected, and I find myself responding to it in a surprising way. I find that I want to sing.

Eric's fingers are still nudging my cranium and I find that there's a note attached to this part of my body. It's a very high melodic note, almost angelic, like the high, clear notes that pre-adolescent boys are able to reach. I try to sing this note, but it comes out cracked and faltering from my aged throat. I can't make the note, but I want to, and I keep trying.

This goes on for some time and it's a wonder Eric can bear it: the broken strains of a middle-aged man wailing at the top of his voice, trying to sing like an eight year old choir boy. But he not only can bear it, he's encouraging it. His deft fingers are working at the sides of my throat, allowing it to open up, allowing the notes to come tumbling from my mouth.

The song I am trying to sing is *Soldier, Soldier Won't You Marry Me* and inside my heart I'm about eight years old.

The work is known as Amanae. It originated in Australia with a woman called Christine Day. She was diagnosed with Lupus Syndrome and given two months to live, but while in hospital she realised that she had created the illness herself. With this came the corresponding realisation that if she could create something to kill herself, she could also create something to heal herself. She began to change things in her life, started on a variety of courses, taking natural herbs and doing bodywork and very quickly brought herself back to health. But it wasn't really the herbs or the bodywork which cured her: it was the realisation of her own innate creativity while she was busy dying in hospital, and the decision that actually she wanted to live.

The blueprint for the work came to her about six months later, during a meditation session. She says it came to her within a 2-3 second period. "All of a sudden one minute I didn't know anything and the next minute I knew a concept of healing that would help people move more completely into who they were."

Later she began teaching it, and later again moved to the United States.

Eric Lipin, the man whose probing thumbs have been making me want to sing, was trained directly by Christine Day.

He was introduced to it by a body worker who was one of Christine's first students in the United States. Eric had been seeing him for a number of years. At some point the body worker had started practicing Amanae, and he introduced it to Eric.

"The work was more intense than other bodyworks I experienced," explains Eric now. But he trusted his practitioner completely and allowed him to get on with it. At some point he was working on his shoulder blades. It was getting almost unbearably intense by now. Eric had a sudden thought, "why am I doing this?" and he began laughing. That was like a trigger. First of all he laughed uncontrollably for about ten minutes, and then, with a slight shift, he began to cry. He'd not cried like that since he was a little child, he says.

After that he signed up for one of Christine Day's 5-day workshops. "That was even bigger," he says. "That completely changed my life. I left that place a completely different person. I left three full suitcases at the workshop. They were suitcases I never knew I'd been carrying with me. I went back to my life, to my office job, and everything was different."

That was about 14 or 15 years ago.

"I learned to trust Christine with my life," he says. Trust is essential.

He decided to undertake the work himself and signed up for a year-long training programme. "I thought of it like one long five day workshop. We were really in the fire the whole time."

After the course was finished there was a series of synchronistic events that lead him the Europe. He worked in Brussels and then in Prague.

"That's when I started waking up to that there's a magic out there in the world," he says. "That there is a force bringing things together at the right time and the right place."

Eventually he decided to move to Belgium, which is where he met his wife.

"I've been here ever since," he says.

For a while he was the only practitioner in Europe. He was invited to London, and then to Holland and to Germany. And some of his trainees went to workshops in Israel, so then there were two more practitioners. These are both in the UK. A number of people have been trained, but only a handful of people have managed to make a practice of it.

The work involves a combination of breath, awareness and points in the body known as "doorways". The breath and the awareness are one thing. You could call it "breathing awareness". The practitioner presses down on the doorways using his thumbs, while the receiver breathes into the sensation, bringing his awareness into any pain that might be locked up there. You are asked to be with the pain, to let it be, and to give expression to it. While the in-breath involves awareness, the out-breath involves a kind of vocalised sigh, opening your throat to allow any sounds to emerge.

And sounds do emerge. It's like these doorways are passages into some primal state of being, something raw and deep and beyond words. Emotional. It's as if deep hidden pain is locked up in the body behind these portals, and by giving voice to them you are letting them loose. Letting them be. It's as if another, hidden part of yourself is being awakened.

I have to say that it can be quite uncomfortable. It depends on the person. For some people it can be painful, for others less so. But it's a strange kind of pain, oddly gratifying. It's like an ache in your muscles. It hurts, but there's a sense of satisfaction that goes with it. You find yourself melting into the sensation in the same way that heavily worked muscles relax after a hard day's graft.

I first heard about it about 2 years ago when a friend of mine had it. The change after Amanae was noticeable and immediate. It was like a great tension had been lifted from her life and she became much less defensive, more relaxed, more joyous and adaptable in her outlook.

I was having therapy at the time: traditional bodywork. My body-worker also had Amanae and had begun training with Eric. And one day she tried it on me.

I almost jumped out of my skin.

It was like she had found some deep node of sensation in my body-structure and she was twanging it. It was tucked away between the bones, deeper than anything I'd ever felt before, an old ache, an ancient pain. It was my pain. And after a while I began to love it. I began to love the ache. My breath and my awareness would move to meet the ache. And then, inside the ache, there were memories.

That's where the Soldier, Soldier song had come from. It was a song I'd sung to a girl I was in love with when I was about eight years old. We were singing the song together in school, in front of the class. She was taking the female parts, while I was singing the male parts, and while I was singing I was looking into her eyes, my heart soaring with every line, with every rise and fall of the melody. Afterwards the teacher commented on how beautiful my voice was.

Later I told my Mum about it, and she teased me. "Was it a girl?" she said, laughing. I was overcome by a sudden feeling of shame, as if falling in love with a girl was wrong somehow, a feeling that lodged itself into my body and has been there ever since.

That was why I was trying to sing on the massage table. I was singing out my secret sense of shame.

I have to say that I felt very supported by Eric. He had the air of a kindly uncle genuinely concerned for my wellbeing. After the session was over he left me on my own for a while, having first offered suggestions as to how I might integrate the experience into my ordinary life. He also offered on-going support via email and the telephone.

Once he had left the room I went back inside my heart. I could feel the hurt little boy in there, still sobbing for attention. In my imagination I cradled him in my arms, as I had my own son when he was the same age.

"That's all right," I was saying, rocking my younger self to and fro. "There, there."

And I carried on rocking him like that till he stopped crying.

2. In the Temple of the Heart: Amanae Receiving Workshop, Brussels, June 3rd - 5th 2011.

"He has blinded their eyes
and hardened their hearts,
so they can neither see with their eyes,
nor understand with their hearts,
nor turn—and I would heal them."

John 12:40

I begin with the quote from John's Gospel because it very graphically describes my own state of being for many years.

I can only speak for myself, and must let others tell their own stories.

My heart was hardened over successive years because of the wounds it received. When we harden our hearts we do so out of love, because we cannot bear our own suffering. We harden our hearts in order to protect ourselves. It is an act of shielding which is an act of protection which is an act of love.

In other words: I do not blame myself.

The corollary of a hardening of the heart is when the heart melts, and my heart began to melt sometime last year, soon after I began receiving Amanae. It was little things at first. Literally little things. It was children. I would see a child playing on the beach, or skipping along hand-in-hand with its parents, or chattering gleefully about everything and nothing, and there would be a kind of ache in my heart, like an ache of longing: a longing for what has long passed for me.

I say, "an ache" but it is also a kind of tingling, a kind of awakening, like the ache of tired muscles that have not been used for a while, like the ache in the body when you first awaken in the morning, which makes you want to stretch and yawn and give praise for the new day. A positive ache. The ache of love.

That seems like a good description of Amanae - "the ache of love" - as the therapy involves working in the deepest places in the body, in the muscle-tissue nearest the bone, at the point where all our deepest hurts are locked away and is, indeed, a kind of existential ache almost reaching to the soul.

The first time my body psychotherapist, Ruth Hoskins, used it on me, I nearly jumped out of my skin. I had never experienced anything like that before. It hurt, but in a strangely satisfying way. Over succeeding weeks on her massage table I learned to stay with the pain, to meet it, to embrace it even, to breathe into it. It was my own pain I was feeling. Maybe it was the pain of being alive.

Ruth had been training with Eric and had attended one of the five day workshops in Brussels.

Very soon things started to happen. For instance, one day Ruth touched a point on my shoulder and my body unfurled. It was as simple as that. I suddenly recognised an unconscious way I had of holding myself which permeated my whole body. There was a kind of tension in my body which came from my mind, and in that moment of recognition I decided to let it go. I let my mind wander over my body and gave each part of my body permission to let go. I let go and my whole body unfurled like a young fern in the undergrowth. I had a clear impression of a young fern unfurling in the dappled sunlight in a wood somewhere. First of all it was my fingers. My fingers unravelled one by one. They stretched out, loosened, relaxed and became free. Then it was my hands and my wrists and my elbows and my arms, until my arms had unfolded, thrown open in an arc of embrace as if I wanted to hold the whole world in my arms and give it a hug. It was exquisite and graceful and surprising and free.

On another occasion Ruth was working on my throat and jaw, and the same thing happened. I was suddenly aware of the self-imposed tension in that space, as if I was permanently "swallowing my words", keeping something in, repressing something, and I let go. Again, my jaw was released and my mouth fell open and I felt the tension lift from every notch and very fibre in that whole area, my throat opening up, as I let go of my unconscious control over that part of my body with a sigh of relief.

And then something very surprising happened.

Ruth had been working on my heart in the way that is familiar to all people who have experienced Amanae. Then she said, "I sense a great rage in you," or words to that effect. She went down to my feet and put all her weight on my feet and told me to push against her weight. I was annoyed at this, irritated. I didn't know what she was doing, and I did what I always do when I'm feeling under pressure: I retreated into a kind of amused insouciance - a learned response - attempting to shrug off the feeling of annoyance. And then it happened. Something suddenly erupted from me, from some place I had never been before, or had forgotten about, and the next thing I knew I was gone. I was gone and then it was as if I was returning from a great distance, from what might have been half a universe away, and I didn't know who I was or where I was or if I had even existed before that moment. It was like I was being born for the first time. I was coming from a place of great intensity and light but I had no idea where I had been or for how long. I was also aware that someone was screaming and with a sudden sense of recognition "the penny dropped" and I realised it was me.

I have since realised that that was the first time that my heart had opened.

And I can tell you now, that every time it happens it is just as surprising, just as intense, just as new. Every time your heart opens it's as if you are being born again for the first time, like you have travelled half a universe to get here, though no time has passed at all, like you have crossed the threshold into another universe and come back unscathed, like you have been plugged in to the Universal Grid and all of your senses have become electrified.

I'm going to give up on the superlatives for now, but I'm sure more will be needed later.

Anyway, all of that is a background to my experience of the Amanae receiving workshop in Brussels earlier this month

By the time I got there I had filed away that experience of my heart opening into the cupboard marked "Imponderables" and had effectively forgotten all about it.

My memories of the first two days are a little blurred.

The first day began with a circle and a "sharing" in which we introduced ourselves and stated our intentions for the day.

I said my intention was to find out what my intention was, which was kind of clever, but also, as I realise now, a mind thing.

I was not speaking from the heart.

After that we were given our partners for the day, and I was relieved that it was a bloke, as I'm a little nervous around women.

He, however, said that he would have preferred it if he had been partnered by a woman.

"Partnering" means that you place your hand on the other's body in the place that is going to be worked on. It helps the person on the table to bring their attention to that place. Also it acts as a kind of reassurance, creating a bond between the two people.

I was surprised at how quickly the emotions started to come up. My partner was on the table first, but very soon I was finding myself sobbing. I had my hand on my partner's back but it was me that was crying. Wouter, a trainee practitioner, came up to me and put his hand on my heart. He said, "it is a very old pain," or, perhaps, "it has been hurting for a very long time," and I was suddenly in tears.

I was remembering a relationship that had ended many years ago but which I had recently realised was still very painful to me.

It was in connection with this relationship that I had come up with the expression about hardening of the heart and got a Christian friend of mine to look up quotes in the Bible for me, which is how I came across that quote from John's Gospel above.

I was also aware, watching my partner's back being worked on, and then putting my hand on the place that had been worked, that my own back was responding, as if, by working on one back the practitioner was also working on the other, or as if the two backs were psychically connected in some way.

Some observations about the process involved.

There are various nodal points on the body, known as "doorways", to which pressure is applied and which connect by some mysterious route to the inner world. You breathe into the inner space, bringing your awareness in with your breath, and attempt to connect to the pressure being applied from the outside. You bring your breath into the inside to feel the hand of the other person on the outside.

In fact there are four distinct elements to the Amanae process. You drink lots of water, you breathe very deeply, you bring your awareness in with your breath in order to feel the sensations in your body. Thus the four elements are as follows: breath, water, awareness, and the body and bone-structure that contains all of these things. In fact, if you want to summarise what makes up a human being, then nothing could be more concise. A human being is a body made of bone and water into which breath and awareness are drawn. We are an amalgam of bone, breath, water and awareness, though I'll leave it up to you to decide which of those elements should come first. Maybe all are equally important.

If we wanted to take this analysis a little further, we might say that these are the four elements of classical thought - Earth (or bone) Air (or breath) Fire (or awareness) and Water – which make up the whole of existence.

We were working on the back on the first afternoon. After the first session was over it was my turn. You lie on your front face-down on the massage table, with your head in a head-rest, with your face poking out. There is a bowl underneath your face, with a few tissues. You soon learn what these are for. You are encouraged not to swallow your phlegm and saliva, which starts to come out in large quantities. At least it does from me. Also there is a particular kind of Amanae breath. You breathe in very deeply through the mouth, but release the breath quickly in a sort of sigh. You don't hold onto the breath or let it out slowly. You simply release it, and let it carry whatever emotion it is you find in your body. The breath becomes an expression of the emotion and very soon you are making primal noises. There is something animalistic about this. You start to growl and whine and shriek and curse and make all sorts of strange noises. Sometimes you chant or croak. Whatever. Being involved in an Amanae workshop is to be immersed in this sea of verbal emotion. It is like waves passing around the room, or like a kind of feedback loop. You pick up on the emotions and start to feel them yourself. You start to mimic the sounds coming from other parts of the room, harmonising with the chants, or echoing the croaks and groans. The sounds pass around the room, washing over you. After a while I was giggling at the absurdity of it. What must people outside have thought? It was like a madhouse in there. No, I thought, correcting myself: it was like an exorcism. It was like we were casting out the demons.

So, then, one of the practitioners was working on my back. There's a kind of movement over the muscle near the spine which feels like a twanging of the muscle. It hurts quite a lot. You bring your awareness in with your breath to meet the pain. Sometimes there are memories locked up in the pain. As you approach it so the memories are released. And then I had a clear image of a person's face. It was someone who had once bullied me. There was a sudden upsurge of rage: all the things I'd not said to this person at the time, all the ways he had humiliated me, made me feel small and worthless. "Humiliated": that's the word. It's from the same root as humus, from the Latin, meaning the earth, the ground. When you are feeling humiliated you want the earth to open to swallow you up. So I shouted out in all my rage, "stop bullying me!" It was not just addressed to this person, but to every person who had ever bullied me. It was a moment of great clarity.

Another thing that came up that first day (or it might have been the second day, I forget now) was that I heard a resounding voice which passed through my whole being like a shiver. "So shy," it said, and I knew that that was me. The voice held no blame. It did not accuse or condemn. It was not judging me. It was not measuring me or making comparisons. It was simply stating what was, and I realised that my shyness is innate, fundamental, not learned, not taught, but a part of my nature, like my brown eyes or my olive skin, my own personal burden in life, or my own secret virtue.

Most of my life has been spent trying to hide my shyness from people, as if I'm ashamed of it, but from that moment on the table I felt that it truly explained me as a person, and I was able to talk about it. It became one of the themes of my weekend.

So that was it: the first day and the second day combined, since whatever was happening on the first day was continued and magnified on the second.

Actually the second day started a little differently as we began with a meditation session. I must admit I was dreading this. "Meditation": the very word has an uncomfortable ring for me as, try as I might, I have never been able to meditate. I just can't sit still. Everything about me wants to fidget. My body wants to fidget, my mind wants to fidget, my heart wants to fidget. Even my nose wants to fidget. I'm a sort of flibbertigibbet of a person, flighty and superficial, with a constantly chattering mind. Meditation, to me, means forcing my mind to be quiet. But, of course, it is my mind telling my mind to be quiet, and, given that I like conversation, especially with myself, so any attempt to talk to myself ends up in a long-winded internal conversation before I even realise the absurdity of the situation. *Be quiet. No you be quiet. I am being quiet. No you're not, I just heard you, you be quiet. Ok I'll be quiet if you are quiet. Ok you be quiet first. Ok, now we're quiet. No we're not, I just heard you...* etc etc ad nauseum.

In fact, Amanae meditation is the exact opposite of this. We were encouraged to make noises, encouraged to move. The session was lead by Judy, an experienced practitioner from the United States. First of all she told us to bring our breath into our body, and to release it in the usual way. Then she told us to move and to stretch. So people were sighing and groaning and moving, and stretching and breathing very heavily. Then Judy broke into a very unusual sounding nasal chant. It had a particular note, like the sounding of a bell. Some people kind of half joined in, but there weren't any rules about this. Other people - Wouter particularly - continued to groan and to sigh and to yawn and to stretch and move about. I found my jaw slackening and the breath coming very deeply into my chest. And then - the strangest of things - I was suddenly still. All those years of trying to sit still in meditation, and then, by not trying, I found myself inexplicably stilled.

By the way, for all of you less familiar with the English language, "flibbertigibbet" is a Middle English word of unknown origin still in use in parts of Northern England. It means a chattering or flighty person. It is also, coincidentally, the name of a demon mentioned in Shakespeare, which brings something else to mind. In my description of yesterday's proceedings I used the word "exorcism", but this isn't correct. We weren't exorcising our demons, we were embracing them. We were giving them expression, inviting them into the fold, allowing them to speak in whatever voice they chose, and by doing this, incorporating them back into our whole being, because, as Khalil Gibran said, "what is evil but good tortured by its own hunger and thirst?" In this particular case it was my Flibbertigibbet – my chattering noisiness – which I had banished and which had then plagued me in meditation. By giving it voice, in fact, it was satisfied, and became quiet of its own accord.

And we see something more of the Amanae working method here: a kind of spiritual anarchy, in which everything is given voice, everything is permitted (short of actual physical violence, that is) and every movement of the heart is invited into the circle, to be embraced, to be celebrated, to be engaged in play: not an exorcism, in fact, more a kind of joyous possession.

So now we have a new concept to play around with: the idea of Shamanic possession, which, if you stop and think about it, is the opposite of exorcism. In exorcism the demons are considered evil and are "cast out" into the wilderness. But, of course, by casting them out we give them power. They work on us from the shade, from the unconscious, from the hidden places in the dark, exerting their influence over us, controlling us without our knowing. But in Shamanism the opposite is true. Instead of being exorcised the "gods" are invited in to the body to take possession, and from there used to heal. In Amanae we invite the demons from the shadows, and into our consciousness, and from there the demons lose their power and integrate into the light of who we are.

In fact the word "demon" – an evil spirit in Christian thought – is derived from the Greek word "daemon", which is a kind of demigod or intermediary in the spiritual world, like the ghost of a dead hero. Benevolent not evil, something to be embraced and called upon, not something to be banished, to be possessed by your daemon is to be inspired from a higher source. It is to locate and communicate with your genius, the source of your being.

So the second day we continued to work on the back. This time I was partnered by a young woman. When we were asked what our first thoughts of our partner were, my partner said she thought I was a sensitive man, which I felt very flattered by.

The day was very long. The woman was on the table first and the session seemed to go on and on. My back began to ache and I had to sit down. Then, after lunch it was my turn. I don't remember anything particular about this. It was all the usual stuff: lots of breathing, lots of groaning, lots of aching, lots of shouting, lots of phlegm, lots of saliva, lots of water. At one point Wouter was working on my legs and I was screaming in pain. This seemed to hurt more than usual. Also, when he was working on my lower spine approaching the sacrum, he said, "it's like a fortress in there. No one is permitted entry."

By now I had taken to spitting into the bowl rather than having dribs of phlegm leaking out of my nose all the time, and it was at a certain point later in the afternoon, after I'd let out one particularly large gob, that my partner suddenly left. She said, "I have a problem with disgust," and she went and sat on the platform at the end of the room.

This was devastating for me. You develop a particular intimacy with your partner, and, in my insecurity, I interpreted that phrase "I have a problem with disgust" to mean "I find you disgusting." After this I couldn't let go of that thought. I'm disgusting. That's why women always leave me. It was like a repetitive loop going round and round in my head. I'm disgusting, I'm disgusting, I'm disgusting. I could hear my partner up on the platform sobbing to herself. I was still linked in with her, but in my head she had rejected me. We had become separated, and I took this as a kind of insult. She came back for the last few minutes, but by now something very dark had got into me. I couldn't stop the resentful thoughts.

I looked around and there were all the other partners embracing each other. I could do with something like that, I thought. My brain was churning over and over. Why wasn't I being embraced? Was I so horrible, so disgusting? I wanted to leave. I started to make plans to leave. I thought, "I can stay here tonight and then leave in the morning." My train was leaving the following afternoon, so I could just hang around in Brussels for the day.

In the sharing circle everyone was talking about their positive experience, but I actively decided not to talk. I sat in surly silence while everyone else went on about the beautiful things that had happened to them on the table that afternoon. My partner decided not to share either, which I interpreted to mean she was being surly too. I kept one thing in mind, however. I thought, "I will talk to my partner." I meant, before I packed up my things to leave.

There were a few minutes before dinner and I spoke to my partner and asked if she would mind talking to me, and she agreed. We went into the garden and I told her that I had felt deserted by her, abandoned, and that I had a problem with rejection, and that I hadn't wanted to say anything in the circle but had decided to talk to her instead. And she said, "I think you'd better talk to Eric."

So we approached Eric and Eric and I sat under a tree while I explained what had happened, and Eric assured me that this wasn't my problem, and I felt relieved.

I decided to stay after all.

I can't speak for my partner, of course. She will have to speak for herself. The only thing this does is to tell you about my own internal dialogue, about what was happening to me. This is as much as I know.

So now we come to the third day, and to the revelations.

Yes, revelations. Things revealed.

According to the Penguin Complete English Dictionary a revelation is:

1a the act or an instance of revealing something. **b** something revealed, especially a sudden and illuminating disclosure. **2** a truth believed to be revealed by God to man, or the communicating of it.

I have chosen this definition as it includes the word "illuminating" and the revelations given to me were indeed clothed in light.

On the third day we lay on our backs and the work was done on our chest. I was partnered by an American woman. I was on the table first.

Before we began we stated our intentions for the day. Earlier, Judy had talked about inviting our mind into our body, an idea I was taken by. I like my mind. I don't like the idea of it being banished or lost. I want my mind to be a witness to all that I see and experience. I want it to keep up its commentary, its analysis, its level-headed thinking. So I stated my intention: "to invite my mind into my body to discover the wisdom that lies there." And this was my first heart-felt statement of intent: an invitation to my mind to partake of the on-going proceedings of the day.

Lying on your back you feel much more vulnerable than when you lie of your front. You have your eyes open and you are looking around at the world. The face is naked and you are looking into the naked face of your partner. You are exposed. My partner was holding my hand and looking down at me from above. There is something archetypal in this. It is the position your mother might take before she tucks you up in bed at night, or the position a lover might take before she bends down to kiss you. Or maybe it is the position a nurse might take before you are wheeled away into the operating chamber and the drugs are starting to take effect. I was looking into my partner's eyes and seeing the eyes of all my past lovers in there. The eyes were sceptical but benign, defensive but compassionate, cautious but kind.

The practitioners were coming over to work on my chest: on my heart area. I was doing what I had stated as my intent. I was inviting my mind into my body to find what wisdom lies there. So I was breathing into the ache in my heart, where whoever it was was working. I found I could go deeper and deeper with this. I could bring my whole awareness into my body to meet the ache coming in from the outside. Judy worked on me, and Wouter and Eric. I don't know how much time was passing. And then Wouter was working on me. He was leaning over me on my right, working on my heart: this small circular motion around my sternum. And....

And then I was gone.

There was no me any more, only light.
I can't say any more about this, as I wasn't there to witness it.

I only know that as I reappeared I felt that I was coming from very far away, from a great distance in time and space, and that I had been bathed in light. It was a place of great energy and power. There was a buzzing in my ears and a rush of energy all around me and as I opened my eyes I didn't know who I was or where I was. It was like being born all over again. I was scared, because I didn't know what had happened to me. I opened my eyes and slowly the world came into focus. Oh yes, I'm on a table. Oh yes, I'm in an Amanae workshop. Oh yes, there is Wouter, leaning over me, just as he had been before. No time had passed. I had stepped through a wormhole into another dimension a universe and a half away, and then returned, in less than a blink of an eye. I guess I was looking perplexed. Wouter said, "your heart has opened," and there was a look of deep compassion in his eye and his voice was gentle and kind and I felt safe.

I had this experience three times on the table that morning, and by the second and the third time I had learned to say "thank you."

The second time was with Judy, who did her strange nasal chant over me, and I disappeared into that. It was like the chant was a trigger for my soul to leap over the threshold into the other world. The third time it was with my partner, who said, "you want to be wholehearted don't you?" and I knew that I did, that my heart had been broken and that I wanted it whole again, and I kind of leapt joyfully into my heart, into that place of light and wonder, to embrace the mysteries that lay there.

As I say, I cannot tell you about that place as each time I became immersed into it my earthly mind became lost. But I was left with certain impressions. Firstly, that it was a place of light, of pure light, of brilliance and intensity, so that it seemed as if I was being bathed in light. Secondly, I had the impression that there was a being there, a being of light. Maybe that was me. Maybe I was the being of light. Or maybe it was an angel or a daemon. It seemed like an angel, or like my higher self waiting for my acknowledgement. It was powerful beyond measure, but compassionate. It cared about me and wanted to heal me. It thought with its heart not its head and it could communicate telepathically, direct from heart to heart. I also felt that there was a symbol on his chest: a triangle radiating lines like rays. Maybe there was an eye in the triangle, like the all-seeing eye of Horus. I had that impression too: of a witnessing eye radiating eternal light.

So there is a place in the heart through which God looks out into the world. The heart is a temple, and the mind must enter it as a supplicant, full of reverence, full of praise, prepared to worship. The heart is the key, because the heart is the mediator. It mediates between God and man. It mediates between the sexual organs and the brain, between instinct and analysis, between sin and redemption, between a hope and a prayer. In the heart lies suffering, and through that compassion. In the heart lies anger, and through that forgiveness. It is the heart that feels. That is why we want to lock it away. Sometimes it feels too much. It aches too much, with all the pain that we inflict in our lives, with all the pain we receive. But because it feels it can also heal. It is the place of the wound where all healing begins.

Judy told me to breathe in through my heart and I said, "it is the angelic breath." My partner said, "what did he say?" and Judy said, "angelic breath." And I said, "yes, because you breathe through the heart and the lungs are like wings and they are unfurling with every breath."

Don't ask me what I meant by that, but it all seemed to make sense at the time.

I could feel the breath like an arrow piercing my sternum and entering my heart. It was like a column of light going directly to my heart. I was brimming with light. All around me in the room I could hear the sounds of other people whose hearts were opening. There was like a shiver of ecstasy passing around the room. The room was stirring with ecstasy. Judy was working on my shoulder and my arms unfolded. My arms opened up so I was in the receiving position. Like Jesus on the cross, but not in suffering, in ecstasy, I lay on the table already receiving what the boundless universe had given.

"You never enjoy the world aright, till the sea itself floweth in your veins, till you are clothed with the heavens and crowned with the stars."

So said Thomas Traherne.

And on that day, I knew exactly what he meant.

Blessings to you all.

Journeys

1. Malta: A journey back to the days when Britannia ruled the waves

In 1798 Napoleon came to Malta. Recognising its strategic importance in the heart of the Mediterranean, he left a garrison of some 4,000 troops to occupy the island. By 1800 the Maltese had had enough of the godless French and called on the British for help. The British set up a naval blockade, and after some protracted negotiations Bony's troops agreed to go.

The way the Maltese tell the story, they were so pleased with the departure of the French that they decided to have a drink to celebrate. They invited the British in to join them. It was a very long drink. It lasted the better part of 200 years.

Malta gained her independence in 1964, and became a republic in 1974. The last British troops left in 1979. Nevertheless there is still a strong British flavour to the island, what with the red telephone boxes and the red pillar boxes, the three pin electric plugs and the fact that they drive on the left. Everyone speaks almost perfect English – it is the official second language on the island - and the Maltese often choose English-sounding Christian names, such as Jim or Joanna.

They also have a taste for bacon and eggs, tea with milk and a Sunday roast.

But there is another way that the people of the two island nations are connected. Generations of British servicemen were stationed in Malta. As one Maltese person put it: they saw the sparkling dark eyes and the glistening black hair of the Maltese girls, and they fell in love. Almost everyone has a relative in the UK, and has visited it at some point. Expect long conversations about your home county while you are there. Chances are that the person you are talking to will have a relative living nearby.

Many British people will have fond memories of Malta, whether of their time as service men and women stationed on the island, or the wives, husbands or children who were brought over to join them.

I'm one of the latter. I was on the island from 1957 to 1959, from age four, to age six, and have many distinct memories of my time there.

Ex service people who were stationed on Malta will find much that they would still recognise. One notable site is the Bighi Hospital in Kalkara, which every British service person will have been forced to visit to receive their inoculations. It is now the Institute of Conservation for Heritage Malta: "a hospital for sick objects" as the manager of the books, paper, textiles and painting conservation section, Joseph Schiro, told me.

It was built in the 1830s to a design by Sir George Whitmore. Work was completed in 1832 and it served as a hospital through all of the major wars after that, when Malta became renowned as "the nurse of the Mediterranean". It is built in the Doric style, and there is much that is reassuringly British about its appearance. It remained in use as a hospital until 1970.

In the centre of the grounds is an octagonal conservatory known as "the smoking shed". It is where generations of sick soldiers and sailors would have repaired for a shifty cigarette. Visitors may walk around the outside of the building and view the grounds, but would have to make an appointment to see inside.

Another important place to visit would be the Malta Maritime Museum, in Vittoriosa. Housed in what was once the fleet bakery, it is an impressively large building: not surprising given the number of ships and men it had to feed in its day. Inside you can find many reminders of the British naval presence on the island, including an imposing figurehead of the HMS Hibernia representing the Irish Dagda, a sea god. You will also be lead through a history of Malta's naval heritage going back more than 2,000 years.

One of the exhibits concerns Operation Pedestal, which is an important reminder of Malta's significance in the history of the Second World War. It shows a photograph of a damaged oil tanker, the Ohio, limping into the Grand Harbour, broken backed and buoyed up by two minesweepers. The ships arrived on August the 15th 1942, the Feast of the Assumption, and was consequently named the Santa Maria Convoy by the ever devout Maltese. The Ohio contained enough oil to re-supply the island, allowing British forces to continue attacking supply ships to Rommel's army during his assault on El Alamein. It is considered by many to be the turning point in the war.

Another place of interest for visitors looking for British naval connections, would be the Ta' Braxia Cemetery in Pieta, where a number of graves of British merchant seamen and their families are located. One particularly poignant grave is carved into the shape of a neatly made bed, with a coverlet and a pillow, with a seaman's cap laid on top. It's as if the occupant has just returned from a journey and has slung his cap on the bed before retiring for the night.

A place that all British servicemen will certainly remember is Strait Street, Strada Stretta, in Valletta, universally known as "The Gut". I say "British servicemen" rather than "men and women" at this point, because it would have been men rather than women who went down this notorious street. It was the city's red-light district. But it was more than this too. It was full of bars and theatres and dance halls, as well as traders and street girls, and it was the place where the Maltese first heard jazz music, and danced face-to-face in the ballroom style.

Unfortunately it is virtually derelict now, a shadow of its former self. There are a few broken neon signs as a sad reminder of its former glory and apparently, according to some reports, some of the bars are still there, behind the shutters and the boarded up windows, the ancient optics still flicker with a ghostly gleam, like reliquaries of the good times gone by.

The only establishment from the old days still trading is a tattoo parlour, run by the third generation of the same family. It fought on as the Royal Navy came and went, through good times and bad. Now, with a new plan to turn Strait Street into a centre for the arts, it could be facing its biggest battle yet.

Malta is a perfect holiday destination, whether you like beaches and bars or baroque architecture, but for a nostalgic journey into British Service history, it is unique.

2. Whitstable: a unique North Kent community

There's something about Whitstable. It's not only its physical appearance - those white-painted, weather-boarded fisherman's cottages in their homely terraces, or the Victorian Christmas card shop-fronts up and down Harbour Street, or even the network of back alleys that embroider the town in a criss-cross pattern of secret destinations (some well-established enough to have acquired names) - but there's something else too, something less substantial, but no less real. It's an atmosphere, perhaps; a mood, a feeling. A sense of history, not as some dry academic thing, confined to the library and a dusty book shelf, but alive, in the very streets, in the lay-out of the town and in the people who choose to live here.

People's first sight of the town is usually coming down the hill from the A299, London to Margate road. You see the town below you, strung out along the North Kent shore at the confluence of the Medway and the Thames, with the Isle of Sheppey dividing them. On a clear day you can see the far-off hotels and tower-blocks of Southend glinting on the Essex coast. But whatever the light, the view is dominated by the estuary, the colours always shifting, from iron-grey, to green, to brown or blue.

I first came here in 1981 or 1982. I was visiting a friend in Canterbury. We caught a bus to Herne Bay, about six miles further along the coast, and then walked to Whitstable along the sea front. It was early Summer. We had cherries and soft cheese with us for lunch. And, when we arrived in the town, we sat down on the sea wall in a place backed by off-balance wooden sail lofts, looking out across the ruffled estuary, and ate our lunch. I knew then that I would like to live here.

Most people fall in love with Whitstable at first sight. I've been living here since 1984.

The first thing you notice about the town is that it is very much alive. It's not like many towns in the South East, a mere dormitory for out-of-towners working in London. The High Street is brimming with bustle and its own particular style. There are enough people left in Whitstable who prefer to walk to the shops to make the High Street still viable. So, along with the obligatory Co-op (at the less fashionable end of town) and a number of quite ordinary butchers shops and green grocers and newsagents, you have the odd glimpse into a forgotten world of gentleman's tailors and oyster parlours with a distinctly nineteenth century feel.

When I first moved here there was a little shop called Hatchard's on the High Street, now sadly closed. It was a gentleman's outfitters of the old fashioned kind, a family business for a hundred years. Prior to that it was a pub.

Stepping through the tinkling front door was like walking back in time. Wooden floorboards and shelves stacked with traditional items: from flat caps to fisherman's smocks, from trousers with turn-ups, made of mole-skin or heavy-duty corduroy, to a rack of fluorescent waistcoats to bring colour to a gentleman's otherwise discrete wardrobe. You would notice that the staff all wore waistcoats too, with handkerchiefs in their breast pockets, and crisp shirts and neat ties. There were three of them, all immaculately turned out. They advertised their ware by wearing it.

Most appealing was the atmosphere. It wasn't just traditional clothing for sale but traditional values too, of politeness and good-service. Alterations to clothing were done free of charge.

Well Hatchard's is gone (it is now a branch of Costa, the coffee outlet) but Wheeler's Oyster Bar is still very much alive.

Oysters are what Whitstable is famous for, of course. As John Hollingshead wrote in "All Year Round" on the 29th of November 1859: "Many important towns in many parts of England exist upon one idea, and Whitstable, though not very important, is one of them. Its one idea is oysters."

That remains a fact. And the one place to eat them is Wheelers. Don't bother going anywhere else. Wheelers is the original oyster parlour, first opened in 1858. We can only guess whether John Hollingshead visited or not, but it's fairly likely that he ate oysters in a place not unlike it.

Behind the bright pink and blue facade, Wheelers offers us a taste of real history, with a parlour that truly lives up to its name. More like someone's living room than a restaurant or cafe, it is homely and comfortable, with plenty more on offer than just oysters: a range of gourmet dishes at reasonable prices. Bring your own beer or wine (there's an off-license across the road): corkage is free. But beware: trade is very brisk all year round, but particularly in the summer and at weekends. We recommend you book well in advance.

I say "ordinary" to describe some of the day-to-day shops on the High Street, but, of course, unlike a number of town-centres nowadays (take Canterbury, for instance) where shopping has become a mainly out-of-town experience, and the High Street is left to chi-chi restaurants and souvenir outlets catering for tourists, the presence of these ordinary shops has become a quite extraordinary thing. Not that Whitstable is entirely free from the requirement to serve out-of-towners. It's just that, amongst the continental delicatessens and croissants caterers - no bad thing surely - you can still buy a plain white loaf, a bag of potatoes and a joint for the Sunday roast.

The reason for the presence of delicatessens and croissant shops is that Whitstable has become fashionable of late, particularly amongst the London media-set. So part of your browsing experience might well be celebrity-spotting, in the process of which - like any good twitcher - you could mark your card with a fine example of the pop-star type (Jarvis Cocker, say), or the comedian type (Alan Davies, who began his career in the town) or even the much rarer Newspaper Editor type, such as Janet Street Porter, who, rumour has it, has a weekend cottage here. Certainly she can be seen occasionally, wearing walking boots and an anorak, striding purposefully out of town on one of her regular rambling expeditions.

None of this is new, of course. Although Whitstable has been a traditional place to visit for day-trippers from the East End of London since the nineteenth century at least, it has always seen its fair share of famous visitors too. Charles Dickens came here, as did Turner - both as famous as any pop-star in their own day - and Somerset Maugham lived here too, and celebrated the town in two of his famous novels: *Of Human Bondage* and *Cakes and Ale*. He called it, not too subtly, Blackstable. And, more recently, that doyen of camp Hammer Horror movies, Peter Cushing, spent his retirement years here. There is a Cushing's View - a platform with benches overlooking the sea – a pub, and even a song to mark his connection to the town.

As for those sea-views: the next thing you notice about the town is how difficult it is to find them. You can drive right through it and never get a glimpse of the sea. This is one of its charms. For a well-known sea-side town it reserves its sea-views with a notable discretion. It's as if, like a huffy pantomime dame, the whole town has lifted its skirts and turned its back on the sea. Finding it is a real adventure involving complex negotiations with back streets and alleys. You can be walking within yards of it and still not know it is there.

But - to give you directions - the sea front is behind Island Wall. Take one of the alleys from the High Street to Middle Wall, and then another from there to Island Wall. Try Squeeze Gut Alley, if you can find it. (Make sure you go before lunch: you'll soon discover how it acquired its name.) From there, slip down any of the alleys cutting through between the cottages, and you'll come to the sea-wall and, at last, your unobstructed sea-views.

And from this position you will notice something else too. There is a pub on the beach. Called the Old Neptune, it is a favourite place to drink and take in the sunset, with tables laid out outside, a welcome resting place for many visitors to the town.

Of course, the Neptune isn't the only pub. Other recommended hostelries are the Royal Naval Reserve, the Ship Centurion and the East Kent (all along the High Street): and my own favourite, the Labour Club on Belmont Road, situated in a classic Whitstable 18th century wooden framed building, and worth a visit, if only for the dry, off-the-cuff humour of its patrons and staff. The beer is cheap too, though you'll have to ask to be signed in.

Finally, no visit to Whitstable would be complete without a trip to the harbour (off Harbour Street, naturally) where you will find the fish market, with a range of local sea-food on sale. This is easy enough to find. You have only to follow your nose. The unmistakable smell of boiled whelks is what gives it away.

All in all, Whitstable is a unique Kent town with a distinctive atmosphere, worth a visit at any time of the year.

3. Angels of New York

We came in on the George Washington Bridge on the Interstate, but you could see the city long before that, from deep inside New Jersey somewhere, the jagged line of skyscrapers flashing between the hills and trees, shimmering in the bright autumn sunlight like some giant bejewelled crown abandoned on the shore by a long-forgotten god. Manhattan Island. Was there ever a more iconic - or instantly recognisable - skyline?

And then we were sweeping in off the freeway along the slow arc of the ramp and down into the bustle of traffic along the highway, making for the Upper West Side.

What is it about New York? Even that phrase "the Upper West Side" is iconic – despite the fact that is no more than a geographical description - sending a spurt of adrenaline into the blood and making the heart beat a little faster. And now there we were amongst the snarling traffic, the mean yellow taxis, the lumbering behemoths of those great American lorries, the limousines, the big-wheel trucks, nudging forward from traffic light to traffic light amidst the blare of horns, the dust and confusion, edging slowly forward in the contending traffic like Darwinian creatures in an evolutionary struggle for survival.

Yes, that's exactly what New York feels like. It's like you've accidentally wandering into some accelerated version of evolution, like the city is urging you from behind – nudging you, pressing you – the whole weight of the city pushing you forward whether you like it or not.

As soon as you step out you can sense it: a kind of hormonal electricity in the air, humanity on a knife edge, an urgency, a drive, crazy, egotistical, vain, but marvellously exciting, as if anything can happen here, and often does, in the grand canyon avenues with the constant blare of traffic and the echoed wailing of police sirens, and people moving to and fro with such a mighty sense of purpose. The hustle. The noise. The constant movement, like a tidal surge of humanity welling up along the straight square streets laid out like graph paper and buzzing with life.

We parked the car, my brother and I, dropped our bags in the hotel, and went out to join the throng.

But first we stopped off for a slice of Pizza.

Throughout the whole of New York State, and probably everywhere else in the world, the New York Pizza is known as that: the New York Pizza. Except in New York, that is, when it is just called "Pizza" and is pretty well the only kind of pizza you can find.

I forget what kind I got. We just went in and pointed, like the foreign tourists we were. "I'll have that one," I said. Mine had olives on it, Rob's had meat. And then we went and sat outside to eat them.

There is an art to eating a slice of New York Pizza. It's actually a piece of architecture. You hold it by the crust, folding it in half, forming a V from which the weight of the pizza hangs, and then load it into your mouth from the pointy end, like a dumper truck loading gravel onto the back of a lorry, positioning your mouth slightly below it to achieve the desired end.

The crust is a bit like the structural arch on a bridge. It holds it together. What you don't do: you don't rip or mangle the crust or the whole thing falls apart.

Which is what I did. I ripped off a bit of the crust to taste it, thus damaging the architectural integrity of the whole structure, so that the pointy end flopped limply forward sending the weight of the topping sliding off onto the plate, which I then had to pick up piece by sticky piece with my fingers.

It still tasted great though. My first taste of New York.

After that we went on the subway.

It was at this point that my excitement exploded and a sense of hyper-reality kicked in, on a train heading downtown towards Times Square, in a carriage of polished aluminium, hanging on to an upright post as the train jerked and screeched and kicked its way along the track. I was humming Downtown Train by Tom Waits quietly to myself, looking round, and it was like I'd been here before, on this exact train, with these exact people: the Latinos and the Blacks and the Irish and the Jews, all these shades of complexion in their various types of clothing, sitting, standing, reading, watching, talking, listening, contemplating the world, one young woman fanning herself with an old fashioned fan, on the inside of a shining silver bullet heading into the heart of downtown New York. The rattle of the train. The rhythm of the track. The train tossing us back and forth. Winding and sliding into the station. The doors swishing open. People getting on and off. Moving round to let more people on. Gripping tight again as the train jolts off. And all those finely delineated faces, all around, their characters moulded in flesh, like animated sculptures worked in various shades of clay. So precise. So alive. So human. People I felt I already knew.

But something starts to niggle me, a feeling which goes on repeating itself throughout the day: the sense that I've been here before, that I've known all this before, in some other life perhaps, in some other incarnation, as if, maybe, I have New York blood running through my veins, a New York soul and a New York sensibility, like some ancient jazz riff in the background of my thoughts, like the musical score from the movie of my life.

Something like that.

And stepping out of the subway into the noise and the traffic and the crowd, streets bursting at the seams and rippling with humanity, Rob says, "there's the naked cowboy," and starts to take a picture. And sure enough, there he is, a guy dressed in cowboy boots and a cowboy hat, but otherwise only Y-fronts, standing on an intersection between traffic lights, with traffic moving either side of him, and people jostling back and forth, singing and playing the guitar. A handsome black dude crossing the road just as Rob is pointing the camera says, "Did you really take a picture of him?" as we head off, and Rob says, "it's not for me it's for my wife," not answering the question and sounding defensive, which makes us all laugh.

But I realise something – not then, later, on reflection – that this naked cowboy guy has placed himself in precisely this spot for maximum effect, the city swirling about him like white water rapids, and that the whole of New York is like that: like a showbiz act, people stepping out onto the streets like they step out onto the stage, the whole huge towering cityscape like a stage set, the people, the actors, the chorus line, the props, like an all-singing, all-dancing, costumed, bejewelled, sparkling, brightly-lit Broadway Musical show: like 42nd Street maybe, where all the buildings suddenly acquire legs and start kicking in unison, like the girls in the chorus line. So now Rob and I are heading into Times Square, doing the tourist thing - well what did you expect, we are tourists — and we're looking up at the lurching, hovering, heaving buildings towering above us, spinning round and round with the intoxication of it, the flash and the span of the building-sized neon advertisements like vast statements of overheated wealth, the whole space a display of conspicuous consumption on a grand scale – I mean, how much electricity is being used here, and for what purpose? – unashamed, unabashed, brazen and obvious, over-the-top and yet viscerally exciting, here at the navel of the world.

It is here that the layout of New York reveals itself, in this intersection, this square that is not a square, where Broadway cuts across Seventh Avenue between 47th and 42nd Streets, because whereas the town as a whole is a relentless series of grids and blocks (avenues running one way, streets running the other) Broadway is this vast sweeping diagonal that cuts across the whole of it, dissecting it at an angle and adding interesting variety to the otherwise straight-up-an-down architecture, forcing buildings into weird, aerodynamic angular shapes to accommodate it, breaking up the rhythm of the streets like the syncopated swing in a dance band number, and adding cool dissonance to the orchestration of buildings, like the blue note in a jazz riff.

And now I hear it – don't you? – sailing in with the sounds of the city: the suave, cool, sophisticated tempo of a Duke Ellington song – *Take the A Train*, written to celebrate the journey through Manhattan to Harlem – this deeply-textured, moving, modern music, but with an edge, a drive, like the rattle of the train on its tracks or the whirring of electricity in the generators, living, alive, accentuated, sweet-stepping, free-flowing, swirling through the cascade of notes in a relentless pulsating chorus of change, riffs and notes scattering like sparks and eddies into the charged air: the perfect musical accompaniment to a visit to New York, this neon electric city of the Jazz Age.

So now it is time for a drink, naturally, and Rob – who's been here a few times now, having moved to Syracuse in the North of New York state about seven years ago – decides to take me to ESPN Zone which is across the way. Now this is crazy. A huge two story bar full of TV screens showing sports channels. Not just one screen, or two screens, or ten screens but – I don't know, I'm trying to count them in my head – maybe fifty screens, maybe a hundred screens, with baseball and American football and ice hockey and basketball and various other sports (one of the smaller screens is showing a British football match) and commentators in studios discussing the action - the whole lot - the largest screen about three times the size of the wall in my living room, a great bank of pixelated colour and light, so much sport it makes your head spin, and, like everything else in New York, way over the top.

So we order a beer and the girl behind the bar says "large or small" and we say "large", thinking maybe it's the choice between a half pint and a pint. Only it's not. It's the choice between a pint and a quart and now we have these two huge pots of beer to drink. Which is fine. We can drink them, though they are a bit on the expensive side, the round being $17. We photograph them, then we drink them, then, at some point, having consumed a quarter of a gallon of beer, I make the inevitable trip to the gents, only to discover that directly in front of every one of the urinals is yet another small TV screen about the size of a cigarette packet, showing yet more sport, so you don't have to miss even half a second of the action. How many screens did I say there were? Well you can double it. Talk about neurosis: this is a whole building constructed around a clinical obsession with the demon of sport.

After this we walk to the Empire State Building and I say, "you can tell the tourists can't you? The tourists are the ones looking up all the time." And it's true, because this is what you have to do, to look up into the soaring vertiginous depths of the sky-high city, between the buildings which suck your gaze forever upwards as they graze the clouds, amazed at the boldness, the confidence, the sheer, brazen self-assuredness of this city's architecture, like monstrous overblown cathedrals dedicated to the megalithic religion of commerce, whose god is money, dwelling places of the economic Nephilim. It's immoral. It's wrong. It's absurd. It's insane. But it's epic too, it's vast, it's intoxicating, it's bold and it's dangerous and you can't help but admire it at some deep visceral level while being shocked at the same time. Who said that life was simple? Or that we can't live with contradictions?

It costs $19 to go up the Empire State building, but you have to don't you? Everyone has to do this once. Unfortunately the whole building is going through a refit at the moment so something of its Jazzy Art Deco sumptuousness is lost – all that layered, multi-coloured marble, the sleek, sweeping staircases, the glass and the stainless steel, the doormen in their smart maroon livery – as we are herded past plywood barriers with posters of King Kong and into the elevator to the 80th floor. And on again to the next elevator taking us the last six floors to the observation point.

OK, and I have to say how exhilarating this is, looking out across the chequered urban landscape from this vantage point, seeing the layout of the town like some vast chess board, with the towering beautiful buildings scattered about. Yes beautiful. These huge, playful, crazy edifices of a deranged imagination, soaring upwards into the sky. Two buildings strike me in particular: the Chrysler building as the epitome of Art Deco on a grand scale, definitely the most beautiful building in New York, not as large as the Empire State, but prettier, nicer, quainter, the model of what a skyscraper should be; and this other building whose name I don't know, which looks like a copy of a Renaissance cathedral, with arches and palisades, a quadrangle and a clock. Yes a clock, a giant clock, maybe fifty stories up. A great big clock. And who can see this clock but the people in the building opposite, or us, up here on the top of the Empire State? : I can't imagine you can see it from the street, or from anywhere else. So what's the point of it, except as a gesture of flamboyance, a grandiloquent statement, a pointless embellishment, a magnificent, ostentatious whim? You can't help but love a city that puts clocks so high up no one can see them. It is a city in which time no longer exists.

So we circle the building about two or three times, looking out in the four directions, towards the four corners of the world, the West Side, and the East Side, downtown and uptown, Brooklyn and the Bronx, and out towards Staten Island and the Statue of Liberty, across this vast, sprawling metropolis - this hub of humanity, this vortex of ceaseless activity, of time and life and psychosis, this city of hallucination and exhilarating insanity, mad like the gods, a modern Atlantis rising out of the waves, miraculous, expansive, fuelled by vanity and electricity, by sex and by greed, breathless, startled, crazy, alive - I can't help but pause and wonder at the works of humanity, how glorious they can be, and think to myself that this city has to be one of the great wonders of the world.

And now I get it – now as I'm writing this, a few weeks later and several thousand miles away – that one of the symbols of New York is King Kong himself, that overblown ape of humanity, trapped within this urban landscape, the instinctual beast raging against the constraints of the modern world, driven crazy by love, tortured by technology, put on display for money, before bursting free of his chains, and then climbing this, the Empire State Building in a bid for freedom, harried by biplanes, before falling to his death in the streets below.

Which is where we are now, of course, on top of the Empire State Building, up in the wild, crashing skies, with buffeting winds blustering in off the Atlantic, gazing out at the City of the Nephilim, surrounded by people taking photographs. Everyone is taking photographs. They're taking photographs of each other. They're taking photographs of themselves. They're asking other people to take photographs for them, positioning themselves in front of the camera with some landmark in the background. So we take some photographs too, and someone offers to take our photograph, so now we too have a photograph of us on top of the Empire State Building with a landmark in the background, just like everybody else. And then you wonder how many photographs there must be from this place, over all these years? How many shutter clicks in how many seconds over how many days, how many years? How many cameras? How many pictures from this weird eyrie, this eagle's perch, high up in the luminescent sky? Will there ever be time to look at them all?

But it's getting as bit cold now so we decide to come down. Down, down. Down through the layers of steel and glass and marble and humanity. Down passed the offices, through the soap opera entanglement of lives, storey by storey, by story, at free fall speed, though we don't know it, to arrive back, padded and cushioned by air, at the ground floor and find a bar so we can drink yet more beer.

There's a bar under the building itself, which we invade with our presence, sliding past a pillar where a bunch of people are nattering away. Only they're not nattering away in New York parlance, but in some weird foreign language only Rob and I can understand. Rob says, "can I hear Brummie accents?" And then standing next to us at the bar, where we are leaning waiting to be served, is a guy wearing a bright red football shirt on which, when he turns around, we read the words "Banks's Bitter".

Banks's Bitter is brewed in Wolverhampton, not more than 15 miles from where Rob and I were brought up in the West Midlands.

"Is that a Banks's Tee-shirt I see there?" says Rob, in his broad Brummie accent. And sure enough, there's a bunch of Midlanders here in the heart of New York with us, and we begin chatting about our respective holidays. They're just about to leave having spent the last five days in New York, just drinking up their last pints – "very expensive," says the man with the Banks's tee-shirt - after which we raise our glasses and bid them goodbye.

After this we head off again, making for Chinatown now. We have a subway map which we've been consulting all day, and the process of finding our way around is a bit like pinning the tail on the donkey. We're just abstractly pointing to bits with nice names we half recognise and deciding to go there.

But first, before we go down the subway, I see this guy with a bouffant hair-do and a $1,000 suit, with buffed immaculate shoes and a crisp, white shirt and a tie, stepping out of the sleek marble lobby of some up-market hotel while the concierge hails him a taxi. He has a woman on his arm – this broad, as we'd say, using the vernacular – with a fur stole and high heels and hair piled high like Audrey Hepburn in Breakfast at Tiffany's, and she's powdering her nose and checking her make up in a little vanity mirror, and I think I recognise them both. Yes, she's Audrey Hepburn all right - Audrey Hepburn as Holly Golightly - and he's Michael Douglas. Michael Douglas in Wall Street. She's a naive socialite who takes a $50 tip for going to the bathroom, and he's this son of a reptile who'll eat your soul for breakfast, two movies stepping out together onto the same sidewalk. So something strikes me now about this irksome sense of familiarity I've been having ever since we got on the subway, that actually I have seen it all before, not in another life, in the movies. 42nd Street and King Kong and Wall Street and Breakfast at Tiffany's. And Taxi Driver and Midnight Cowboy and Naked City and the Fisher King. All these movies. All these scenes of streets and people. The crowds, the taxis, the subways, the shops, the diners, the bars, the streets, the avenues, the buildings, the bridges. Tracking shots down Broadway to Times Square and Fifth Avenue. Aerial shots from helicopters swerving in and out between the skyscrapers. Long shots along wind-blown dusty streets with a solitary sheet of newspaper bustling in the wind. Night shots though a windscreen in the rain with the wipers swishing back and forth. All of these shots. All of these scenes. All of these stories. Being in New York is like walking about inside a film set. It has to be the most filmed city in the world.

So I wonder what kind of movie Rob and I are in? Hopefully none of the above.

Finally we make it to Chinatown where we stop off for something to eat. $5 each for a meal. Can't be bad. And then, just as the sun is starting to go down, we head off to Battery Park near where you catch the Staten Island Ferry, which is the nearest point on Manhattan Island to the Statue of Liberty, where Rob takes some great photographs of the statue with the sunset blazing in the distance.

After which we start walking back passed the National Museum of the American Indian as night is gathering in the streets and the lights are flickering on in the skyscrapers, and nearby there's a bunch of cop cars gathered in a car park, and they start to move off slowly, each one just giving us a short burst of its siren - wee-ow: like that! - and a single red-blue flash of its lights as they crawl out into the city in a funereal procession one at a time. How many are there? I don't know, maybe 20 or more. What is this about? Are they all just going on shift? Is this like some sort of a daily ritual? Or is it a protest of some sort or an actual funeral? We never do find out.

And after this it is Grand Central Station with its bustle and noise – I'm reminded of a scene in the *Fisher King* where everyone begins to waltz while Robin Williams is following his girl - then back to Times Square, and after that to a series of bars along Amsterdam Avenue on the Upper West Side between 80th and 86th I think, which get cheaper and cheaper the further we go along, till we fall into our cheap hotel room sometime after midnight, after a night of ogling the barmaids, which beer and tiredness and lust and age had made me decide were amongst the most beautiful women in the world.

If only I was thirty years younger.

4. Along The Pilgrim's Way From Winchester to Canterbury

There are many words for walking. We amble. We stroll. We march. We trudge. We perambulate. Best of all, perhaps: we saunter.

This last word is from the French, "Saint Terre" meaning "Holy Land".

It derives from the Middle Ages, when pilgrimage was all the rage. Everyone was going to the Holy Land. Some people took it up as a profession. They would wander from town to town, from church to church, begging for alms, like Sadhus and Holy Men do in India today. When asked where they were going, they would say, "to Saint Terre"….. to the Holy Land.

They would never actually get there. It was the journey itself that mattered. Perhaps they were already in the Holy Land in some sense. Perhaps it was the walking that took them there.

It certainly felt like that to me.

We were on the Pilgrim's Way: the ancient pilgrimage route hemming the line of the North Downs through Kent and West Sussex, a long, wavering ribbon of battered tarmac and chalky track that stretches out between the great Cathedral cities of Canterbury and Winchester; and beyond, from Dover to Stonehenge.

It was late April and the Bluebells were out. We sauntered along country lanes through wooded hills as dappled sunlight played down upon us, as the road unravelled and birds sang, scurrying about in the treetops. Hardly a car passed. There was hardly a reminder that we were in the 21st century at all.

I was with my friend, Paul. We were about three days into the journey by now, up an isolated track by a wood. We were talking about walking, about the way walking changes things. "You get to know the world you're walking in," said Paul. "It's more intimate."

"Yes," I said. "You get to know the faces of the trees."

This is true. In our 21st century world we circumscribe the landscape. We surround it. We look in on it from the outside, from a distance, from our roads, from our cars, from our cities, from our houses. When you walk, on the other hand, you enter the landscape, stepping across a threshold as if through a doorway into another world. You become immersed in the landscape. You become a part of it.

A journey that might take 20 minutes by car would take three days on foot. The whole world changes with this change of pace. England is another country, an undiscovered land, one you have only ever glimpsed from afar. The trees are like sentinels, guiding you on your journey, guarding you on your way. And each tree has a character, a personality. Soon you find yourself talking to them, like long lost friends.

It had been a variable journey so far. We'd caught a train to Winchester, but, arriving late, had had to take the first bed and breakfast we could find. It was a scruffy, dirty little room above a pub and didn't bode well for our trip. It didn't even provide a proper breakfast. And the first day it rained heavily all day, making walking impossible. We visited the Cathedral - which we got in for nothing, telling the cashier that we were on a pilgrimage and wanted to say a prayer at the start of our journey - after which we decided to skip ahead by bus, to Farnham, where we found a welcoming pub and a much more hospitable B&B. And the following morning, the weather being suddenly bright, we set out on foot at last.

We were following the North Down's Way, the well marked English National Trail which approximates the route of the old Pilgrim's Way. You leave Farnham on a wooded footpath which parallels the A31 - which intrudes upon you with its incessant roar at first - but very soon you swerve away into open countryside.... And into silence, expansiveness and beauty.

I think this is what is so remarkable about this route: the fact that in this most crowded and built-up corner of England, the South East, you can travel for hours, even days, at a time, and hardly cross a road or meet another soul.

As well as the white acorn signs which point the way, you also encounter the occasional more eccentric marker. Decorated trees. You don't often see this in England. But here, on the Pilgrim's Way, we came across two in the space of less than an hour. Later, in the village of Puttenham, we found a pub, The Good Intent. It was lunchtime now. We'd been walking since early morning, so you can be assured our intentions were very good as we stepped in for some welcome refreshment and a chat with the locals.

It was in here that we heard about the Watts Mortuary Chapel.

"You'll be surprised," said the patrons of the pub, mysteriously. "It's like nothing you have ever seen before."

We set out on our walk again, and about an hour further on we found ourselves approaching the monument.

It is a few hundred yards off the route, near the Watts Gallery in the village of Compton, up a lane and around a bend. We'd been walking for most of the day and were very tired. When the monument failed to jump immediately into sight we almost gave up. "If I don't see it soon I'm heading back," I said. But then, there it was.

At first sight it is very plain: a domed, red brick chapel set on a wooded hill. Closer up you can see that it is elaborately decorated, with intricate terracotta forms weaving in and out of the brickwork and a fine, ornately carved wooden doorway. But it is on stepping through the doorway that the magic hits you. As the people in the pub had told us, it was like nothing we'd ever seen before. It very nearly took our breath away.

If the outside is a monochrome terracotta red, inside it glows with the richest of hues, reds and greens and purples and browns and blues, all the colours you can imagine, with images of fiery Angels making secret hand signs, with code words woven into the design and deeply resonant quotations from the Bible. It is like an Art Nouveau temple in there.

A notice at the door explains its origins.

It was built as a memorial to the Victorian portraitist George Watts by his wife Mary Fraser Tytler, who designed the building, and includes a painting by Watts himself, which he completed just months before his death.

The whole thing is a stunning, awe-inspiring, mystical work of art, which would be worth a visit even without its connection to the Pilgrim's Way.

Aldous Huxley is buried in the graveyard.

The Watt's Mortuary Chapel is in Surrey, but, over the border in Kent, there are further surprises. One of these is the Coldrum Stones, a Neolithic chambered Long Barrow near the village of Trottiscliffe not far from Sevenoaks.

I've lived in Kent now for 25 years but had never heard of this ancient place until recently. It is one of Kent's best kept secrets, hardly more than half an hour's drive from Canterbury.

It is perched just off the Pilgrims Way on a spur of land over looking the Weald of Kent, where the River Medway cuts through the Downs, facing East towards the Vernal Equinox sunrise.

Excavations show a number of burials in this place, including the skull of a woman who may have been ritually sacrificed, which stood on a raised shelf inside the burial chamber. Some of the bones had been painted in red ochre. These are now situated in Maidstone Museum.

And from beside the chamber, looking East, you can just make out the site of another Long Barrow, Kitt's Coty House, about five miles away, also situated on the slope of the North Downs along the Pilgrim's Way.

It's as if, in locating these two monuments within sighting distance of each other, the ancient builders were marking out this venerable track for travellers to follow. Possibly a ferry crossing on the Medway would have lain in between. Possibly, also, they were standing in defiance of each other across the spacious landscape, marking out rival territories.

It was May Eve by now, Beltane, the perfect time to be here. There was a circle of flowers in the grounds where previous visitors had made their offerings. Paul burned incense and did some rituals, while I said my prayers to the ancestors, absorbing the atmosphere of peace and tranquillity which pervades the place.

It felt as if, in following this ancient pathway, we were being led, not only through the physical landscape, but through a psychic and historical landscape too.

There's something about this road, something indefinable but alluring. It calls to you, beckoning you along the way. Every so often the way is cut or broken by a stretch of modern road, with the traffic rushing by, fuming and roaring; but then you'd catch sight of the Pilgrim's Way in the distance, a dark little funnel through the greenery, luring you into its peaceful shade.

I always knew instinctively when I was on the Pilgrim's Way. I could feel it in my bones.

This road could represent the earliest evidence of human activity on these Isles, being not only a medieval Pilgrimage route, but a part of a much earlier track-way too, stretching all the way from Dover to Stonehenge: from the most important crossing point for the continent, to the very heart of Britain.

It is the natural route from the East to the West, avoiding the mires and the bogs of the marshy valleys, and the forest entanglements of the heights (full of wild animals and hostile tribes) keeping a level course, sheltered from the wind, on the sunny side of the slopes, overlooking the vast expanse of the landscape stretching out below.

It was once a great trading route, with people bringing goods and raw materials to and from Europe. Perhaps it is the road taken by the great megalith builders when they first set foot on these Isles, bringing with them their high culture and their knowledge of the stars. Perhaps, too, the first metals were brought in along this road.

Hunter-gatherers used it to track their prey. Farmers used it to bring their crops to market. Nomads used it to move their herds.

The Celts used it, the Romans used it, the Saxons used it.

Medieval pilgrims rode along it at a canter (at the Canterbury pace) to visit the bones of their sacred dead, just as Neolithic travellers had before.

John Bunyan lived nearby, and wrote his Pilgrim's Progress as an allegory of its spiritual meaning.

Hilaire Belloc in The Old Road speaks of the archetype of *The Road*. "It is the greatest and most original of the spells which we inherit from the earliest pioneers of our race," he says.

The Road leads us on. It is *The Road* itself which guides us, taking a level course, avoiding the traps and the dangers lying in wait either side, taking the simplest and most natural route through the landscape. *The Road* knows the crossing points for every river, for every hill. It knows the best way over every obstacle, and all along it there are places to stay, for rest and refreshment.

Here, in the early part of the 21st century, it sometimes feels as if the whole of the human race is lost.

Once on *The Road* you cannot get lost. It is *The Road* that guides us home.

5. Riding With Lady Luck: A journey across Europe in a Grand Cherokee Jeep

It was at a toilet-stop somewhere in Hungary that the song came to me. This drear place of nothing by the side of the road, just a pull-off with a scrubby bit of grass bordered by a fence, with a grey toilet block in the middle, two metal doors, one for the Ladies and one for the Gents, but the same filthy, smeared toilets inside. In the end I decided to go against the fence. Then I got back in the car and sat down, exhausted.

There were several cars lined up beside the road. A couple of lorries. Almost everyone was asleep.

A lorry pulled up about 50 yards ahead. The driver got out and went to look in the toilet block. He looked in the Gents and he looked in the Ladies. Then he went back to his cab and got some toilet paper. He saw me clocking him. We both knew what the situation was. These disgusting toilets. But he had no choice. He disappeared into the Ladies and came out several minutes later feeling a whole lot better I expect. He washed his hands with bottled water, got into his cab, then he drove off.

I was so tired. I'd been travelling now for nearly a whole day, with just a short break in some service station somewhere in Germany. All those miles of ravelling road from Calais to wherever I am now. The whine and hiss of the traffic. This world of ceaseless movement, of ceaseless distraction, of cars, of lorries, roaring and racing in either direction, from somewhere to somewhere else. No one wanted to be here. A kind of dead world, dusty grey and full of danger, always moving, always raging, always screaming, like a terrified monster in its death agony.

You have to keep your wits about you all the time, especially in Germany where there is no speed limit and they're driving these vicious machines that rush up from behind at 140 miles an hour, lights flashing, and you have to get out of the way quick. You're watching all the time, checking your mirrors, staying alert, focussed, concentrating on the road ahead.

Every so often I'd find myself drifting off into a thought and I'd have to stop it. You can't afford time off in that lethal world. There's only you, the road, and the other cars. Everything else is superfluous. It's a kind of moving meditation on mortality. One slip and you could be dead.

I'd driven through the night, through the darkness and through the rain, hearing the squeak of the windshield wipers rubbing back and forth sluicing diamonds from the glass, watching the lights from in front and from behind, mile after mile of road in this great arc across a continent, sweeping though invisible landscapes and the shadows of mountains, like dark, unseen presences, through Germany and through Austria, through unknown borders between sleeping nations, through dreams and night time stirrings, through the first flickers of light on the horizon, the rising dawn, to this place - not even a name on a map - a toilet-stop in Hungary.

I phoned Stuart, my constant companion on this journey, a friendly voice on my mobile giving me instructions. "Hello mate," he said. I'd had about three nervous breakdowns so far, having missed the hotels he'd told me about, and having wandered off the road and getting lost, once near a MacDonald's near an erotic supermarket where I'd eaten a burger and lost my wallet, and always Stuart's voice was there, disembodied, distant but reassuringly familiar, offering sound advice. Now he was telling me about the next leg of my journey, past Budapest towards Szeged, and the most dreaded part of the journey so far, into Szeged itself, my first attempt to drive through a city with traffic.

This was the first time I'd driven on the right hand side. It's easy enough on the motorway. A cinch. But those couple of times when I'd come off and got lost had frightened me. I just didn't know what to do at a roundabout. I kept having visions of taking a wrong turn and smashing in to the on-coming traffic. Every time I got to one I'd have to talk my way through it. "That's right, Chris, veer right. That's right. Keep to the right. OK, so now you come off here. Keep it steady." Breathing deeply to hold my concentration. "OK, so that's it, you're approaching the motorway. Down the slip-road. Watch for the traffic on your left." Driving a UK registered right-hand drive vehicle. Looking out from the passenger mirror. Seeing the traffic surge and loom as I indicate, speeding up to position myself between lorries, pulling out. "There you are Chris. Back on the road. That's it, that's it. Heading in the right direction again. Good boy Chris. You made it," before putting my foot down to slip into the fast lane and passed the lorries that were hemming me in.

That's why I was still travelling all these hours later. It was easier to keep going than to have to go through all that trauma every time I came off the road.

I was still sitting in the car, a Grand Cherokee Jeep, all black, with tan leather upholstery and tinted windows. It was Stuart's car. I'd agreed to drive it to Romania for him. It had cruise control, which meant you could set a speed and then sit with your feet off the pedal. That was good. You would position yourself between two cars going at approximately the right speed, and then set the cruise control. After that you'd just be sailing, guiding the car with occasional jerks on the steering wheel, though it had very sloppy steering which meant you were adjusting it all the time. My right hand ached from gripping the wheel. Every so often I'd change hands and do these tai chi patterns with my spare hand, like floating magical gestures in the air, pointing at the road, just to relieve the tension.

But I wasn't driving now. I was just sitting here in this anonymous place of nothingness, watching small birds dart and weave between the traffic signs. There was one little bird close by, oblivious of me, pecking in the grass. I was just watching it blankly, letting my tired muscles relax a little. Letting myself unwind. Tired. So tired. I really could do with some sleep. I closed my eyes, but sleep wouldn't come. I was too wired-up with the journey. Too wired into the road.

I had all these CDs with me. Nothing special. I hadn't selected them for the journey. They were just some CDs I'd grabbed hold of the last minute to keep me going. The first was a compilation from Uncut magazine specially selected by Keith Richards of the *Rolling Stones*. That was the one I'd played ultra loud as I'd descended the ramp from the ferry and taken to these European roads for the first time. Amos Milburn, *Down The Road A Piece* , this boogie-woogie piano reeling and rolling like a fast car careering down the motorway, followed by Jackie Brenston, *Rocket 88*, which is about a guy singing the praises of his new car, its V8 engine and how fast it is. I screamed with laughter at the appropriateness of these songs, banging my fists on the steering wheel and singing along at the top of my voice. Later, in the night, it had been Leonard Cohen keeping me going with all his wry, unsentimental, cynically acute observations about the meaning of life. I'd gone through the entire collection, one by once, ten CDs in all. There was only one left, *Closing Time* by Tom Waits.

Now there's a history to this album for me. A sad history. A lost romance. There's one song on it I can't bear to hear. It's too full of loss, too full of heartache. But it was my last record and I had no choice. It had been years since I'd last heard it. I slipped it into the CD player, put the car into gear, and nudged out onto the slip-road, heading straight for the dawn. It was about 6.45 am. I'd been on the road for 22 hours.

The sound of a sentimental mushy piano filled the car as I indicated into the traffic on the motorway, picking up speed, and hustled my way into the general flow, Tom Waits' familiar voice rising up over the piano, full of lonely regret:

> *Well my time went so quickly, I went lickety-splickly out to my*
> *old '55 As I drove away slowly, feeling so holy, God knows, I*
> *was feeling alive.*

And that's me now, pulling away slowly into the traffic, feeling holy and God-knows alive.

> *Now the sun's coming up, I'm riding with Lady Luck, freeway cars and trucks,*
> *Stars beginning to fade, and I lead the parade*
> *Just a-wishing I'd stayed a little longer,*
> *Oh, Lord, let me tell you that the feeling's getting stronger.*

Ha! And the sun is coming up, yes! And I'm riding with Lady Luck, yes! And there's a freeway, cars and trucks, yes! And the stars are beginning to fade, yes! And I don't know about the parade or wishing I'd stayed longer, but, yes, yes, yes, the feeling is getting stronger.

> *And it's six in the morning, gave me no warning; I had to be on my way.*
> *Well there's trucks all a-passing me, and the lights are all flashing,*
> *I'm on my way home from your place.*
> *And now the sun's coming up,*
> *I'm riding with Lady Luck, freeway cars and trucks,*
> *Stars beginning to fade, and I lead the parade*
> *Just a-wishing I'd stayed a little longer,*
> *Oh, Lord, let me tell you that the feeling's getting stronger.*

You know how it is with music in a car. I wasn't consciously listening at first. Too busy driving. Too busy keeping my eyes peeled for danger, for BMWs and Mercs with flashing lights coming up from behind. It took a minute or two for the words to sink in. And then, there they were: this exact description of my situation, as if Tom Waits had written them for me all those years ago, just waiting for this moment, as if this moment was written into history, complete with its own theme tune.

It was that line about Lady Luck that struck me the most. That's exactly what I was doing. Taking my chances on the road of life, driving into a future I didn't yet know, my heart pounding with fear and anticipation, cautious and alert, watching the changes. It wasn't just this drive. The drive was the beginning of the journey, the prelude to an adventure. Me, driving from the UK to Romania to try my luck with the changes. Yes, me: Riding With Lady Luck.

And there was something about this car too. I can't remember at what point I noticed it. It might have been here. It might have been before or later. The car had a note. As you drove so it played a single note, quite musical, quite distinct, like the high tone of a flute or an organ, and as you speeded up so the note rose, and as you slowed so the note dipped, and at some point I found that I was accelerating the car to hit exactly the right harmonious note to go with whatever song was playing - in this case Tom Waits' *Ol' 55* - and it was this note that determined the speed. Yes. Riding With Lady Luck. In harmony with Lady Luck. Even the speed of the car was down to luck. The tunes I was listening to. None of it was determined. It was all part of some flow I was caught up in, some movement like traffic on the edge of the world.

And now this car journey was symbolic. It was all symbolic. Life was a series of ever changing symbols, a movement through time. All that concentrated energy of the road. That focus. That determination - my determination, my choice, not forced on me, freely chosen - that movement through space, all leading somewhere, to something, something not determined by a pre-written fate, but undertaken as an adventure, by myself, interacting with the rest of the traffic, careful not to let it mislead me or misdirect me, concentrating on my part of the road, careful to play my part and not slip-up, careful not to put myself or anyone else into danger, staying awake despite the weariness, keeping going in spite of the time.

Later I pulled off the motorway and into Szeged near the Hungarian-Romanian border, and it was easy. No problem. I just followed the signs and the flow of traffic, sticking to the right hand side, and the traffic told me what to do, and an hour or so later I was coming up to the border itself, the first time I had been stopped in the whole of this amazing, relentless journey through space and time, this journey into the depths of a continent, into the depths of myself.

6. Landscape and Possession

> "At present, in this vicinity, the best part of the land is not private property; the landscape is not owned, and the walker enjoys comparative freedom. But possibly the day will come when it will be partitioned off into so-called pleasure grounds, in which a few will take a narrow and exclusive pleasure only, — when fences shall be multiplied, and man traps and other engines invented to confine men to the public road; and walking over the surface of God's earth, shall be construed to mean trespassing on some gentleman's grounds. To enjoy a thing exclusively is commonly to exclude yourself from the true enjoyment of it. Let us improve our opportunities then before the evil days come."
>
> **Henry David Thoreau**: Walking

People ask me what attracted me to Romania. It had something to do with the landscape.

There are four photographs that show the process. Two are of the landscape itself. There's a valley surrounded by wooded hills, with a scattering of cottages in small, fenced enclosures, with a few of those characteristic Romanian haystacks dotted about: the ones that look like witch's bonnets. Drifting wood smoke. Small barns. A hint of shepherds with their flocks. It's very picturesque, in a picture-postcard sort of way. It looks like a painting. But the thing you notice, beyond the small-scale farmsteads with their enclosures, there are no fences: just woods and hills reaching to the horizon. I think this is what touched me so deeply when I looked out upon it and which I found so difficult to describe: this landscape isn't owned. It is the landscape that encloses the human, not the other way round. The picture is one of human beings being occupied in a landscape, not one of human occupation. It is a landscape without possession. The land doesn't appear to be owned by anyone. Perhaps it is the landscape that does the owning: perhaps it owns all the creatures, human and otherwise, who dwell within it. After all, the landscape is bigger than the rest of us, and it has been around much, much longer.

Does the land belong to us, or do we belong to the land?

The next two photographs are of me and a friend in the place where the first two photographs were taken from, maybe two or three minutes later.

Stuart is looking cool and relaxed, as usual, with his shades and his skinhead cut, in a tee-shirt that shows his tattoos. In the first I'm standing next to him in my leather jacket, looking slightly hunched; in the next I'm embracing him and he is joking with me. In both I have this look on my face. I'm smiling, but about to cry. It's a look of deep intensity, as if I've just seen a ghost.

In a way, that is exactly what I have seen. I have seen the ghost of a different time out there in that landscape. I have seen the ghost of another kind of mind.

That is what I mean by possession.

When a ghost enters a man we say he is possessed.

But what if he is already possessed and he no longer knows it?

What if the mind that he carries around in his head isn't his real mind at all?

What if it isn't just one man, but all of humanity that is possessed? Possessed by the demon of possession, in fact, by the mistaken belief that anyone can ever own anything. What if there are people, even now, casting dark spells over you, in order to possess your mind. What if the god you worship, all unknowingly, is in someone else's power?

Can a man be possessed by his own possessions? Can the objects he owns own a man? The ghosts aren't things but thoughts. They are in the relationship between a human and the world he inhabits. Does he see the world, or does he only see what can be bought and sold? How does he make the world his own? By sealing it with money, or by animating it with his thoughts? By planting it with keep out signs, or by planting it with seeds? With the dead hand of legal obligation, or with the embrace of physical graft? By signing contracts or by building a home?

We have "ownership", we have "possession", we have "occupation" and we have "belonging". All of them are words with more than one meaning.

So "occupation". It is occupation that occupies a man. We have our jobs, our occupations. We are occupied. But then, when one country invades another we call that "occupation" too. Occupied France in the Second World War. The Occupied Territories in what were once Palestine. Occupied Iraq. Occupied Afghanistan. The question then is, when we say that the landscape is occupied by humans what do we mean? Occupied as in an occupying army - a band of foreign invaders in the landscape imposing an alien culture upon it, degrading it, destroying it, murdering its inhabitants, exploiting it, marching all over it with storm-trooper boots of oppression? Or as human beings merely working in the landscape, working with the land, being occupied within it?

And when we say we "own" something, how do we own it? You can own a thought. You can own knowledge. You can "own up" to things. None of these involve a legal relationship. Ownership here is just the acceptance of responsibility. It doesn't imply possession at all.

It is the same with "belonging". We can belong to a club, or to a tribe, or to a culture. We don't say that the club "owns" us. Belonging, in this sense, is a relationship with something, the way we say two people belong to each other, the way a child belongs to a mother, or a man belongs to a women. It is a relationship over time: a be-longing, a being-over-time. A longing. A longing to belong.

All cultures have a sense of ownership in these terms, as relationship, as knowledge, as commitment, as work. But most cultures until very recent times did not have a sense of possession in the way we now have it: of a legalised and exclusive ownership, of an ownership that implies that what belongs to one cannot therefore belong to another. Common ownership was once the norm. This is what has changed. And the joke here, of course, is that when you look at who owns what in these legal terms, most people in the world own very little, or nothing at all, and a very few people own almost everything.

This form of possession is invisible, like a ghost. It is exactly like possession in that other, occult sense. A man does not need to have done anything to have this form of ownership. He does not need to have built a farm, or raised crops, or raised a family. He does not need to have worked the land or to have maintained it, to have tilled the soil, to have built fences, to have planted seeds, to have reaped the harvest. He does not need to have hunted on it. He does not need to know where the wild creatures go. He does not even need to have visited it. He need not know where it is. All he needs is a bit of paper that says he owns it, and when he wants to dispossess the man who is actually living on it, and who has raised crops and a family and built a home, he can. The joke is that we have all been sold into this form of possession, and yet all it has achieved is to have dispossessed us all.

Possessed and dispossessed, all at the same time.

And who, now, truly "owns" the land in which he lives? Who, now, owns it in the form of knowledge, in the form of belonging, in the form of being occupied within it, of being occupied by it? Who, now, can hear the land talking to us? Who can hear its secret words of wisdom, in the wind, in the trees? Who, now, knows the rituals of the landscape, it's cycles and its seasons, and the potent alchemy that plants perform to turn soil and air into food? Who knows its secrets? Who knows its charm? And who, now, knows how to charm it and be charmed by it? Who knows its magic?

The hint out there in that Romanian landscape is of a time when a legalised form of possession was the exception, not the rule, when lands were held in common, and when humans took their abode in the landscape as passing strangers in the sacred dimension of time; when we shared the land with the other creatures of the landscape, with the wolves and with the bear, with the snake and with the eagle, and when we allowed the landscape to enter us and possess us with it's abiding, ancient presence, and never tried to claim but temporary ownership of what can never, in the end, belong to anyone.

Let's face it: death takes all possession away, but the landscape will remain forever.

Bear Nation

1.

As we came over the mountain we could see the storm clouds gathering in the distant hills, dark and ominous looking. Attila was angry. "Fucking hell," he said.

"Why are you angry?" I asked.

"Maybe we don't see the bears," he said.

I'd met Attila a few days before. He's this small, pale, intense character with jet-black hair and light blue, questioning eyes, always in a sort of fury of activity bordering on hysteria. When he got out of the car he was clutching a beer. He shook my hand and said, "excuse me this beer. Yesterday was a holiday in Romania, but I have to work, so today I will have my holiday instead. That is why I am drinking beer."

Later he admitted that it was because he was nervous about having to speak English with me. He speaks good English, very correct. "Oxford English" as he calls it. But this is part of the problem, that he is intensely aware when he makes a mistake, when his grammar is not up to his own high standards. This was why he was nervous. He felt the beer would make it easier to communicate.

He had Huni and Szabi with him, the cameraman and the guide. They were all in their twenties, henceforward to be known as "the boys".

Attila said, "I hope you don't mind it that we are so young."

"Why would I mind that?" I asked. "I'm young too, I just don't look it."

Huni is muscular and handsome, with sparkling eyes and a cool, relaxed, self-aware presence. He is obviously very comfortable in his own skin. Szabi is tall and dark, with a hooked nose like a bird of prey and a sense of the wild about him. He was the guide. It was he who would be taking us into the forest later to see the bears.

We met in a car park. Then we went to a restaurant and ate. We drank some beer. It was very relaxed. We talked about the Aves Foundation, their organisation. We talked about the problems with the bear in Romania. We talked about the wildlife in general. I took to them all immediately. My face still bore the scars of a party the night before, when I'd fallen over in the dark. I had angry-looking scabs all across my forehead. In the restaurant I pointed it out (although it was obvious). "Palinka," I said. Attila said that Huni had said it was the first thing he had noticed about me when he had got out of the car, and that he had said the same thing. "Palinka," he'd said. "This man likes to drink."

Later we drove to the far side of Brasov to a bear sanctuary called Libearty. It was full of bears that had been in captivity, in zoos or in cages. The bears were in compounds behind fences, but out in the open, in a forest.

Attila said, "these are not real bears. They are more like dogs. You will see when you get there."

At one point he was struggling for a word. "This is not good for the bear... the bear..."

He was trying to find a word to describe the family of bears as a whole.

He said: "This is not good for the bear nation. That is not the right word. The bear nation. What is the right word please?"

I said, "I think you mean species, but, I tell you what, I like 'bear nation' better."

We drove up a steep gravel track on a hillside overlooking some spectacular mountain scenery till we came to the gate. The gate was a tree branch strung across the road. Then we parked. Everyone except Huni (who was the driver) had been drinking beer, so we all stopped for a piss by the side of the path. After that we went into the compound.

Huni had his camera out and was filming everything.

There was a gravel path between high link fences, behind which was an electric wire. We were in the forest by now, albeit one fenced off into compounds. Even so there is a particular sound associated with the forest. A kind of hush. A whispered ripple of wind through the leaves. Your voice takes on a certain quality. It's not an echo, the opposite in fact. A kind of muffling of the sound, a closing-in, as if the forest is drawing close around you, as if it is wrapping you in its presence.

Suddenly Attila said, "there is a bear!"

It was walking on all fours with its back to us, maybe thirty feet away in the forest, this slow, ambling walk. It was my first sight of a bear. We came to another compound on the left and there was another bear, only much nearer. Attila made a clucking noise and it turned and came to the fence. So now it was barely three feet away, this huge, furry creature with a wet black nose and claws.

"See," said Attila, "I told you they were not real bears."

It looked like a real bear to me.

We carried on walking. We passed another compound, this time on the right, and there was a medium-sized bear inside.

Attila said, "so this is the last chance for bears." He said, "it's not a bad thing for a bear in captivity to live here, but it's the last chance."

The bear had tan coloured fur on its back and was strolling up and down near the fence.

Attila said, "that's Lydia."

"Lydia?"

"She is another female. And that one there is Cristian."

I looked and there was another very large bear behind.

"He is a real big bear," continued Attila. "But you can see like dogs they are coming here. That is the difference."

Szabi said: "That's a bear!"

"Cristian?"

I couldn't get over the fact that these bears had names.

"He is about 400 kilos," continued Attila. "So that's a bear. And they are very good friends. He spends together winter, Cristian and Lydia, and, you know, I know all these bears. When Lydia came here she was psychologically absolutely down, was moving like that, like that, like that" - miming a distressed bear stepping backwards and forwards on the spot – "and now you can see, no problems…"

But Cristian was huge, a great hulking thing, twice as big as a man, at least eight feet tall at a guess, though it was hard to say as he was on all fours. But he had broad shoulders and a rippling, muscular back, and you wouldn't want to meet him if he was in a rage. He could tear you to shreds, could kill you with a single blow.

"How old is he?" I asked.

"It's about 24 years old," said Attila, and he lives about 40 years. So it's like a 40 years old man. So it's in the best time. On the top, on the top. The strongest bear. And you know, if you shoot a bear like this as a hunter you pay about €10 or €15,000. If you shoot a bear like Lydia you pay about €7,000."

"That's a bear," said Szabi. "It's needed in the nature. The number is very low, just, I think, maybe about 20, 50 bear. Could be about 30, 40."

He was referring to the fact that fully mature adults like Cristian are a rarity in the wild, precisely because they are the greatest prizes: the biggest and most dangerous, the most impressive as trophies.

"This is the problem that I told you about, that the most part of the big bears are hunted, are killed, and this is the problem. It's good if we have got a little bit more bears, but I don't think it's true. But it's good if we have got a little bit more, but we have to select them, not just to kill the biggest."

"What I was say," said Szabi, "we could reintroduce in other parts that bears…"

"He's absolutely fantastic," I said. "Cristian, you say his name is? Why do they call him Cristian?"

"He is from the circus in Bucharest, and they gave him that name," said Attila.

It was after this that I first heard a bear speak. It was Lydia. She was walking up and down by the fence making this noise. It is a unique and unmistakable sound, like a plaintive nasal cry, slightly wistful, slightly melancholic. The Latin name for bear is "Urs" and that is exactly the sound they make. "Ur?" It's a question. There's a questioning tone to it, like a philosophical query you might ask of the mountains, of the wind. Something slightly sad. "Why have you left me, Ur? Where have you gone, Ur? Why do us creatures have to die?" You can hear the peaks of the mountains in its voice. You can hear the hollowness of the wind. You can hear the echoes of the forest. You can hear the lonely miles of travel. You can hear mortality and loss.

We carried on walking. Attila said that it was a pity we couldn't see bears in the trees. "Now is too cold," he said. "When it's warmer they are climbing the trees and playing in the wind to cool down," he said.

It was like fate. No sooner had he said this than we turned a corner and there was a bear in a tree. It was kind of perched there, lodged in the branches halfway up a tree, its forelegs jammed into the v of some small braches, its back legs wrapped around the trunk, holding on with its claws. It was swaying in the wind, this incongruously heavy creature on a thin stalk of a tree, like a great fat cat with a black nose. Did I see contentment in its face? Probably not. But I saw a bear in its natural environment, halfway up a tree, kind of rubbing itself up and down against the bark.

It was growling at another bear which was prowling up and down on the ground. Szabi said, "it was probably say something like, 'go away'."

Attila said, "I don't agree." The boys started talking in Hungarian, and then they were laughing.

Attila translated for me.

"We was talking about the bears sexual habits. I was saying it was not 'go away', it was something like 'what are you doing there? Why don't you come here?'"

You may have noticed by now that Huni never speaks. Attila speaks, and Szabi speaks, but Huni never does. That's not because he can't speak English. His English is as good as anyone's. It's because he's filming, non-stop. Everywhere I go I have this camera pointing at me, at my face, at my back. Or he's filming from behind, as we walk. Or he's filming each of us as we talk, first Attila, then me. Or he's filming the bears as we look at them.

So now he came up very close and was focussing on my face. I was obviously looking delighted at the sight of a bear up a tree, which must have made an interesting picture. But I was slightly annoyed. "Not at me," I said, putting my hands up to cover my face. "At the bears."

"Ignore him," said Attila. "He's working."

Huni said, "I film you. I film the bears later."

It was only at this point that it occurred to me that they wanted to put me on TV.

2.

We are in Harghita county, a wild, volcanic, mountainous region in central Transylvania. It is a Hungarian speaking part of Romania. When the boys are not speaking English to me they are speaking Hungarian to each other, which is the strangest language in the world. It has forty four letters, most of which are unusual vowel-sounds with an uncanny resemblance to someone having sex in the bathroom. Eu! Nyuhn! Yuh! Ouieh! Aoh! Uihnh! Owuh! Uh! Oh Yes! Uh! Yes! Give it to me big boy. Unyunhn!

The language as a whole sounds like someone talking backwards down a drainpipe. It has four tenses - past, present, future, and infinity– and all the different parts of the language – the tenses, the verbs, the various grammatical parts – are stuck onto the back of the word in a string of additional letters, meaning that all the words are at least a hundred and forty letters long. And that's just asking if you would like to have sex in the bathroom. It shares no common words whatsoever with English, or any other language on Earth.

No, that's not true. It has about forty words in common with Finnish – for which reason the language group is called finno-ugric - and another few hundred in common with Turkish, the traditional enemy, and they do share one word in common with English. They say "hello", by which they mean "goodbye".

The odd thing is that they shared an Empire with the Austrians for a few hundred years, but that Hungarian has no German words in it. And while many of them speak German, you can bet your life that no Austrian ever bothered to learn Hungarian. Also, they didn't quite share an Empire as such. They were the junior partners. They got to do all the fighting, while the Austrians got to keep all the treasure. They got to do all the dying while the Austrians got to swan around in elaborate golden carriages, wearing wigs and doing the waltz. They were the foot soldiers of the Holy Roman Empire, the cannon fodder. Brave but foolhardy you might say. Szabi told me that they invented underwear, and he was immensely proud of this odd little fact. But they are a strangely reserved, strangely diffident people. I was in a restaurant once with a friend and it was a children's birthday party, and the children all sat at the table and whispered to each other. I think one have them might have giggled once. It was hard to know as it was drowned out with the sound of polite whispering. I've never seen such a bunch of well-mannered children in my life.

But it's not as if they beat their children around the head to get them to act like this. They ARE like this. Polite. Well-mannered. Decorous. Disciplined. Restrained. It's in their blood. So it's hard to picture the fact that historically they were warriors, that they stood on the borders of Europe defending it against the Turkish invader. Perhaps it is these very qualities that define the warrior. Restraint in peace-time but all-out commitment in war. Disciplined because discipline is the first rule of an army. Decorous because they like to wear uniforms. Well-mannered, because this is another word for discipline. And polite because politeness is the mark of a person who has seen the savagery of the battlefield, and who therefore knows where to draw the line.

Actually they are not quite Hungarian either. They speak Hungarian – though a specific local dialect - and they identify with Budapest as their capital. They live in Transylvania which was once part of Hungary before it was ceded to Romania after the First World War; but they call themselves Szekelys and the region Szekely Land, and claim to have been here since Attila the Hun first passed by in about the fifth century AD. So they are the last born children of Attila the Hun in Europe, Attila being the most popular name for a boy.

This is disputed of course, as is every fact in history. But it is their myth. It is what they believe about themselves and therefore, in this sense, entirely true.

So they are a stoic, hardy, self-reliant mountain people with the breath of the forest in their veins, practical and hard-working. It is mountain-forest air they breath and they share their lands with wolves and bears. They were all schooled in the outdoors. They know how to make fires and how to barbeque meat. Meat is their favourite food. Meat in any form. A Hungarian meal consists of meat and two meat. Meat followed by meat followed by more meat.

Well that's not quite true of course. They do eat some vegetables. My favourite meal was something called a Hungarian platter. It consists of a large pork steak, two huge smoked pork sausages, two neat slices of some tangy, salty village cheese, with half a tomato and some shavings of onion and with a great, fat rubbery slither of pork fat perched on the top. And that's it: meat and meat, with cheese, and with meat fat. The tomato and the onion are like an afterthought. Just in case there aren't enough vitamins in the meat. I ate everything but the fat.

So their language is almost impossible to learn, but you soon pick up one word. Igen. They say it over and over again. Igen, igen. It punctuates their language with the regularity of a common verb. It's the first word they say when they answer the phone. Every sentence contains it, and when they say it they usually repeat it several times. Igen, igen, igen. And again. Igen, igen. It is their favourite word. It means "yes".

Which is the quality that is most admirable in them. They are an open-hearted generous people and their favourite word is "yes".

So now it is time to go back to the beginning, and how all this started.

A few weeks before I'd been staying in the region with some friends. We'd gone out for a meal with a young gypsy called Marton who was acting as my friend's caretaker at the time. Later we went to a bar. Marton was very drunk and was slurring and repeating himself in Romanian. Romanian was probably his third language, his first being Romany, his second being Hungarian. One of my friends, Aurelia, was Romanian, the other was English. So Aurelia was having to translate. Marton spoke no English and was hardly coherent in Hungarian, let alone Romanian, and he kept saying the same things over and over again.

At one point this wild Hungarian music burst on over the speakers. It was very fast, frantic, like savage punk music played on violins and accordions. This middle aged guy with a moustache and Wellington boots leapt up and started to dance, a crazy Hungarian dance. It was all elbows and knees and head-bobbing angular frenzy, accompanied by yelps and shrieks. His feet never seemed to touch the floor. Then he was joined by a young couple who were spinning each other round looking into each other's eyes, and after that everyone joined in. The whole bar was going crazy with this music. There were fights breaking out all over the place. They were kind of playful, and kind of not, slaps and jolts to the back of the head. You could see it all getting out of hand. And there was something in their faces too, like angry winds blowing over vast plains. Something elemental. Something tribal. You could definitely imagine they were descended from the Huns, and you could picture any one of them on horseback, wheeling and fighting his way across the steppes.

Suddenly Marton said something to Aurelia. She'd mainly given up bothering to translate by now since it was all variations of the theme, "you are my really good mates you are." He kept wanting to shake my hand.

"He said do you want to see a bear?" said Aurelia.

"Pardon?"

"Do you want to see a bear?"

Marton was rattling on excitedly. "He said he can take you to see a bear tomorrow if you like," continued Aurelia.

"Of course we would like to see a bear," I said. "You'd like to see a bear too wouldn't you Stuart?"

"Yes, I'd like to see a bear."

"He said it's a bit dangerous because the bears all have cubs now. But he can take you to see a bear if you like. He knows where one is."

"Yes," I said. "Yes. Yes, tell him we would like to see a bear."

The following day Marton came up to visit, but he was looking sheepish and strained. He obviously couldn't remember anything about the night before. We were all too tired anyway, even assuming he really knew how to find a bear, so we left it for the time being.

But the thought had excited me and when I got back to where we were staying in Timisoara, I did an internet search. I came up with a preliminary report from the Aves Foundation about the number of bears they had estimated were still in the wild. The report said that the official numbers were grossly exaggerated. There were not 6,000 bears, as was claimed: it was probably more like 2,500. There were also photographs with a contact address and an advert for bear-stalking holidays in the Transylvanian mountains. I sent off a note to the e-mail address and within a couple of hours had a reply from Szabi, which included his telephone number, and soon after that we spoke.

3.

It was after that we'd arranged this meeting, for the week of the bank holiday when I was back in Harghita anyway. It turned out that the boys were based in Harghita too.

At the time I thought they were a campaign group. Later I discovered that they ran nature tours. But they were also a monthly nature magazine and a TV company. Hence the constant filming. They were planning to put me on Hungarian TV.

Actually the TV company belonged to Attila. He was the one running the show. He said that the previous week the BBC had been there too, filming a piece about the Romanian wildlife. They'd been to Libearty, but it was only at the last minute they realised they didn't have any footage of wild bears.

"So we gave them some of ours," he said.

"Did they pay you?" I said.

"No."

"Well they should have paid you," I said. "They are the BBC. They have lots of money. Why shouldn't they pay you?"

Anyway it was on the back of this that Attila was constructing his programme for Hungarian TV: this sudden interest in the West (in "the West Part" as he consistently described it) for the Romanian wildlife. He had film of the BBC while they were filming at Libearty. And then he had film of me. Now he wanted more. So we were working together on this. I was trying to write an article about the Romanian wildlife, and he was trying to make a TV programme about western journalists being interested in the Romanian wildlife.

The following day I went out with Attila and his father (who is a hunter) to a private hunting ground to meet the gamekeeper.

This is so I had all sides of the story.

We drove out in the early evening along the most potholed road I have ever seen in Attila's dad's Russian jeep, till we got to a village where we met the gamekeeper, Istvan, and then up the hill and into the woods.

I have to say I loved that Russian jeep. We were driving along rutted, skidding tracks slimy with mud, up fierce inclines, through stream beds laden with rocks, through thick undergrowth and dense funnels of foliage, with tree branches springing back and scraping the roof, bouncing over the broken landscape, and at no point did that sturdy Russian machine waver, not for a second. Attila's dad said: "they are cheap, so you don't mind if it gets scratched." I sat in the front next to Attila's dad, while Attila and Istvan sat in the back. We were all drinking beer.

I also have to say that I loved Attila's dad and his gamekeeper friend even though they were hunters and I was trying to write an anti-hunting story.

Attila's dad, a doctor, spoke English exactly like Bela Lugosi in those 1930s vampire movies: the same deep, rich, rounded, sonorous vowel-sounds, the same sombre expressiveness. He also had Hungarian eyebrows, thick and luxurious, and the air of a man who knew exactly who he was meant to be.

Istvan – whom they had described before I met him as "a simple and a good man", and who spoke no English at all – had this deep, ruddy, weather-beaten complexion and a look of true kindliness about his face. It was hard to believe that he made his living from killing animals; or not from killing animals as such: from selecting which animals from the stock are to be killed, from pointing them out to the huntsmen. But, I realised, there was a kind of quiet reverence in the soul of this man; a commitment to the very environment that gave him his living, and that he truly loved his beasts.

He had on a tweed hat and Wellington boots and was wearing binoculars.

After a while we came to a shady clearing in the forest. There was a metal container full of corn near a hide. It was then that I realised that this was a managed process. It was not "natural". This was not wilderness. They fed the beasts. They fed the beasts in order to shoot them. Istvan got out a bucket of corn and was spreading it around by hand. He showed us Wild Boar tracks in the mud. After that we got back in the jeep and there were more twists and turns and skidding manoeuvres through the dense forest undergrowth, until we broke out into a ploughed field in the middle of which was a raised platform hidden in a tree. We parked on the edge of the field.

I thought the platform looked like one of those watchtowers you see in films about concentration camps.

They told me that Istvan had ploughed the field himself, had brought a tractor up to do so, and that it was planted with Barley. It was for the Boar to feed. So this was even less like a wilderness. They were planting crops for their "crop" of meat. But Attila's dad said that they had to plant grain up here in order to stop the game going down into the village below. He said that the hunters had to pay if the game ate the crops in the village.

Then he added, in that deep, rich Hungarian voice of his: "I like to come here. Here is natural. I am not a doctor. He is not a teacher. We are all hunters here. It is an ancient feeling."

He was referring to himself and the other hunters and their relationship to the wild. There are no professions here. Everyone is a hunter. The hunting takes over. It is like being thrown back into some ancient part of your soul.

After which he took a bucket of corn which Istvan had given him and was casting it about by the handful either side of a trodden track through the middle of the field.

That's when I had a realisation, as I watched Attila's dad spreading corn about a planted field for the Wild Boar to eat.

I thought there never was a time when the landscape wasn't managed, not as long as there have been human beings on this earth. Hunters manage the landscape. They always have. Even the most apparently wild places are marked by human intervention. From the most ancient times hunters have lured their prey with food and built platforms to watch them by. Maybe there is no such thing as wild nature, not as long as there are human beings in it. Maybe it is wild only so long as humans haven't touched it. As soon as humans enter the landscape, it becomes managed. It is always managed, always bounded, always circumscribed by human activity. It is the human who defines the wilderness. The wilderness is where the human hasn't interfered.

Or perhaps it is the other way round. Perhaps it is the wilderness that defines the human.

The human is what the wilderness hasn't entered with its presence. It's all that's left over once the wilderness is gone.

4.

Ok, so Attila, his dad, the saintly Istvan and I are still halfway up a mountain in the middle of a forest in an incongruously ploughed field.

It was about eight o'clock by now, and the sun was beginning to dip near the horizon, giving a blush of colour to the evening sky. Attila's dad had scattered corn about, and then we were told to be quiet and to not say anything from now on, as we began trudging our way to the concentration camp watchtower in the middle of the field, which we climbed, being careful to place our feet at the ends of the rungs where they were nailed, it being a very rickety platform. And then we stood and waited, four of us on this tiny platform hardly bigger than a toilet cubicle, huddled together like schoolchildren in an ice cream queue. And it was funny because, although I'd been told to be silent, the other three were all chattering together in excited whispers, exactly like schoolchildren, laughing and passing the beers around. At one point Istvan placed his tweed cap on my head, I guess because my grey hair would be visible from a distance. And we were just scouring the forest's edge for any sign of the boar.

This went on for what seemed like a long time. I kept thinking I could see the shadows of the forest moving. It was an optical illusion. Between the trees was a darkness which shimmered. I kept thinking it was Wild Boar.

And then, suddenly, it was Wild Boar. They sort of emerged from the darkness: darkness becoming darkness, darkness that moved, stillness merging into movement, a stillness that became alive.

It was Attila who saw them first. He pointed them out to us, these shapes emerging from the trees, muscular and huge with hulking shoulders and craggy heads like great black rocks, with curling tusks and wet noses, snorting and trotting up the hill with a sort of hungry wariness, cautiously looking around them for any possible danger. They were a family group of about ten individuals, snuffling about and rooting in the soil for the corn.

I immediately had a sense of them there, not just physically, but psychically too. There was an alertness, a bright keenness like a spark, hidden in that dark, mean-looking form. I was suddenly aware of being in the presence of another kind of intelligence than my own. I felt that they were communicating with me on some level that I have yet to access with my ordinary mind.

Istvan handed me the binoculars and I watched them, fascinated, for about ten minutes.

Attila was filming them, but he decided he needed another angle, so he climbed down the platform, and did a wide, circling sweep around the back of the platform, to a small clump of trees nearer to the Boar. He was stepping slowly and carefully as this was a dangerous move, edging towards the protective shade with deliberate caution. The Boar got wind of his presence and scattered. Then they came back. There was one extra brave one who moved nearer than all the rest. So it was mutual caution on both sides. Attila got to his shaded spot, and the Boar returned for their corn, but they were spooked and kept scattering and then re-grouping, wheeling and turning in unison: all except this one, who was keeping a wary eye on what was going on. They knew Attila was there, of course. That was why they kept running away. That one was the outrider busily appraising the situation. The scout. Obviously the fastest and the meanest.

You had to admire the bravery on both sides. For all those Boar knew Attila's camera was a gun. And Attila, meanwhile, was facing a severe mauling, and possible death, for the sake of a nice camera angle. Wild Boar are a powerful creature, made out of black granite and engine oil with tusks like axe-heads and a formidable charge. They would break all of your ribs if they hit you at full pelt.

But eventually the Boar had eaten all the corn and made their way from the clearing and it was time for us to go home.

So we drove back down the hillside to Istvan's village, where we stopped off for a beer in the local bar. It had a charcoal portrait of a naked woman on the ceiling – half finished and with nipples framed like targets - and multi-coloured fairy-lights that flickered on and off. It was like being at a disco. A disco in the Wilderness, only there weren't any wild women to contend with.

Which was a pity.

5.

It was the day after this that my brakes failed.

Between Odorheiu Secuiesc, where the boys live, and Lazaresti, where I was staying, there is a mountain. You go up one side of it and down the other. It's about 60kms, a good thirty of which are on a twisting careening mountain road, with hairpin bends overlooking sheer drops. Up and up and up, round and round and round, then down and down and down. After that you go through Miercurea Ciuc – which has a crazy bridge which is never finished, and where the by-pass appears to take you through some people's back yards – and onto the road to Baile Tusnad and Sfantu Gheorge. Lazaresti is about halfway to Baile Tusnad.

It was along this road that the brakes failed. There was a sudden smell of burning, and then, when I tried to brake, nothing happened. I went sailing on. I was approaching a village, so I geared down, and then pulled into the side, allowing the van to coast to a halt.

I stopped outside someone's gate.

It was only as I was drifting slowly to a halt along the dusty track by the side of the road that I realised – with a sudden burst of adrenaline that sent my heart pounding – that had they failed as I was coming down the mountain I would now be dead.

On the other side of the gate was a little boy on a bike. I tried to speak, but he ran away scared.

I rang Attila. A teenage girl passed and went to go in the gate, so I called out and handed my phone onto her. Attila spoke to her. I was trying to find a mechanic. She was too young and didn't have any idea what it was I wanted. After that I went through the gate where the father and mother were sitting on a step outside their house. Attila spoke to the father and then the father was ringing round for a mechanic for me, while I rang a friend. I wanted to know if it was possible to drive without brakes. He said it was, if you drove slowly and kept your distance and used your gears to brake. After that I decided to try my luck and try to get the rest of the way home. It was only once I started out again – having thanked the man for his help – that I found out I was in the next village but one to Lazaresti.

So I drove home without brakes, and then, the next day, I drove back to Miercurea Ciuc to meet Attila to get the brakes fixed. It was afternoon, and the drive was all on this side of the mountain: that is, it was all on the level. We left the van in the garage, and then drove back over the mountain in Attila's car. We were going to see bears in the wild.

It was at this point, as we breasted the peak and were coming down the other side, that Attila said, "fucking hell!" and pointed out the ominous black clouds sprouting rain that lurked over the distant hills.

"That's where the bears live," he said. "In the forest in those hills."

Back in Odorheiu we met up with Szabi, who had Attila's dad's Russian jeep, and Huni, who had his camera. The clouds were looming in the late afternoon sky, like huge black turrets, with the sun bursting out from behind them, sending sprays of golden light into the air.

Szabi said that this was a good sign. "Bears love rain," he said. He said that there was more chance of seeing them after a storm.

And now we were driving back along that same potholed road we had followed to see the Boar, till we came to a valley and took a turn. The valley was deeply wooded and full of new Swiss-style chalet buildings. There was a stream running through it, full of tumbling water. We took another turn and were going up a hill, on a gravel path now, as opposed to a road. At some point we stopped outside a compound, and Szabi got out to talk with the forest warden. I was watching. Attila said, "don't look. Maybe they are doing some business." Szabi got back in and we continued up the track, which got steeper and steeper, till we came to a barrier.

Szabi got out, unlocked it, got back in, drove through the barrier, parked up again, and then locked the barrier behind.

After this the Russian jeep was in its element again: a rutted forest track wet with leaves.

After about half an hour we parked up and stepped into the hushed cathedral of the forest. It was like we were stepping into sacred space.

We were walking in a line, stepping over tree trunks and wading through slurries of mud. Szabi told us not to talk. Eventually he indicated with a gesture that we were to stop. He got out his binoculars and looked into the distant clearing. He made another gesture, a flick of the fingers that said that we were to duck in behind the trees. Then he passed me the binoculars.

That's when I saw it, peering out from behind a tree as I brought the binoculars into focus on the sunlit clearing ahead: the brown fur tinged with black quivering with flies, the long nose, the tiny myopic eyes.

I gasped for breath. It was as if the breath was yanked from my body. It was my first sight of a Bear in the wild.

After that Szabi led us step by cautious step from tree to tree. A twig cracked. The Bear heard us and stood on its hind legs to sniff the wind. It was at least seven and a half feet tall. It seemed to be looking straight at me.

I was caught out in the open. I was crouched down in the undergrowth holding my breath. Luckily Bears have bad eyesight and the wind was in the wrong direction. It went back down on all fours and continued its feeding.

The process took about fifteen minutes, stopping and starting like this, ducking behind trees, melting into the undergrowth, but eventually we made it into the hide on a raised platform, from where we could see the whole clearing, with the Bear and a family of Wild Boar snuffling and feeding, not more than twenty feet away.

As the Bear approached the Boar would scatter. He was definitely the king in this realm. You could tell by the walk, muscular and ambling, full of regal self-assurance.

The rain had stopped by now, but the Bear was wet. It shook itself and raindrops sprayed from its back. Szabi said it was a young male, about four or five years old. He handed me the binoculars and I watched it with intense fascination for at least thirty minutes. I couldn't take my eyes off it, not for a second. After that it slowly ambled its way from the clearing and was gone, closely followed by the Boar.

Huni said, "you were a little bit afraid I think."

He must have heard the intake of breath.

But I wasn't afraid. I was awestruck. I was wrenched to the very roots of my being at my encounter with a creature of such awesome, magnificent, majestic power.

I'm using a lot of superlatives here. They are all true. It was as if a part of me leapt from my body in that instant and went to join the Bear in the wild.

Was this a "spiritual" experience?

Of course it was.

Take that expression "an intake of breath" for instance: it's another term for spirit. It is inspiration. In that moment I breathed the spirit of the Bear on the wind. The Bear and I were in communication. The word "spirit" is from the Latin and means breath or air. Every inspiration leads to expiration: to expression. I am expressing my feelings now. What is spiritual is the silent, invisible communication between beings carried on the breath of the wind.

Just like this story.

6.

I can honestly say these were amongst the most exciting days of my life. It was like I was on a magical journey to somewhere, an adventure, as if my life had just turned into a magical tale from a book. From abjectness and loss to high-flying romance. As if the spell cast into the fire on May Day a week or two before had done its work and was transforming my life and my being by the minute.

That night I was put up in a pensiune with a warning. We would be going out again at 4am.

And then there was the 4am phone call, and I leapt out of bed, and we were on our way into the wild again, Szabi, Huni, Attila and me.

It was still dark, but people were on the streets.

I said, "how come people are out and about at this time?"

Attila said, "this is Romania. This isn't the decadent West-Part. People here are happy to get up early for work."

A little later we met up with our contact, another game-keeper, an associate of Istvan and Attila's dad. He had his gun with him, and was wearing a tweed hat and Wellingtons. We clambered into his Russian jeep (the vehicle of choice amongst the hunting fraternity) me in the front again, with that rifle lodged behind my back, and were off: back along that pitted road, through the village, and up the hill where we'd seen the wild boar a day or two before.

Only now we weren't going through the woods, but were skidding about through open grassland. It was light by now, the sky a fragile blue, pocked-marked by dusky clouds.

This was the strangest of journeys. It took a while for me to realise what was going on. We were belting through the hills, swerving and sliding on the wet grass, and every so often our game-keeper driver would skid to a halt and leap out to look at some creature or another. Mainly it was deer. He was saying, "look, look, Reebok. What is that in English?"

"Roebuck?" I ventured.

And we get out and look at these soft-eyed, delicate creatures with the strange bouncing spring bounding about all over the place. This kept on happening. We'd leap back in the jeep and go sailing and swerving once more, zigzagging between trees full of blossom, over ditches and along tracks, and then into open country again, where we'd make new tracks in the dew. And then we'd skid to a sudden halt, and come scattering out onto the wet grass, where we'd look at another Roebuck pirouetting about on the hillside, while the gamekeeper made clucking and cooing noises in order to attract its attention. Which worked, it has to be said. The Roebuck would stop and stand transfixed looking at him for a second or two before beyoinging off again.

We were doing this for about an hour maybe. It was only after about thirty minutes that I realised we were going over and over the same bits of ground, skidding about on the same bit of hillside. Round and round and round. In and out, in and out. I had no idea what it was for.

But – eventually – we drew up in a field by some woods and got out, and our gamekeeper friend leant on the roof of the jeep with his binoculars and pointed:

"Wolves," he said.

My heart leapt, but we were too slow to see them. They sensed the breath of us and were gone, like fleeting shadows, into the forest cover. Like swift grey ghosts they had melted back into the trees. The gamekeeper said (but in Hungarian, Attila translating for me): wolves are the most difficult to spot, the cleverest of them all. They are very swift and astute and they don't like to be near humans. But down in the trough of the valley where they had been there were the old bleached bones of a cow and I realised that this was food provided by the hunters, that this was, once again, a managed environment. And then we saw the tracks, by a muddy pool, just inside the wood: like large dogs, a kind of tangle of footmarks by the pool.

"Look, look," said Szabi, "two of them. Large male, small female. You can tell they are wolf not dog by…"

And he indicated the difference with this display with his hands. Pad, pad. Pad, pad. Dogs walk splay-footed, feet landing side-by-side – pad, pad with the palms of his hands - whereas wolves walk one foot in front of the other, like tightrope walkers along a wire - making a more delicate display with his fingers to show us.

Dogs are clumsy. Wolves are elegant.

"Like ballet dancers," he said.

And now we were all walking in single-file into the tangled woodland cover, like a party of hunters on an expedition, slow step by slow step, through the dense, wet undergrowth, the gamekeeper with his rifle slung across his back, and Huni with his equally predatory camera. On and on, through the muffled hush of the forest, only the occasional twig crack or the swish of a branch amidst the trudging footfall through the leaf-mould and ferns, till we came to a place with low-slung branches and the tangled foliage of trees....

Why here?

What strange ritual were we to perform in this out-of-the-way spot, where wolves lurked in search of prey?

We were going to be on the telly.

This was the first time I'd got a picture of the plans. Attila was going to interview the gamekeeper, Szabi and I as representatives of different interest groups around the subject of hunting. I was the western journalist interested in wildlife. Szabi was the representative of the conservation lobby, and the gamekeeper was there to speak for the hunters.

So it was the gamekeeper first. He had his rifle slung across his back as a prop, and Attila went into TV interview mode, with his microphone lead wrapped about his hand, with the name of the TV company, Hungarian TV, as a blue clip around the stem of the mike to be kept in camera shot, and then he was shooting questions, waving the mike back and forth in front of the camera, with Huni standing behind him, occasionally adjusting his position to get a better shot.
I have no idea what was said.

Then it was my turn too.

I have no idea what I said either.

I've seen the film since, but it has a voiceover in Hungarian translating my words, so I could transcribe them into Hungarian if you like. All I can say is that in the film my eyes are burning with a kind of fire, as if I am speaking for the bears and the wolves.

There's only one thing I remember, and that's what I didn't say, because Attila cut me off before I had time.

"Why do you Romanians allow foreign hunters to come here and kill your wildlife for money?" I was going to say. "Why do you place such little value on your heritage? If a person's only power is money then he don't deserve to hunt."

I was very fired-up.

Afterwards the gamekeeper started talking to me in his broken English. I had obviously said something that had stirred him to communicate. He was saying – something like – under communism it was in some ways good and in some ways bad. Under capitalism, now, it is in some ways better and in some ways worse. But it is bad for the hunting. And he said he had been out hunting in Belgium at the invitation of some of his foreign clients. "Not wild, not wild," he said. "was like a park, you know. Like parkland. Not wild like this" – indicating the broad tangled expanse around us. "It was like industry. Like industrial park for killing. I not like this way of hunting."

Later that day I was driven back to my pensiune where I fell asleep seeing the lush green of the hillside bouncing along in front of my eyes as in a countryside road movie. Green on green on green on green. I thought, "this is food for my eyes."

7.

I'd told the boys that I was hoping to sell this story to *the Times* newspaper. This was true. I'd had a sort of tentative letter of encouragement. "Once you are out in Romania let us know if you have any story ideas." But I was clear with them that this is all it was. An expression of interest.

And I wasn't using them. Or rather: it was mutual relationship. I was serving a story idea of theirs while pursuing one of my own. I was fully convinced that *the Times* would want to buy this story. How could they not be interested?

This was made even more convincing by the fact that by now Attila had secured me an interview with the Minister of the Environment, Attila Korodi.

He was a Hungarian speaker, a Szekely, a local to this region, having been brought up in Miercurea Ciuc, only 30kms from Lazaresti.

So we drove over to Bucharest to his office to meet him.

We picked up the Manager of the Libearty bear sanctuary on the way - a clean-cut, healthy-looking guy in a safari shirt, who also wanted to ask some questions of the Minister – and then we were driving to the capitol.

There's not much need to go into this here. We got caught up in traffic in Bucharest and were about half an hour late. The offices were in the centre of the city, not far from Ceausescu's crazy oversized people's palace, the current parliament, and, once we were parked up and walking Huni asked if I had my press card with me. I hadn't thought of it. It was in my jacket back in the car, but no one asked in any case. We went into a cool, echoing building with a sweeping marble staircase, found the offices – which were panelled in dark wood in the usual governmental style - and waited. Then we were ushered in to see the Minister, who was this youngish-looking Hungarian with glasses and a tie. I did my interview and he was typically evasive and then Attila did his on camera. The Minister didn't want my interview to be on camera as he felt his English was not good enough. Afterwards the manager of Libearty asked some hard-hitting questions about the legal status of the sanctuary – it was in a sort of legal grey area, being neither a reserve, nor a zoo – and that was it, we went home. On the way home I interviewed the Manager about the history of the sanctuary and then spent another night in my favourite pensiune.

The reason there's no point in going into this is that, in fact, *the Times* never bought my story, so my interview with the Minister was never used. Attila's interview went into his film, and the Manager of Libearty had been given some reassuring answers. The journey wasn't wasted. But nobody wanted my story.

After I got back to Timisoara I was writing proposal after proposal and sending them off to all the English newspapers, but all I got were rejections.

I couldn't understand this.

Are we so parochial as a nation that issues in a foreign country aren't of any concern to us? Are we really that arrogant, that stupid?

What got to me at the time – what still gets to me – is that this story is of huge concern to everyone in Europe.

Remember: the official estimates reckon on there being about 6,000 bears in Romania. The Minister had said as much. However, according to Szabi and the Aves Foundation, this might be an exaggeration, an overestimation due to the fact that the same people who make the estimates also want to sell hunting licences. There may be only 2,500 bears left in the wild, with perhaps only 50 or so of those large males that are of such vital importance to the genetic stock. Even now the bears may be being hunted to extinction. Surely this is an issue worthy of our attention: the possibility that soon there may be no bears left in Europe?

These are European animals, not only Romanian animals. Once upon a time bears roamed all over these lands, including England. Bears and wolves and wildcat and lynx. They are our own wild heritage.

Maybe, when the human race finally wipes itself off the face of the planet by our own stupidity, short-sightedness and greed – which is a distinct possibility right now – then these Romanian creatures will be the ones who will return to fill the gaps. It is from Romania that the rebirth of Europe will begin.

Or maybe – if we can wake up from our current nightmare and start to think clearly like human beings again – we can begin the rebirth right now, and include ourselves as part of it.

That's the only choice that's left.

The Home Front

Accommodationally challenged after a disastrous foreign trip in 2007, CJ Stone was forced to take refuge with his parents. It was the first time he'd lived with them since his teens, and he was surprised to find himself in a war zone. Following are CJ's bulletins from the front line in the eternal war of age and sex.

1. Bangers 'n' Mash

It was bangers 'n' mash night. Bangers 'n' mash and the six o'clock news. Mum said, "What did you used to do before there was telly?"

"Are you getting at me again?" Dad squeaked in an offended tone, almost banging his knife and fork on the table. "I used to read and listen to the radio if you'd like to know."

"Well I'm fed up with looking down your ear'ole," she said.

There's three of us at the kitchen table: Mum on one side, with her back to the telly, Dad on the other - even now craning his head around again to catch some local news item about a mother-of-two who's won a modelling competition, giving Mum a glorious view down the hairy funnel into his inner ear - and me, opposite, trying not to laugh.

"So what did YOU do before there was telly Mum?" I asked. "You're always watching the telly too."

"I used to talk," she said. "He never had anything to say even back then. Always just sitting there like a great big fat lump."

Well it's true... or partly true. Dad watches a lot of TV. He'd turned it on in the kitchen even as his dinner was being laid on the table. He does the same thing every night, making a great to-do about the process, turning it on, picking the channel, adjusting the volume, even as Mum and I are tucking into ours. Until then he'd been watching a program in the other room. Mum said, loud enough for him to hear, "He hangs around like a schoolboy waiting for me to call him in for his dinner."

He doesn't like silence our Dad. He always likes to fill the empty spaces with something glaring and noisy. Generally that thing is the TV. If he's not catching the news, or watching an afternoon movie on Channel 5, then he's playing something he recorded last night or the night before or something he recorded while he was watching something else. But then, what else is he supposed to do? Sometimes he just looks very tired. Tired to his bones.

They are both in their late seventies now. Still squabbling after all of these years. It's the squabbling that keeps them alive. But it's the rule of the house: Mum is always right.

She has a certain tone. A certain way of looking at the world. For years I used to think it was me. I'd lived in fear of that withering look, that note of scorn. Even when I was a grown-up that look would have me quaking like a schoolboy before the headmistress' office. It's only in the last couple of months that it's struck me. She can't help it. It's just the way she was made.

I'm a middle-aged man living at home with his parents.

I'm thinking of joining one of those on-line dating websites. I'd put it up as my personal ad: "Middle-aged bachelor living at home with his Mum."

The women will be queuing up in anticipation.

She even does my washing for me. I try to stop her but she's always rifling through my drawers when I'm out, fiddling with my underwear.

If you ask me she has an unhealthy interest in the state of my underwear.

She's also always asking me if I've got a woman in my life yet. Once she asked me it in Tesco in a very loud voice. Everybody turned round to look. I must have flushed a healthy state of scarlet, shushing her as I did.

"Please, Mum, not here."

I've refused to go to Tesco with her since.

I say, "No Mum, there's no woman as yet. Who would want me? You'd be standing outside the bedroom listening in."

"Well I have to know what's going on in your life. It's my duty."

You're probably wondering how I got here. I won't go into all that now. Life has so many twists and turns, so many ups and downs, it's like a rollercoaster ride at times. The rollercoaster of mundane middle-age. Even six months ago I had no idea that this is where I would end up: that very soon I would be living back at home with my Mum and Dad.

I also had no idea that it was a war-zone. So I'm a war-correspondent now. These are my domestic bulletins from the home front.

It's a kind of trench warfare rather than an all-out attack. Dad is usually sniping from a fox-hole. The big guns are all on her side. He keeps his head down mainly, defending himself with hobbies and with routine. He has a lot of hobbies and a lot of routines.

Turning the TV on as he's sitting down to dinner is one of them. Is it a hobby or is it a routine? It's hard to tell with our Dad. Both have the same quality about them, a kind of dogged persistence, a head-down, measured, unswerving sense of purpose, an unwillingness to adapt to change. Everything he does he always does it in the same way, at the same time, in the same order.

After dinner is over Mum gets up and starts putting the dishes away. Dad says, "You go and sit down love, I'll do this," but she carries on anyway, just long enough to annoy him. This is also part of the daily ritual.

Dad likes to have control over the washing up machine. So Mum sticks a few plates and cups in, rattling them about, and then he very pointedly takes them out again, one by one, unloading it completely before reloading it again. There are certain places for certain dishes and no one else knows where they're supposed to go. Only him. This is his territory.

So Mum gives up and goes into the living room and I make her a cup of tea while Dad fills the washing up machine. The cup of tea is my contribution to the routine.

After that I go upstairs to play with my computer.

Can you see how undignified all of this is? Not only am I living at home with my Mum and Dad, but I'm turning into a bored teenager at the same time.

2. A Surprise Attack

It was about 8 o'clock in the morning when Mum came down the stairs. Dad was late. But there was an extra twinkle in her eye. You could see she was relishing the morning's adventures.

She said, "He's in for a surprise when he gets up this morning. I'm going to make him change his own bed." And she let out a throaty chuckle, rubbing her hands with glee.

She'd obviously been planning it.

"I'm going to say, 'When I made those marriage vows I don't remember promising to make your bed for you.' He'll hate it. No matter how many times I show him how to change the duvet cover he always gets himself into a knot."

This must have been a Tuesday or a Sunday. All the other days are already occupied by Dad's impenetrable defensive routines.

Monday and Friday it's golf. Wednesday it's bowls. Thursday he makes his wine. Saturday it's the shopping. Monday afternoon he goes to the bank to collect cash from his account.

Always from the bank, never from a cash-machine. Always the same amount.

The night before golf he goes to bed early - at ten o'clock rather than his customary 10.15 – but not before he's made all his preparations. The car has to be loaded with his electric trolley and his golf bag, and the car put away. This is usually done in the afternoon, which puts the car out off commission for the rest of the day. He doesn't like to leave the car on the drive or go anywhere in case someone notices the clubs glinting temptingly in the back, so he tucks it up neatly in the garage instead.

Then, just before he goes to bed, he lays out his flask, his gloves, his mobile phone, and a banana. I always know it's golf day when I see this enigmatic assemblage in a little bundle on the kitchen table, like some sort of a surrealistic commentary on the meaning of existence.

Why a banana? Why anything?

It's a kind of warning to the rest of us, like one of those triangular road signs indicating hazards ahead. "Warning!" it says. "Routine in Progress. Move Carefully. Do Not Distract Golfer From His Arrangements."

In the morning, he gets up at precisely 7.15, gets dressed, comes downstairs and makes himself a cup of coffee while filling the flask with boiling water; after which he goes back upstairs to clean his teeth and collect his e-mails.

I think this is what describes my Dad best. Not the routines. We all have our routines. It's that hot water in the flask while he gets on with the rest of his business – not wasting a moment of his precious morning - so that the coffee later in the day, on the green, or wherever it is he drinks it, will be at the optimum temperature when required.

This is both my Dad's genius and his weakness. He plans everything like a military campaign. Meticulous down to the last detail, calculated and precise, you know that he's worked this all out in his head years ago, each move being timed and slotted in with an exact formula, like forward planning in a battle strategy.

The problem is that once he's set these plans in motion it takes an almost supernatural effort to break him out of them again.

Take breakfast for instance. Breakfast on non-golf days takes place at 9.15. It consists of cornflakes, tomato juice, and a handful of pills, both medical and dietary. It's at this point that he'll watch one of his tapes: a cowboy movie with John Wayne, say, with lots of shooting and shouting, the volume turned up to some unbearable level (he's quite deaf these days) or some creaking 1950s stop-gap animation movie which Dad still thinks is the height of cinematic sophistication.

This takes place in the kitchen. But you have to be very careful if you walk in on him. He's in such a state of concentrated abandon – completely lost in this other world - that he physically jumps with surprise, like he's forgotten your very existence. He IS John Wayne at this moment, the tough guy with the heart of gold, growling out some laconic, pithy commentary while he shoots down all the bad guys in a blaze of guns and glory.

This is where Mum can launch a surprise attack. She has her own routines, of course, but she's much more adaptable, much more open to change. So while Dad plans his day like a military campaign, she uses guerrilla tactics to undermine him, ambushing him in the midst of his drill like a rebel army sweeping down from the hills.

Hence the bed-changing arrangements today. Hence the look of mischief on her face.

"Eddy," she says, walking in on him even while John Wayne is engaged in a standing battle with the man with the scarred face, "I want you to change your bedding this morning." And she goes into the well practiced routine about what she did and didn't promise in her wedding vows.

Dad, meanwhile, is completely surprised, completely flummoxed, unable to resist or argue or even to think of anything to reply.

What would John Wayne have said?

Something strong and clever, no doubt, something menacing, grinding his jaw and looking the other guy straight in the eye while he goes for his gun. But that tough guy has nothing on our Mum.

The best our Dad can come up with is, "can't I watch my movie first?"

But, of course, she's completely ruined it for him now.

Later on I see him, red-in-the-face and flushed to his roots, his hair all awry, after struggling with the duvet cover for half-an-hour, a look of defeat in his eye.

"Mary," he squeaks despairingly, "I can't get the cover over. Can you help me?"

And she tuts and takes it off him, bundling on the duvet-cover with quick efficiency while casting me a glance that speaks of triumph.

3. The Wrong Bus

I was lying on my bed when they came in, huffing and clattering and rattling the doors about.

When I came out of my room Mum was on the landing, flouncing, swinging her arms and hips.

"We got on the wrong bus," she said. "It was awful! It went all around the houses. One and a half hours on the bus. The worst of it was not knowing if it would get here or not."

I said, "Why didn't you talk to the bus driver?"

"We didn't like to," she said.

"What do you mean, you didn't like to?" I laughed. "You only had to ask him where the bus was going."

"We thought he might be cross. Anyway it was his fault," she added, with a backward nod over her shoulders while drifting into the bedroom to get changed, "he made us get on the wrong bus."

Meanwhile Dad was labouring up the stairs behind her looking flushed and exhausted.

"It was her fault," he said conspiratorially, with a wink, once she was out of ear shot. "I knew it was the wrong bus before we got on."

"So why didn't you say something?"

"I was just following your Mother," he said.

I went down stairs to make them a cup of tea.

Eventually they joined me. They were still huffing noisily but good humouredly, the ordeal over at last.

Dad said, "I just spoke to Roy next door. I told him we'd got on the wrong bus, so it'll be all up and down the street by now. 'Eddy and Mary got on the wrong bus!'"

Mum said, "there was this little fat boy pushing in in front of me. I was all confused. You can't smack little fat boys these days, can you? More's the pity. I was too busy watching what he was up to."

There's two buses from the nearby city. They do a loop in either direction. One of them comes straight here, the other one goes the long way round via Herne Bay, taking in half of the countryside on the way. You can tell which is which as soon as you leave the bus station. One turns right, the other one turns left.

I said, "why didn't you get off once you saw it was going the wrong way?"

Dad said, "I thought it might be going a different way. I thought we should wait to find out."

This is what they're like. Mum gets on the wrong bus. Dad follows her, even though he says he knows it's the wrong bus, and then keeps them on it because he thinks it might be the right bus after all but going in the wrong direction. Both of them blaming the other and neither of them daring to ask the bus driver.

But they've moved on by now. All this talk about buses has led our Mum onto a conversation about another time they caught the wrong bus, which has led to a discussion about their various friends - some of whom had been with them when they'd caught the wrong bus the last time - which has led her on to thinking about one of their friends in particular who they went on holiday with once.

"Never again," said Mum. "She goes to bed too early. Do you remember Eddy? Eight o'clock and it's, 'Oo I'm tired, I must go and lie down.' What's the point of that? What's the point of being on holiday and going to bed at eight o'clock? It was a beautiful hotel too. It was like a holiday camp only more up-market. We didn't go in the chalets, but they were beautiful. And the food was lovely. And then she says, 'I don't like this,' looking down her nose at it. And I said, 'So where did you used to go when your Alfie was still alive,' and she said, 'We used to go camping.' But, like I said, she wouldn't be going camping now would she, not at her age?"

Dad just nods sagely to all this, smiling to himself. He knows he's not expected to join in.

But this reminds me. They're going on holiday again soon. I mention this and then make a joke.

"Now you'd better be good boys and girls," I said. "I don't want you spending the whole of your holiday squabbling like a couple of school children."

Mum rears up, glaring.

"It's not me, it's him," she says, with sudden sharpness. "We wouldn't have to argue if he did as he was told. Most men do as they're told you know."

Later we've got the TV on and there's a reference to social services and to being taken into care. Mum always does the crossword while she's watching the TV, glancing up from the paper to do so.

There's a sudden glint in her eye.

"I could have you taken into care," she says, looking at me.

"That's a good idea," I say. "I could do with being taken care of."

"What's that?" says Dad, looking slightly puzzled. He's always a little slow on the uptake, this being a consequence of his partial deafness. But whenever he hears us laughing he always thinks we're laughing at him.

"Into care Dad. She wants me to be taken into care," I say, raising my voice so he can hear. "It was me last week," he says. "She said she was going to have me taken into care."

"Yes, and you know what you said? 'You're my carer,' you said. Well excuse me Eddy, but I'm not your carer."

And she starts laying into him again about all his little foibles, his quaint little habits, his this's and that's, while he tries to defend himself lamely, giving her more and more ammunition with every bruised reply.

"You know we got on the wrong bus today?" she says.

"Yes?"

"Just like our wedding day. I got on the wrong bus that day too."

4. A Bad Cold

It's about 2.30 in the morning when I bump into him, padding out of the bathroom in his slippers, still half asleep. He always seems ready to jump when we cross paths at such a late hour, looking timid and confused.

I step back a pace to allow him to pass, but rather than going back to bed he fumbles his way downstairs instead, groping with his arms like a zombie on its midnight crawl.

The following morning there's no sign of him at his usual time. A dour silence emanates from his room.

Mum says, when I get downstairs, "Have you been going through the medicines?"

"No."

"Only they're all out all over the place."

Sure enough, there they are, all those brightly-coloured bottles of pills and potions for every imaginable ailment (and some which don't yet exist) scattered about on the kitchen work surface like a toddler's discarded toys.

Dad's obviously been going through them in the night. What can be wrong?

A hour later and he still isn't up. Mum decides to wake him up with a cup of coffee. She takes it in to him, tiptoeing into the darkened room, to be greeted by a heart-rending groan of anguish.

"I'm not well, Mary," he says, his voice quaking with self-pity. "I've got an awful cold."

There's something gloriously pathetic about our Dad when he's ill. You'd think he was dying of some terminal illness rather than just suffering with a cold. He shuffles about like an invalid, his voice a thin croaky whisper, full of barely suppressed emotion. He wants you to feel sorry for him. You WILL feel sorry for him.

Mum just tuts and rolls her eyes. "He makes such a fuss," she says.

That evening he refuses to eat his dinner, and in the morning, when I get up, there's his customary glass of wine lying abandoned, untouched, on the kitchen table, looking forlorn and lonely.

He must be ill, I think. I've never known him to leave his wine.

Later he goes to the doctor. After he gets back I find him in his bedroom room playing computer games.

"How was the doctor Dad?"

"I wanted antibiotics but she said I'd be better in a couple of days," he says, tetchily. "All she does is give me lectures about my diet. I'm not interested in hearing lectures." And then he adds, with terse finality, "She's not a very good doctor."

Her failure to properly comprehend the depths of his pain is proof enough of her complete lack of medical expertise. He gives a thin little cough of discomfort, as if to confirm the reality of his illness.

The trouble is you can't really tell if he's ill or not. Mum gets ill but you know she suppresses it. She bears it with womanly fortitude. With Dad it's all on display. That cough gets worse and worse. He takes to holding a handkerchief in front of his face and coughing into it, going bright red as he does so. Coughing at the dinner table, just as we're about to eat.

"Oh Eddy! Do you mind? Not at the dinner table."

"I can't help it," he says. "I'll go and sit in the other room if you like."

"No you won't. You'll sit there and eat your dinner. Just try not to cough over the food."

And so it goes on, for several more days. Dad is unable to move a muscle, he feels so ill. He confines himself to his room, that persistent, niggling little cough the chief evidence of his existence, only emerging every so often to take some food or to get a drink, shuffling down the stairs and into the kitchen like a tortured ghost on its eternal wanderings through the afterlife.

"I don't know what's wrong with me," he whimpers, as we pass in the hall one day.

I say, "It can't be a cold, otherwise why hasn't Mum got it? Why haven't I got it?"

"I don't know," he says.

Eventually he makes another appointment to see a doctor and comes back looking pleased.

"I got Dr Collis this time," he says.

Dr Collis is a male. In my Dad's terms, that means he's a real doctor.

"He's given me antibiotics. He said I might have heart palpitations. I have to go for tests. He said we have to be sure. I knew something was wrong."

You see, the illness wasn't the real problem. He was depressed too. No one ever takes him seriously. Having his illness confirmed has obviously cheered him up. He can really enjoy being ill now.

But heart palpitations! He's taken to stopping on the stairs halfway down and clutching his heart.

"I think I'm having heart palpitations," he says, in a voice like a wounded soldier just returned from the battlefield.

So even as he's getting better, he's getting worse. The cough has gone away to be replaced by something more sinister, more undefined.

Mum is finding it all too much and has taken to talking about his illness in a loud voice whenever he leaves the room.

"He always did make a fuss you know. We went on holiday once and he just lay in bed all the time saying he was ill. He was in bed for four days watching the TV, leaving me on my own. I didn't know what to do."

And then Dad pops his head a round the door, looking like a guilty toddler – you know he's overheard - and, in a low, pathetic whisper, asks her if she wants a cup of tea.

"I feel terrible, you know," he adds, turning to me, as if to counteract her attack.

"Do you remember that Eddy, when we went on holiday and you went to bed for four days leaving me on my own?"

"No, I don't remember that."

"Well you did. Four days on my own. It was horrible. And you just lying on your bed groaning all the time. I'm fed up with your illnesses."

"I can't help it if I'm ill Mary," he croaks.

"Well you'd better hurry up and get better," she says.

Miraculously he starts to get well after that.

5. Mum Goes On Strike

Most of the time it's more a state of stubborn siege rather than all-out war. Dad has his routines, Mum has hers, and as long as they don't contradict each other or get in each other's way there's no problem. An uneasy peace reigns throughout the territories. She might lob an explosive comment like a hand grenade at his defences every so often, but this is more for her own amusement than for any strategic purpose. She does it because she can't think of anything else to do.

But – occasionally - something comes up which has them at it again: in a full-scale bloody battle, no prisoners, all-out war.

The last time I saw this was when my sister was preparing to go on holiday and they'd agreed to look after the dog.

Mum wanted the carpet cleaned. It's a cream carpet and, she's right, there were shadowy stains and scuff marks creeping about where people had, very inconsiderately, put their feet down: using it like a carpet of all things. It's something they do about once a year. They hire a carpet cleaner and Dad pushes it around and about, up and down the living room and into the hall, shoving back the furniture to do so. It's a great big effort, I know - it's a hefty piece of machinery - and Dad is dreading the work. I can't help as I'm going away.

Dad said, "Let's wait till after we've had the dog."

"No Eddy," she said. "I can't wait till then. The carpet is in a horrible state. Look at it. It's in a mess. I want it cleaned now."

"Be reasonable love," he said, before launching into a long, complex and entirely logical explanation of why it made more sense to wait a week or two. He needn't have bothered.

It was that "be reasonable" that did it.

"'Be reasonable,'" she repeats, scathingly, mocking his tone, while he's in the kitchen clattering about in the dishwasher. "'Be reasonable.' I don't like it when I'm told to be reasonable."

Well I can see my Dad's point-of-view. What if it's raining that week? The dog will be running in and out with muddy paws all over their nice clean carpet. They only have to delay it for a while. And Mum sounds like a petulant teenager with her "I want it NOW" attitude.

But she's right about one thing. It has nothing to do with reason. Since when did reason come into it? "To love, honour and be reasonable." The reason reason is not in the marriage vows is that it's a contradiction in terms. Not like chalk and cheese. Chalk and cheese at least share the same planet. Reason and marriage, on the other hand, are two entirely separate entities, from two completely different universes.

A bit like men and women really.

"I'll show him," Mum was saying quietly, her legs crossed, her arms folded, tapping her foot with rhythmic agitation, keeping her words to herself and not letting him hear. "If he can't do his job, then I won't do mine."

Uh-oh. I knew that look. It was time to duck out of there.

It only took a day or two. As soon as I stepped through the front door two days later I could see it. There were crumbs and bits of fluff all over the carpet in the hall, and a scattering of toys where the granddaughter had been playing. Her toy push-chair and her doll were heaped in the middle of the floor. The door mat was all scuffed up and in the wrong position. I stepped over the rubble and into the living room and it was even worse. Leftover crockery on the coffee table. Bits and pieces lying all over the place. Discarded cushions. Cake crumbs. Biscuits crumbs. Scuff marks. And two carved wooden ornaments which normally sit neatly either side of the grate lying abandoned in the middle of the floor.

I picked one of them up and put it back before sitting down.

Mum came in.

"What have you done with the ornament?" she said, noticing straight away.

"I put it back."

"Well you can just move it back to where you found it," she said. "I'm on strike."

"I thought so," I said. "I could see it when came through the front door. Does Dad know?"

"No. He hasn't noticed yet. But he will," she said menacingly. "I will not be told to be reasonable. He'll see how reasonable I can be," she added with an entirely unreasonable-sounding cackle.

After that she wouldn't let me touch a thing and it was a few more days of having to pick my way through the debris. The washing up got done, as usual, but that's because the washing up is his job anyway. He always does the washing up. As for the rest, it just got worse and worse.

Even the washing wasn't done. There were piles of clothes creeping out of the clothes basket like some alien disease come to smother us all.

Dad just carried on regardless. Several days had gone by and he still hadn't said anything.

I went away on my business trip.

About three days after this Mum rang me up.

"The strike's over," she said.

"Oh good. What did Dad say?"

"Nothing. He never noticed."

I laughed.

"So what happened then?"

"I couldn't stand it any more. So I said to him, 'I've been on strike.' 'Have you?' he said. He drives me up the wall he does. But I said, 'I want that carpet cleaned or else,' and he agreed. So that's it. I'm getting the carpet cleaned tomorrow. You can come home after that."

So that was that. I got home and everything was back to normal. The carpet was clean, the washing had all been done and Mum and Dad had returned to their state of customary – if freshly laundered - siege.

As for the battle, I think we'll have to call it a draw. Yes, Mum got the carpet cleaned. But she was on strike for a week, and he didn't even notice.

At least he pretended he didn't.

6. Matalan Family

It was coming up for Christmas. My sister was staying with us, consequently I'd been relegated to the spare room, while Mum was having to share the bed with Dad. If they were perturbed by this new-found, enforced intimacy, then they were pretending not to bother.

My sister is the last member of our family to smoke. She lives in Tenerife, where cigarettes are very cheap. She's comes over loaded up with cigarettes by the suitcase-full and smokes almost continuously, hovering round at the kitchen door to blow her smoke into the back garden.

Mum packed up smoking a year ago, but unlike me, she still misses it. You can see her sniffing the trail of Julia's smoke as she passes by, and every so often I catch them huddled together at the kitchen table trying to look all innocent. I just know that the cigarette that my sister is holding has recently been at my mother's lips.

"If you're going to smoke then smoke Mum. There's no point in pretending," I say.

"Just don't tell your father," she says, rescuing the recently abandoned cigarette from my sister's fingers. "It's just the one."

Oh yes? I'm not sure at what point I got landed with the job of moral enforcer, but I don't like it. There seems to be some role-reversal going on here: me trying hard not to look disapprovingly at her weakness; her trying hard not to look found-out and guilty, like a toddler caught with her fingers in the sugar bowl.

But the house is very jolly. Helen, my other sister, who lives just down the road, is over for a visit. It's a family get-together.

The sisters are on the settee, bathed in the pale light of the winter sun, while the parents are upstairs getting ready. They are all going Christmas shopping. Helen is flicking idly through the newspaper, rattling the pages as she does so, looking for bargains.

Suddenly she says, having spied an advert: "You can buy a dinner suit from Matalan for £40."

"Come on," I say. "£40 for a dinner suit. It's got to be crap."

Helen says, "That's how much it would cost to hire one. So you can buy a new one and just wear it one night."

Meanwhile Julie, mishearing, says, "Some people wouldn't mind laying out forty quid so that it matches the rest of the table."

Pardon? Everybody laughs. "So they make dinner suits in co-ordinating colours to match your table cloth and napkins now?" I say. "How very modern."

She thought we'd been talking about a £40 dinner service.

The whole family are great fans of Matalan whose original shop was situated not more than forty miles from where we were brought up. It's cheap and cheerful, just like our family.

It's where they are planning to go today: to the brand new Matalan store in the Westwood Retail Park in Broadstairs, where they will be doing their Christmas shopping for the next twenty years I suspect, buying matching dinner suits and napkins for the Christmas table, along with other useless knickknacks that will fall apart on the very first use.

I must say, I don't like Christmas myself. All that enforced jollity. Right now I had this annoying tune going through my head: The Most Wonderful Time Of The Year, by Andy Williams. No it's not. It's The Most Irritating Time Of The Year. What other time of the year will you be subjected to sleigh bells in the supermarket and Andy Williams at the dinner table and other dreary seasonal offerings all day every day without so much as a by-your-leave?

Another problem is that in your desperation to get all the shopping done you go into some form of a blind frenzy. This is a bit like that battle frenzy that Viking Berserkers were said to experience, where they saw red and wanted to kill everything in sight. Only you don't see red, you see bargains. And you don't want to kill everything in sight, you want to buy it.

I'd already bought a wooden dragon made of cut-out shapes from a market stall in Canterbury. It was only on reflection that I realised that I had no one to give it to. My son is far too grown up for wooden toys.

How many more bad buys was I going to make before the season was out?

Meanwhile the ageing parents had got themselves ready at last and I was busy hustling them out of the door. I didn't envy Dad. He was going but this was definitely a girl's day out. I imagined him trailing behind looking lost and disconsolate, like a schoolboy dragging his feet on his way to school.

It's his punishment. He is made to go through this every year. It's punishment for something he did one year which Mum will never let him forget, and for which he will forever be in debt.

It was Christmas a few years back. Just like today Mum was hustling about trying to get everything done. Every year it's the same. Mum does most of it, the shopping, the preparations, the decoration. She buys all the presents, selecting them carefully to suit the various relatives. She's usually spot on. Dad has only two jobs. He writes the Christmas cards and he buys just one very important present: the most important present of all.

And every year he makes a fuss about it. "I don't know what to get you Mary," he moans.

So this particular year she was a little fed-up with this on-going mantra. "If you can't be bothered to go into Marks and Spencer and look in the women's clothing department for something in a size fourteen," she says, exasperated, "then forget it."

So come Christmas day they were handing out the presents. She bought him a nice pullover, all wrapped up in shiny paper with a bow.

He must have been feeling very uncomfortable by now. He had nothing to give her.

"You said to forget about it," he said.

You can imagine the look on Mum's face. She was staring at him furiously.

An ice-cold silence descended. He's been paying for it ever since.

7. A Disapproving Look

Mum used to scare me. There was a certain look she would cast down upon me, like a wicked witch casting a spell, which would stop me in my tracks. It was a look of severe disapproval. She would glance from under knotted eyebrows and pierce me with her gaze, sharp and shining like a polished blade. There was nothing I could do to resist its fierce condemnation. I would have to stop doing whatever it was I was doing and obey her unstated command, whatever that happened to be.

I used to think that it was a form of telepathy, that I could hear her thoughts.

I'm not sure how old I was. Anywhere from about 12 months old till I was a teenager I would guess. In all those years the effect was exactly the same, she could always stop me dead with a glance. I suspect now that my rebellion, in my teenage years and beyond, arose from the fact that I didn't want to admit that this woman had ever had such power over me. My rebellion consisted mainly of doing all the things of which I knew she would disapprove.

Later I forgot about this look and the effect it had upon me. Maybe I buried it. I left home to go to college. I travelled about the world a bit. I moved from city to city in an ongoing search for life and adventure. I grew up. I was married. I had a child. Eventually I ended up here, in Whitstable, and settled down.

I used to go back and visit them, of course, a couple of times a year, sometimes at Christmas, sometimes for one or other of the birthdays. The rebellion faded away and I became a responsible adult at last. Having a child changed my relationship with them. They stopped disapproving, and I stopped doing things to make them disapprove.

Then one year – it was Mum's sixtieth birthday – there was a party at their house, organised by the whole family. Everyone was there. My sister, Helen, had arranged for a stripogram. There was a knock at the door and a man dressed as a policeman stepped in. He was asking for Mum by name. Mum has always had a desperate fear of all things pertaining to the Law. You could see the look of shock and confusion on her face when he came into the room where the party was, saying that she was under arrest, looking at his notebook, his cap tucked under the crook of his arm. And then, suddenly, he yanked on his belt and his clothes started to come off. Mum's eyes became round and she flushed. She didn't know where to look. He stripped down to a g-string and gyrated in front of her face, making her get on her knees in front of him and take a rose out of his pants with her teeth. She was a furious shade of scarlet by now. It was all painfully embarrassing.

After he'd gone Mum was storming through the house.

"I bet you had a hand in that," she said, staring at me.

And there it was again, that look, sharp as a razor. It was like I'd been cast back over forty years and I was just a naughty boy again doing something of which she disapproved. I was stopped dead in my tracks, unable to move, pinned there by her forensic gaze, a child once more, busy making excuses: "No, Mum, um, it was Helen, honest Mum, it wasn't me."

Who says we ever grow up?

Later they decided to move to Whitstable. This was at my suggestion. They'd been planning to move to the West Country to be near my brother but then he had a job offer in America. He couldn't turn it down. Dad was happy in his retirement, having lots of hobbies and lots of friends, but Mum was frustrated and isolated in their suburban ghetto. There was nothing there, just a row of shops and a dusty road laden with traffic.

Something profound shifted in our relationship. I remember walking the streets looking for houses and I had a powerful sense of protectiveness towards them. I wanted them to be safe in their retirement. I could feel the protective arms of the town, like my arms, encircling them. Whitstable is a nice place to be.

They moved in some months later and were transformed by the place. All that sea air. Walks to the beach. Shops, cafés, bars, restaurants. Lots of exercise. Maybe even a touch of romance in the air. They became more tactile with each other. Sometimes, indeed, you'd see Dad sitting extra close to our Mum, looking flush-faced and relaxed. I suspected some hanky panky had been going on.

I remember sitting in a pub with them one evening and Dad was jovial and laughing with one arm crooked casually around Mum's shoulder and I suddenly realised that the gloom that had descended on Mum's life had lifted. It had taken its toll upon him too. He'd been the sacrificial victim for all her quiet frustration. Now she was happy she could afford to let him be happy too.

They joined the bowls club and gained a new circle of friends. Their lives were full. Well Dad's life had always been full, but now they had some shared interests too. They were in the bloom of life again, busy going out and getting on with things, having fun, like a couple of school kids on an extended summer break.

That was seven years ago now. I still had a flat of my own. I would visit them regularly to make sure things were OK. We shared the same town but we still retained a relative distance.

It was a liminal time, a time of transition.
And now here I am, in their house again, cast up on their doorstep like a shipwrecked survivor, and everything has changed once more.

I came in late from the pub one night, but I was very careful not to make any noise.

In the morning Mum said, "where were you last night?"

"I was at the pub," I said. "I didn't wake you did I?"

"No," she said, "But I don't approve." And she threw that look at me again, the one I recognised from my childhood.

And you know what? It only made me laugh.

Postscript: Still dancing at 80 – then gently sailing off.

My Mum, Mary Stone, passed away on Saturday, the 20th April 2013.

It was a gentle death. She kind of sailed off, like a boat which has slipped its moorings and which drifts away on the current.

It was my Dad who gave me that image. He was sitting next to her as she died. He said it was like she had sailed away.

I won't tell you about her illness. It wasn't very nice. It was ugly and painful, and in the end I'm certain that she was glad to be free of the body which had turned so humiliatingly against her.

She died at home, which is what she had asked for. She wasn't properly conscious for the last few days. She didn't speak, but she did open her eyes, and I know that she knew where she was, and it was this fact which allowed her to relax enough to finally let go.

My Dad is devastated, of course, as are my sisters, Julia and Helen, and my brother, Robert. We know that we have lost a Mum like no other, and that we shall never see her like again in this world.

She was a unique individual, always funny, even in the midst of her illness. She had a way of rolling her eyes and sticking her tongue out when she thought we were nagging her about eating, which she was refusing to do towards the end. It was like she was a naughty, stubborn little girl defying her parents wishes and that our roles had mysteriously reversed.

My most abiding memory of her is from about two years ago. It was a sunny Sunday, and she was out in the kitchen preparing lunch, listening to the *Gypsy Kings* on the CD player, and she just started to dance. The sun was streaming into the kitchen at her back, and she was swivelling her hips and swaying like a young girl at a rave party.

Still dancing at eighty, that was our Mum, listening to this wild, romantic guitar music, completely in love with life.

Eulogy

*This is the text of the eulogy I gave for our Mum on the day of her funeral,
May 13th 2013.*

This could be the hardest thing I have ever done, to stand here before you now saying my goodbyes to our Mum.

I say "our Mum", rather than "my Mum", not only because she belongs to all of us, to all the brothers and sisters here today, to the children and grandchildren, and to our Dad, but also because that is how we always spoke of her, as "our Mum."

It's a Birmingham expression. We never talk in the singular in Brum, but always in the plural. So it's "our Mum" and "our Dad" and "our house" and "our family". It's a generous way of talking and it includes all of you here today, even those who are not related and for whom Mum was a more recent friend.

Shall I tell you what it was about our Mum? She never grew old. I remember her saying, only a year or two ago, that she was always surprised when she looked in the mirror, to see that old lady looking back at her, because she didn't feel like an old lady at all. She said she felt just the same as she always felt, when she was a little girl growing up in Birmingham, under the ever watchful eye of her beloved father, Arthur.

This last year has been very hard for our family. We've watched our Mum go from the peak of health to someone who was, finally, bed bound and helpless, incapable of doing anything for herself.

For this reason I say that, while we can't help but grieve, we should not be sad.

Mum is glad not to be on this Earth any more. She is glad to have escaped the pain. She hated what had become of her body. She hated the humiliation of it. In the end she only wanted to be free. In the end, it is the best gift that we can give her that we let her go.

The last few days with her were a privilege, however. She was at home, which is where she wanted to be. She was pretty well unconscious most of the time, but she did wake up occasionally, and I know that she knew where she was, and it was this fact that gave her the strength to move on.

The day before she died there was a sudden storm as I was driving round to see her. It was really dramatic. The rain burst from the heavens in a veritable deluge, while, at the same time, the sun came out, and, turning the corner into Downs Avenue there wasn't just one rainbow, but two, one above the other right over our Mum's house. It was the first time I'd ever seen a double rainbow. And then, later that day, there was the most beautiful sunset over the Isle of Sheppey, like someone had set the sky on fire.

Mum always used to say that that was her view. Whenever we got to the top of the hill and looked out on the estuary below, she would say, "how do you like my view?"

So I'm going to say, and no one is going to tell me otherwise, that Mum had arranged that for me, that sunset and that rainbow. It is how I will always remember her. She chose her moment, in a glory of light and colour, like the light that she gave to all of us, which will live now forever in our hearts.